Pogrom

Pogrom

*Kishinev and the
Tilt of History*

STEVEN J. ZIPPERSTEIN

LIVERIGHT PUBLISHING CORPORATION

A Division of W. W. Norton & Company

Independent Publishers Since 1923

New York   London

For information about permission to reproduce selections from this book, write to
Permissions, Liveright Publishing Corporation, a division of
W. W. Norton & Company, Inc., 500 Fifth Avenue, New York, NY 10110

For information about special discounts for bulk purchases, please contact
W. W. Norton Special Sales at specialsales@wwnorton.com or 800-233-4830

Manufacturing by Quad Graphics Fairfield
Book design by Helene Berinsky
Production manager: Julia Druskin

ISBN 978-1-63149-269-3

Liveright Publishing Corporation, 500 Fifth Avenue, New York, N.Y. 10110
www.wwnorton.com

W. W. Norton & Company Ltd., 15 Carlisle Street, London W1D 3BS

1 2 3 4 5 6 7 8 9 0

For Hans Rogger, my teacher

CONTENTS

NOTE ON TRANSLITERATION, DATES, TERMS, AND PLACE-NAMES

In transliterating Hebrew and Russian I have followed the Library of Congress rules except that I have eliminated most diacritical marks and have presented the names of those known in the Western world (e.g., Alexander Pushkin or Hayyim Nahman Bialik) in their most familiar form. Yiddish transliteration is based on the system devised by the YIVO Institute for Jewish Research. Personal names appear in different versions depending on the geographic or cultural context in which the individual was most active. Place-names are identified with the spelling used at the time (e.g., "Vilna," not "Vilnius," and "the river Byk," not "Bîc").

The Julian, or Old Style, calendar was until the turn of the twentieth century twelve days behind the Gregorian calendar—and thirteen days behind it at the outbreak of the Kishinev pogrom.

PREFACE

"God is in the details," wrote the art historian Aby M. Warburg.[1] How is it that a particular detail looms or recedes? How can we chart the interplay between the trivial and the essential, the idiosyncratic and the historical? How should we understand those slices of the past that are far less momentous—on their surface, at least—than others, yet are able to imprint themselves onto history, to define their time and place?

This book explores a dreadful moment—albeit by no means worse than many others at more or less the same time—that would define for many Jews and others, too, the contour of Jewish fate in the half century before the Holocaust. Prior to Buchenwald and Auschwitz, no place-name evoked Jewish suffering more starkly than Kishinev (Chişinău since the emergence in 1991 of an independent Moldova). Israeli textbooks of the 1950s and '60s often dated the start of the Nazi campaign against the Jews from the Kishinev pogrom. In the early 1940s it was commonplace for Jews to insist that Kishinev had in its day garnered more attention than Hitler's war against the Jews. The historian Ben-Zion Dinur, Israeli minister of education in the 1950s, would declare that every aspect of the Holocaust had been anticipated by the Kishinev pogrom.[2]

Still today, with the city's massacre having receded into obscurity, the lessons learned from it remain among the most deeply ingrained in Jewish life. It would leave an indelible imprint on how Jews and non-Jews, too, viewed life and death in Russia, which was at the time the largest Jewish community in the world.

Pogrom: Kishinev and the Tilt of History sets out to defamiliarize a familiar story. Even those who know nothing of Kishinev are nonetheless likely to have encountered some of its fallout—a belief in the complicity of the Russian government in anti-Jewish violence, for instance. Kishinev was that rare event of the time embraced by all in a singularly fractious Jewish community, racked by debate over emigration, Zionism, Jewish socialism, and the like. The lessons that spilled from the pogrom's rubble would enter squarely into the day-to-day beliefs of contemporary Jews, with echoes, still time and again, in the speeches of Israel's prime minister Benjamin Netanyahu and many others. Kishinev, barely known beyond its immediate region before the pogrom, would quickly become the inspiration for some of the most powerful—and resilient—metaphors in Jewish life, ones that have seen little diminution in their timeliness or ferocity.

The reasons for Kishinev's lingering residue may at first seem unsurprising. Forty-nine Jews died in the pogrom, many were raped, and much of the city overrun. The massacre occurred at the dawn of a new century and was inspired by the darkest of medieval-like accusations—the so-called blood libel, which charged Jews with the use of Christian blood for ritual purposes. And most troubling of all was the evidence that surfaced after the riot ended that officials at the highest level were themselves culpable. Kishinev—little more than its name was now needed to evoke horror—would be seen as among the world's bleakest locations.

Yet little if anything regarding Kishinev's riot would be either clear-cut or simple. Meticulously documented then and later, it would inspire a veritable thicket of myths extending well beyond the confines of Jewish communal or political life, its impact—surprisingly enough—felt on endeavors as varied as the prestate Haganah, or nascent Israeli army, the NAACP, and *The Protocols of the Elders of Zion*.

Simple this story would *not* be—even in terms of its most obvious details—from the moment it occurred. Hence the pertinence of the account of Sergei Urussov, appointed governor general of the Bessarabia province—Kishinev was its capital—to replace his disgraced successor soon after the pogrom. He relates in his memoirs how at the time of his appointment he knew as little about the region as he might have about faraway New Zealand, and felt fortunate that a guidebook to the area had just been published. He pored over the book during his journey from St. Petersburg and carried it with him on his first few days in the provincial capital. He had the volume in hand as he made his way into one of the worst of the city's neighborhoods, known as Lower Kishinev, or Old Town, the epicenter of the April anti-Jewish massacre. There, he writes, he sought the river that was reportedly nearby:

Nearing the end of town, I vainly tried to see the river mentioned. . . . For a long time I could not bring myself to identify it with the little, ill-smelling pool, in places not wider than a yard, without current, and with no green on its banks. Thus, the first statement I gained from the experience of others—that Kishinev is located on the river Byk—proved to be incorrect. There is no river . . . or even a brook in Kishinev.[3]

The river Byk does indeed exist. A modest extension of the Dniester River, in the hot months of summer when Urussov first saw it, it would in fact have been reduced to little more than a swamp. Still, the passage haunts because the object of Urussov's frustration is a guide to Bessarabia, published in Moscow in 1903, written by one Pavel Krushevan, who was soon also to publish—and likely write or cowrite—the first version of the most infamous forgery in modern history, *The Protocols of the*

Photograph of the Byk taken by the author in September 2016.

Elders of Zion. The image of Urussov, a well-intentioned Russian official quite sympathetic to Jews, hunting on a sweltering summer day for a river described in a book written by one of the world's most notorious fantasists, provides a bracing entry point for our tour of Kishinev, too.

■

I construct this book in a series of essay-like chapters. The first chapter explores how Kishinev's riot would come to serve as the bedrock for so much subsequent knowledge—accurate and inaccurate—about pogroms and their origins and significance. I explore how the term, soon among the best-known Russian words in the world, would garner a new, chilling infamy in Kishinev's wake. "Pogrom" was now embraced as the most relevant of ways to understand the condition of Russian Jewry.[4]

I then examine Bessarabia, which was annexed by Russia in the first years of the nineteenth century and still coveted a century later by Romania, whose borders were only a few dozen miles west of Kishinev. It was a poor, mostly illiterate region, rich in agricultural resources but inadequately farmed, where Jews played a visible role as shop owners and artisans in the cities and towns and as middlemen in the countryside. I also look closely at Kishinev and the place of Jews in its communal and cultural life, and I explain why its Jews were truly shocked by the severity of the 1903 pogrom. Little in the daily rhythms of life there would have predicted that an outbreak of this sort was in the offing.

The next section looks at the pogrom itself through many different eyes. Likely the best-documented event in Russian Jewish history, the sources on it are vast. These include transcripts of victim testimonies, court records of those accused of crimes during the riot, and journalism in Western languages as well as

Russian, Yiddish, and Hebrew. This material offers the opportunity for an hour-by-hour exploration of the pogrom. Kishinev was the first instance where the inner life of Russia's Jews was laid bare for Western audiences; books about the pogrom were written and published within a few short months of its eruption.

This is followed by a description based on material in Israel and in Ireland, revealing how the pogrom was captured in the two most influential works on it. The first is the Hebrew poet Hayyim Nahman Bialik's "In the City of Killing," which is widely considered the most influential poetic work written in a Jewish language since the Middle Ages. Its laceration of the cowardice of Jewish males during the massacre remains a flashpoint in Israel for politicians, educators, and others. Alongside Bialik, whose five-week investigation of the pogrom yielded what remain the most detailed descriptions of its impact, I examine Michael Davitt, whose book, based on his newspaper reports titled *Within the Pale: The True Story of Anti-Semitic Persecutions in Russia*, set the standard for Western descriptions of Russian Jewish life for the decade to come.

I then analyze the connection between the Kishinev pogrom and the writing of the first version of *The Protocols of the Elders of Zion*, which was published—under another title—by Krushevan shortly afterward, in September 1903. This chapter is based largely on archival material previously in private hands. I explore how this event—understood by Jews and their sympathizers as laying bare the reality of Jewish powerlessness—was seen by Krushevan and those close to him as proof of just the opposite. As they viewed it—and captured in *The Protocols*, which remains, of course, the most widely cited antisemitic tract in the world—the unprecedented attention lavished on Jews in the pogrom's aftermath revealed more transparently than ever before their dangerous capacity to manipulate and control. Kishinev, as they saw it, was an ideal launching pad for Jewish designs on world domination, with the city's local Zionists little less than the Svengalis of such efforts.

Finally I explore the pervasive impact of the pogrom in the United States, which was the epicenter of pro-Kishinev relief campaigns and demonstrations. My focus is on how the pogrom shifted the politics of Jews on the Left, like Emma Goldman—whose rise to prominence was buttressed by her work as the promoter of a highly successful Kishinev-themed play—as well as others who would set in motion the National Association for the Advancement of Colored People, or NAACP. The NAACP's start was energized by efforts to align the Russian pogroms against Jews and the American lynching of blacks as tragedies of comparable importance. This campaign was pioneered by a remarkable now-little-known couple, William English Walling and Anna Strunsky. Both were intimately familiar with Russia: Walling's book, *Russia's Message,* would be the most widely read English-language account about Russian radicalism before the appearance of John Reed's *Ten Days that Shook the World.* Returning from a two-year stint in Russia in 1908, just in time to cover as journalists the Springfield, Illinois, race riot, the Wallings were the first to champion the cause of treating black lynching no less seriously than Russia's anti-Jewish pogroms. The founding meeting for what would soon emerge as the NAACP took place in January 1909 in their New York City apartment.

■

Based on research in Tel Aviv, Dublin, Chişinău, Moscow, New York, and elsewhere, *Pogrom: Kishinev and the Tilt of History* explores the extraordinary shadow cast by a riot lasting scarcely longer than a day and a half. Indeed, the worst of its violence transpired over some three or four hours on a cluster of intersecting streets that were little more than alleyways. More would soon be known about these streets than about anywhere else in Russia where Jews lived.

Not examined in this book is Kishinev's impact on the politics of the Jewish Socialist Labor Bund, then the largest Marxist group in Russia. This influence, while undoubtedly significant, proved too difficult to substantiate, given that the Bund's keen preoccupation with the pogrom was silenced by its insistence on its internationalism. The lingering impact of Kishinev on the formation of the Haganah is also left unexamined; this would be a fascinating story worthy of another book. The various ways in which Kishinev inspired the activity of the Territorialist movement, launched in the pogrom's wake and breaking from Zionism with its relentless search for anywhere on the globe in which to establish a Jewish national home, has recently received attention in several superb works. The impact of visual evidence—the photographs of the dead, of torn Torah scrolls, and of devastated city streets—on knowledge of Kishinev's pogrom is a theme discussed, but no doubt deserving greater attention. A brilliant analysis of Kishinev's impact on the politics of New York City's Lower East Side left-wing Jews can be found in Jonathan Frankel's study *Prophecy and Politics*.[5]

I dedicate this book to the memory of my UCLA teacher Hans Rogger. His scholarship on the Russian right and late imperial Russia's preoccupation with Jews remains crucial. All that has been done on these subjects since his death in 2002, including this book, is built on its shoulders. Hans was a man of rare sensitivity and wisdom, a teacher who treated his students as peers, and a historian who understood how achingly difficult it is to try to tell the truth. I sorely miss him.

Pogrom

Alexandrovskaia Street, 1889.

1

Age of Pogroms

The sheer surprise of the Lindbergh nomination had activated
an atavistic sense of being undefended that had more to do
with Kishinev and the pogroms of 1903 than with New Jersey
thirty-seven years later, and as a consequence, they had forgotten about Roosevelt's appointment to the Supreme Court
of Felix Frankfurter and his selection as Treasury secretary of
Henry Morgenthau, and about the close presidential adviser,
Bernard Baruch.

—PHILIP ROTH, *The Plot Against America*

"Pogrom": The word's origins can be traced to the Russian for
"thunder" or "storm." A dark remnant of the Old World, it
retains the capacity to feel as immediate as yesterday's outrage
on morning services in Jerusalem: "The sight of Jews lying dead
in a Jerusalem synagogue, their prayer-shawls and holy books
drenched in pools of blood, might be drawn from the age of
pogroms in Europe."[1]

When a bird flies into a Lower East Side apartment in Bernard Malamud's 1963 short story "The Jewbird," its first words are, "Gevalt, a pogrom!" Mary McCarthy described the explosive response to Hannah Arendt's *Eichmann in Jerusalem* as a pogrom. In *Annie Hall*, Woody Allen has Alvy Singer insist that his grandmother would never have had time to knit anything like the tie worn by Annie (Diane Keaton), his non-Jewish lover, because "she was too busy being raped by Cossacks." The quip is at once alert to its own crudeness and to its capacity to sum up an astonishingly sparse historical repertoire. Explaining why art impresario Bernard Berenson's family abandoned Vilna (Vilnius today) for Boston in 1865, the author of a recently edited edition of the historian Hugh Trevor-Roper's letters to Berenson writes that it was because they "were fugitives from anti-semitic pogroms"—despite the fact that the first pogrom wave erupted more than fifteen years later and even then, with rare exceptions, far away from Berenson's native city. Irving Berlin recalled how in 1893 in his birthplace in Mogilev Province—"suddenly one day, the Cossacks rampaged in a pogrom . . . they simply burned it to the ground." His family fled, smuggling themselves "creepingly from town to town . . . from sea to shining sea, until finally they reached their star: the Statue of Liberty." Here as elsewhere, pogroms are shorthand for cataclysm, misery in a dark, abandoned place.[2]

For a readily accessible way to comprehend the diverse grab bag of such references, see Franz Kafka's letters in the 1920s to Milena Jesenská; they speak of unease on Prague's streets as a precursor to pogroms. The 1929 Hebron riot, Kristallnacht in 1938, and the anti-Jewish riots in 1941 Baghdad were similarly described. Arthur Koestler, in his novel of the late 1940s, *Thieves in the Night*, compares British Mandate officials in prestate Israel to pogromists: "I am a sincere admirer of Jews," says one of them.

"They are the most admirable salesmen of the world, regardless of whether they sell carpets, Marxism, psychoanalysis, or their own pogromed infants." Pogroms were how Arab attacks against Jews in prestate Israel (and later) were often depicted; curiously enough, this was a source of solace, since such violence could thus be dismissed as artificial—the concoction of manipulative, reactionary Arab authorities.[3]

Pogroms continued to weigh heavily decades later in the deliberations of the Kahan Commission, which was chaired by the president of the Israeli Supreme Court. In those discussions, Israel's behavior in 1982 during the Sabra-Shatila massacre in Lebanon was likened to that of malevolent Russian and Polish authorities during pogroms. In 1993 the New York mayoral candidate Rudolph Giuliani would accuse the city's incumbent mayor, David Dinkins, of the same sins with regard to the Crown Heights riots: "One definition of a pogrom," declared Giuliani, "is where the state doesn't do enough to prevent it." In the sixth season of Showtime's *Homeland*, airing in 2017, the Israeli ambassador to the United States fears an Iranian nuclear bomb and asks pointedly, "Should we go back to the ghettos of Asia and Europe and wait for the next pogrom?"[4]

Sturdily portable, the term "pogrom," like none other in the twentieth century, was believed to capture accurately centuries of Jewish vulnerability, the deep well of Jewish misery. And in stark contrast to the Holocaust, pogroms would never—despite their Russian origins—be tethered to a particular time, place, or dictator. In Malamud's "The Jewbird," once the bird opens its mouth and utters the word "pogrom," the response from those in the Lower East Side apartment is, "It's a talking bird. . . . In Jewish."[5] What *else* would a talking Jewish bird say if it were able to speak?

■

The word's imprint was a by-product of the widespread, ever-escalating anti-Jewish violence in the last years of the Russian empire and the mayhem following the empire's collapse. It was then that *pogrom* entered the world's lexicon as one of the tiny cluster of Russian words—alongside *tsar* or *vodka*—no longer considered foreign. This trend solidified as anti-Jewish attacks criss-crossed Russia amid the 1905–6 constitutional crisis, in which eight hundred were killed (six hundred in Odessa alone). Such massacres were frequently the work of roving bands of Jew-haters, the so-called Black Hundreds, whose commitment to saving Russia from constitutional rule was translated into anti-Jewish brutality. The Yiddish author Lamed Shapiro described a son witnessing his mother's rape: "Wildly disheveled gray hair. . . . Her teeth tightly clamped together and shut. They had thrown her onto the bed, across from me."[6]

Once the empire finally crumbled in 1917, such attacks spiked amid the anarchy, banditry, famine, and ideological fervor of new, raw Bolshevik Russia. The dimensions of this savagery, involving Ukrainians and White Army Poles as well as Bolsheviks, have yet to be comprehensively calculated, since so much of the slaughter was registered only sporadically. Attacks on Jews now reached fever pitch, with Russia's Bolshevik leaders seen by their foes as part of a Jewish conspiracy. It seems clear that no fewer than one hundred thousand Jews were murdered in these offhandedly brutal horrors, and at least that many girls and women raped and countless maimed between 1918 and 1920.[7]

Although pogroms would come to be seen as no less a fixture of the region than impassable winters or promiscuous drunkenness, until the early twentieth century the term was just one of several used for attacks of all sorts without specific linkage to violence against Jews. "Southern storms" would be how the riots of the early 1880s (largely in Russia's southern regions) were spoken about; *besporiaki*, a generic word for "atrocities," was still more commonplace. In the copiously detailed *Correspondence Respecting the Treatment of Jews in Russia*, issued in 1882 by the British Parliament on the massacres of the 1880s, atrocities are spoken of as "serious riots" or "disturbances," with no mention at all of pogroms. (Responsibility for the riots, as described in that document, was placed entirely on the shoulders of Jews because of their allegedly oppressive commercial practices, their control over liquor, their usury, and their habitual radicalism.) When "pogrom" first appeared in newspapers in Europe or the United States—in the early years of the twentieth century—it was typically either defined or placed in italics. Jews were already familiar with it, of course, but it did not yet carry the incomparable burden it would soon take on. In Harold Frederic's fierce exposé *The New Exodus: A Study of Israel in Russia*, published in 1892 and based on articles written by the *New York Times* London correspondent, the word "pogrom" never appears.[8]

This would soon change, something that occurred at the very moment when the wider world first took serious notice of the huge Russian Jewish community, then accounting for half the world's Jewish population. Their migration westward since the 1880s or earlier, their concentration into dense, increasingly squalid urban clusters in New York, London, and elsewhere, their resultant poor hygiene, and their propensity for crime—all these, exaggerated or not, had been noted before, of course. But now, for the first time, the world's attention turned resolutely to Russian Jewry and the discovery that there was no better way to understand the rhythms of that community than through the prism of pogroms. Synagogue prayer in the United States would begin to introduce hymns honoring a pogrom-ridden Russian Jewry, the first best-selling books about it in Western languages would be devoted to pogroms, and plays depicting the effects of such massacres would inundate the Yiddish- and English-language stages as far away as Australia.[9]

True, sympathy gave way in many quarters to mounting concerns in the wake of an unprecedented escalation in immigration, ever-shriller calls for restrictions, literacy tests, or other strategies to stem this deluge. The political radicalism increasingly associated with Jews struck fear or contempt in the hearts of many. This extraordinary visibility, however, was very recent. Until the first years of the twentieth century, Russia's Jews were seen, if at all, in the West as mostly a dark, unfamiliar continent. "We are amazed," wrote the literary historian Benjamin Harshav in 1993 in *Language at a Time of Revolution*, "at how wretched, degenerate, illiterate, or ugly our ancestors looked—only three or four generations ago." *Baedeker* guides of the region as late as the first decade of the twentieth century offered no details regarding Jews in cities like Brody, just beyond Russia's western border, where the vast majority was Jewish, except to say that they were loathed by the gentiles.[10]

Jews were clustered mostly in Russia's western provinces, known in the English-speaking world as the Pale of Settlement and historic Poland, an area that stretched from a few hundred miles west of Moscow to the borders of Germany, Austria-Hungary, and Romania. When they were thought of at all in Russia or abroad, it was mostly in terms of their economic proclivities—petty commerce, the making of cheap clothing, trade in liquor or grains—and their distinctive religious practices, which were considered mostly arcane, sometimes suspect. Their diet, language, and clothing, their secrecy despite their obvious volubility, and their many mysteries—perhaps, above all, their purported capacity to resist liquor's allure—set them apart. They were often thought of as wealthy despite their ubiquitous poverty; they were seen as unnaturally adept at making money while excoriated as unnaturally susceptible to political radicalism. They were loathed for their unwillingness to be absorbed into the fabric of Russian life, though conversion did not necessarily rid them of the taint of Jewish origin. It was often assumed that public figures sympathetic to them had been bribed or otherwise strong-armed. It was commonplace for those so attacked—such as Prime Minister Sergei Witte, and later Rasputin—to be the target of accusations that they were paid off or were engaged in other nefarious activities.[11]

Since the mid-nineteenth century, Jews in large numbers had acquired a formal education, with Russia's cities within the Pale of Settlement and elsewhere packed with university-trained Jewish doctors, lawyers, pharmacists, and notaries. Leon Pinsker, long the head of the Palestinophile movement, based in Odessa, was a beloved doctor and a cholera specialist who was eulogized at his 1891 funeral by more non-Jewish colleagues than by the Jewish nationalists whose organization he ran for nearly a decade. Russian-language books, not those in Yiddish or in Hebrew, were the ones most sought after in the many dozens of small-town libraries set up by Jews in the last decades of the nineteenth century. It was only once Hayyim Nahman Bialik's brilliant Hebrew poem on the Kishinev pogrom, "In the City of Killing," was translated into Russian—by Vladimir Jabotinsky, later the founder of right-wing revisionist Zionism—that it captured a widespread devoted following. Jews then emerged among the masters of Russian prose, with Isaac Babel and so many others beginning illustrious literary careers amid the twilight of imperial Russia.[12]

A startling example of Jewish integration can be seen in the infamous Mendel Beilis affair, in which a Kiev brick-factory manager was jailed despite no credible evidence, tortured, and eventually put on trial in 1913, charged with having killed a Christian boy for Jewish ritual purposes. The prelude to the trial—Beilis was first jailed in 1911—pitted many of the regime's most vocal antisemites (who insisted that the whole endeavor was a farce) against a motley crew of fanatics who failed, in the end, to convict Beilis. The accused himself was absurdly miscast: Largely indifferent to Jewish ritual, he had served without complaint in the Russian army, befriended Russian neighbors who testified on his behalf at the trial, and made good friends of gentile prisoners he met in jail. Once declared not guilty (though the jury insisted that a ritual murder had taken place but not at Beilis's hands), he became something of a local celebrity, his fame so great after his exoneration that tram conductors would as a matter of course call out, "Take number 16 to Beilis."[13]

Nonetheless, even on the cusp of the twentieth century, Jews would continue to be widely viewed as they had been many decades before. Little less resonant than earlier were images comparable to those aired in the privately printed traveler's book by the Englishman John Moore, *A Journey from London to Odessa*. In the summer of 1823, on an unnamed diplomatic mission, Moore kept a record of his trip through East Galicia with its "dirty, busy" towns "full of plunderers"—which was his description of Brody. "On looking over my journal, I find the following memorandum: . . . first litter, Jew, or Devil, fleas, etc. etc." Here and elsewhere: "Their costume, features—movements—all produce a singular effect . . . as I walked out amongst them . . . and observed their grave, yet anxious countenances." Time and again, he was struck by the uncanny energy of these dark figures: "Several lank Jews, in their black gowns . . . flitting about, making divers energetic appeals to me, and jarring with each other—enforcing their arguments by almost frantic gestures." Still, no matter how much money Moore offered his wagon driver, the latter refused to travel on the Sabbath. The wagoner's devotion to family life was no less admirable. His leave-taking outside his "mean habitation" was done without "parade—not acting. The marks of mutual affection were unequivocal."[14] Moore took in synagogue services, which he found hauntingly moving. Still, most Jews were intolerable:

> No sooner had I arrived at [an inn] than a host of Jews entered my apartment, with all sorts of goods for sale. The weather was exceedingly sultry, and the odour of the exhalations from the filthy persons . . . was almost insupportable. I was obliged to call in the aid of the facteur [porter] of my hotel who by persuasions, threats and something approaching to blows succeeded at length in clearing the room.[15]

Against this complex backdrop, pogroms would come to be seen as the most transparent of ways in which to describe the condition of Russian Jewry. Proof of the term's relative obscurity soon before it became commonplace may be seen in a London *Times* column appearing in December 1903. The piece opens by acknowledging that confusion probably exists as to what "pogrom" means, thus requiring a definition that distinguishes pogroms from mere massacres. It is then explained that pogroms come with the following features—these "well-established and characteristic rules."[16] They begin with rumors, hints that Jews soon will be punished with authorities looking the other way. Such rumors will surface a few months before Easter, with anti-Jewish propaganda circulated in taverns or cheap restaurants.

Nearly always stoking the fire are accusations of deplorable Jewish economic practices or their dreadful killing of Christian children for ritual purposes.

Easter arrives amid this ever-toxic atmosphere, in which the smallest mishap can readily precipitate an explosion. This could be a fistfight between a Jewish carousel owner and a customer, which might lead at first to seemingly aimless mischief, perhaps boys tossing stones at Jewish buildings. Police then arrest a few of them but show little initiative to do much more. Now rioters have the signal they have been waiting for, prompting them to roam freely and go on the attack. Jewish houses are broken into, furniture is smashed, belongings are carried away, and plundered streets are strewn with feathers: "The Jews are very great consumers of poultry, and they carefully keep their feathers."[17] Once the authorities finally intervene, only on the morning of the third day, fear of any reprisal has evaporated, and rape and murder are now commonplace. All this, "from the very first pebble thrown by a small boy to the last murder committed, . . . is absolutely under the control of the Government." These details—the fight with the carousel owner, the riot starting with the pelting of rocks by children, the feather-strewn streets, the rumors of ritual murder— were all drawn from newspaper reports of the Kishinev pogrom of 1903. It was this tragedy that, as the *Times* column put it, ushered in the start of pogroms as "a national institution—not a massacre in the ordinary sense of the term."[18]

"Before Kristallnacht there was Kishinev," as the journalist Peter Steinfels observed in 1998 in the *New York Times*. "A finger of God" is how contemporaries would refer to it; "an earthquake," in the words of the Israeli historian Anita Shapira. "Kishinev" almost instantly became shorthand for barbarism, for behavior akin to the worst medieval atrocities.[19]

No Jewish event of the time would be as extensively documented. None in Russian Jewish life would leave a comparable imprint. The young Joseph Hayyim Brenner, the closest counterpart in Hebrew literature to Fyodor Dostoevsky, wrote in a letter of September 1903: "In the world there is certainly news. Kishinev! If we were to stand and scream all our days and our nights, it would not suffice." Kishinev managed to push the Dreyfus Affair to the margins, and it dominated the headlines of American newspapers for weeks. The Jewish press would lead with it for months: "We write and write about Kishinev," opened an editorial in *Forverts* (the *Yiddish Daily Forward*) in early May, "we talk and talk about it."[20]

Moreover, it would become the only significant event embraced by all political sectors of the severely fractured Russian Jewish scene. And yet, like so many politicized lessons, these were as often as not the products of half-truths and untruths, of mythologies morphed into certainties, and of forgeries stitched together in the pogrom's wake. And more than a century later many of these continue still, as we will see, to instruct generations of Jews and others regarding the essential condition of Jewish life in the past and present.

Pogroms would thus enter the lexicon of Jewish life as little less than a contemporary analogue to Egypt's biblical plagues, the dark before the most momentous of modern-day Jewish exoduses. This occurred against the backdrop of the certainty—long suspected and finally buttressed with what now appeared to be incontrovertible proof—of government complicity. The knowledge that Russia's officials fomented these attacks would prove decisive in consolidating long-standing Jewish political inclinations—most pronouncedly the marriage of Jews and the Left. Much else would, to be sure, cement this relationship, including the allure of revolutionary Russia, worldwide depression, and the rise of fascism, but no ingredient proved more formative than the commonplace that Europe's most conservative empire unleashed hoodlums to beat, rape, and kill Jews.

Pogroms would provide the stuffing for lessons as diverse as distrust of conservatism, the urgency of radicalism (eventually liberalism, too), the return to Zion, territorialism, and, arguably, the fight for black civil rights. Kishinev would also be built squarely into the history of prestate Israel's defense forces, and it would inspire the call for assimilation into the democracies of the world so different from autocratic Russia. This was foregrounded most resolutely in Israel Zangwill's much-celebrated 1908 play, *The Melting Pot*, which its Anglo-Jewish author insisted was "the biggest Broadway hit—ever." Its protagonist, a brilliant, tortured violinist unable to rid himself of recollections of Kishinev's brutality, struggles with whether the best response to these demons is the use of a gun or a violin. Choosing the latter at the play's end, he muses, "I must get a new string." Indeed, so must all Jews, as Zangwill's play teaches, with the New World beckoning and Russia forever damned.[21]

Amid a cacophony of outrage, instant relief projects, and protest meetings in more than a dozen countries (with some two hundred such gatherings in the United States), Kishinev's pogrom became a stand-in for evil, a jarring glimpse of what the new century might well hold in store. "I have never in my experience known of a more immediate or a deeper expression of sympathy," President Theodore Roosevelt declared at the time.[22]

Chronology explains some of its resonance, the shock that such "medieval-like butchery"—these terms were repeatedly recycled at the time—had intruded on the dawn of the new century. The explosion in worldwide communications networks—in particular, the proliferation in the United States of the William Randolph Hearst press empire, which embraced Kishinev as a cause célèbre while highlighting it with the lavish use of photography—further contributed toward setting it apart. That all the slaughtered could be captured in a single widely reprinted photograph—with the forty-five shrouded Jewish dead stretched out on the floor of the local Jewish hospital—went a considerable distance toward consolidating this as a tragedy unlike any other.[23]

And then there was the role of ideology: The pogrom occurred at a moment of singular coherence, of overall popularity for Jewish political movements, including the Jewish Socialist Labor Bund, the Zionists, and many others. Kishinev was the rare—perhaps the only—item on the Jewish communal agenda embraced by all. An indication of how strikingly unusual such a consensus was is the Bund's first response: that only poor Jews figured among the pogrom's victims, with the wealthy fleeing the violence by hiding in local hotels or leaving by train for Odessa or Kiev. Crucial to Kishinev's continued impact was Bialik's famous pogrom poem, which emerged as a clarion call for Jewish activists of all stripes, Zionist as well as socialist. It would be built squarely into the repertoire of Jewish self-defense in Russia and was no less an inspiration for Jewish socialists than it would be in Palestine for the Haganah, which even today traces its start to the poem's explosive impact.[24]

Kishinev's impact was felt deeply at the time even in settings where it was left unmentioned. Its influence on the deliberations of the Social Democratic Party's Second Party Congress, held in July and August 1903 in Brussels and London—the meeting that first consolidated Vladimir Lenin's Bolshevism and its commitment to the rule of a centralized party—was decisive, despite the fact that the pogrom was barely touched on. In Kishinev's wake, with the Jewish Socialist Labor Bund all the more intent on being recognized by the party as "the sole representative of the Jewish proletariat," such preoccupations helped Lenin paint it as hopelessly ethnocentric. The charge rendered the Bund in this internationalist setting all but tongue-tied, vigorous in its (ultimately unsuccessful) resistance to Lenin and his allies but hopelessly vulnerable when confronted with such invectives at a moment when Jewish tragedy weighed so heavily. The Bund's exit from the congress provided Lenin, much as he had hoped, with the majority he sought—and with Kishinev's pogrom the dark cloud hanging over the single most formative gathering in the history of Russian Marxism.[25]

■

"Even Hell is preferable," proclaimed Kishinev's Jewish communal leader Jacob Bernstein-Kogan at the Sixth Zionist Congress in Basel in the summer of 1903.[26] This slogan was soon adopted by those supporting the prospect of Jewish settlement in East Africa, an idea proposed by Theodor Herzl and now floated by the British. Elsewhere the insistence by Russian apologists after the massacre that pogroms in the empire's southern region were no more containable than lynching in the American South prodded Jewish radicals in the United States, in particular, to take a much closer look at the persecution of blacks. The confluence of Russian pogroms and antiblack riots would become one of the age's most formative lessons in American Jewish radical circles. An eventual by-product would be the formation in 1909 of the National Association for the Advancement of Colored People (NAACP), which was launched in the New York City apartment of Yiddish-speaking Anna Strunsky and her husband, William Walling, who became the NAACP's first chairman. At much the same time as they were galvanizing support for a national organization to protect African Americans, Strunsky was struggling to complete a manuscript that she would describe in letters to her family as her "Pogrom" book.[27]

A still greater influence than the pogrom itself was the document that would cement Kishinev as a catastrophe unlike all others. This was the letter signed by the Russian minister of the interior, Vyacheslav Konstantinovich Plehve, that surfaced a few weeks after the pogrom. Plehve was known for his antipathy toward Jews, whom he undoubtedly loathed, and his letter, dated just before the pogrom's outbreak, instructed Kishinev's authorities to avoid all use of force once the massacre erupted. Hence the proof that Russia was unsafe for Jews set it apart from all European countries—except, perhaps, for Romania.

This document was deservedly shocking, and yet there is little doubt, as we will see, that it was a forgery written by those—whether Jewish or not—who sincerely believed its sentiments to be true if impossible to substantiate conclusively. No evidence exists that Plehve wrote the letter, and there is considerable evidence that he did not. (Russian conservatives like Plehve shared an intense distrust of Jews—of their economic rapacity, their radicalism, their incorrigible separatism—but had a much deeper fear of unrest on the empire's streets.) Nonetheless, widely believed at the time to be true, even by some close to Plehve, the letter rapidly became the prime bulwark for Jewish distrust of conservatism, the most emphatic of all counterarguments to restriction on Jewish immigration, and the most powerful of all justifications for why Jews must flee Russia or fight to bring its government down.[28]

Oddly, Kishinev's pogrom would come to occupy a roughly comparable prominence for those on the Russian Right. For them it represented a gruesome moment far more harmful to Russians than to Jews and, like so many others, massaged by Jews for their own benefit. Because of such machinations, world opinion would turn against the regime, and moderates inside Russia would abandon it—all because, as the Right saw it, of outright lies set in motion by Jews and their allies in newspapers throughout Europe and the United States. Shocked by this unprecedented outcry, Krushevan, Kishinev's most prominent antisemite, rushed into print (in a newspaper he owned) the first version of what would eventually be called *The Protocols of the Elders of Zion*. Scholars now concur that the text was almost certainly his own handiwork in cooperation with a small clutch of far-right figures close to him, nearly all from Kishinev or nearby. Linguistic fingerprints unique to Bessarabia and adjacent regions are studded throughout the original text, though all of these were excised from the better-known, book-length versions published soon afterward. Much as the pogrom proved to Jews and their supporters that the long, wretched arm of the Russian government was behind it all, *The Protocols* provided no less conclusive proof to antisemites of the limitless power of worldwide Jewry.[29]

■

With its imprint so multifaceted, Kishinev's memory continues to be widely embraced, in contrast to that of tragedies far more murderous that have faded into oblivion, pertinent to few beyond survivors or their relatives. Reviewing in 1923 the first of a projected two-volume work on the pogroms of 1918–20, the Yiddish literary magazine *Bikher-velt* (*Book World*) insisted that the book was all the more welcome since these massacres, so devastating at the time, were then disappearing into the mist of history.[30] In contrast Kishinev stood there on its own, hugging the beginning of a new century, unmoored to the constitutional crisis of 1905–6, and with its many lessons believed to remain relevant—an unforgettable ingredient of Jewish culture and politics.

How is it that an event so resolutely enters into history that it defines the past and how to behave in the future? What we see here is an inverse relationship between the sheer quantity of available information and a veritable mountain of teachable lessons, many of which at best are only sketchily based on the events themselves. Kishinev's pogrom may well be the best known of all moments in the Russian Jewish past and the one most persistently, lavishly misunderstood.

Moreover, despite its vaunted standing in contemporary Jewish memory and elsewhere, it was made of so many moments so random, so circumstantial. Had the early-morning rain—which stopped at around six in the morning on the riot's second day—persisted, the pogrom almost certainly would have ended before the worst of its violence. (Pogroms, like revolutions, occur almost invariably in temperate weather.) Kishinev's location at the most porous edge of the Russian empire—Bessarabia was the easiest of all places from which to smuggle goods or, for that matter, information—meant that the world was informed of the pogrom's atrocities with rare dispatch. Had the same events occurred a few hundred miles to the east, it is unlikely that they would have had a comparable impact; the details would have been reported on fleetingly and peppered with fewer updates, and the tragedy, like others then and later, would have almost certainly been mourned locally without much resonance beyond the town itself.

■

The pogrom revealed Russian Jewry's inner recesses on the front pages of the world's press, distilling a coherent set of beliefs about modernity itself. And much of this was the by-product of half-truths, of poetry read as journalism, and of "facts" passed from generation to generation with little basis in fact. The uncanny longevity of beliefs that tumbled from Kishinev's rubble are crucial to its story; this mix of mythology and countermythology was inspired by a riot in a city barely known of before and rarely spoken about since except as a synonym for devastation.

For example, in the grand, lyrical autobiography of Israel's first president, Chaim Weizmann, *Trial and Error*, published in 1949, he describes how as a student and Zionist activist in Geneva in 1903 he had been so crushed by news of the Kishinev pogrom that he rushed immediately to Gomel (in present-day Belarus), where that September he organized the town's widely lauded Jewish self-defense effort. But in fact it was radicals associated with the Jewish Socialist Labor Bund, with the help of Marxist-Zionists, who organized those efforts. At the time Weizmann was in Geneva, having just returned from Russia. His letters to his fiancée, postmarked Geneva, attest to his whereabouts. Even if Weizmann was not intentionally lying, he told the same story for much of his life. For Weizmann, eventually a towering figure in Russian Jewry, it likely felt quite natural to insert himself into what was the most defining of all contemporary Russian Jewish sagas. He returns time and again in the book to lessons learned from Kishinev—for instance, how to recognize the imprint of mendacious officialdom: "Just before the [1937 Palestinian] riots broke out I had an intimate talk with the [British] High Commissioner. He asked me whether I thought troubles were to be expected. I replied that in Tsarist Russia I knew if the Government did not wish for troubles they never happened."[31]

For Noam Chomsky, too—the distinguished linguist and outspoken anti-Zionist who would have agreed with Weizmann on very little else—Kishinev's lessons are all but identical and no more accurate. In a 2014 National Public Radio interview, he lambasted the Kahan Commission's comparison of the Sabra-Shatila catastrophe to Kishinev's pogrom for its failure to take it far enough: "The Kahan Commission, I think, was really a whitewash. It tried to give as soft as possible an interpretation of what was in fact a horrifying massacre, actually one that should resonate with people . . . who are familiar with Jewish history. It was almost a replica of the Kishinev pogrom of pre–First World War Russia, one of the worst atrocities in Israeli memory. . . . The tsar's army had surrounded this town and allowed for people within it to rampage, killing Jews for three days. . . . That's . . . pretty much what happened in Sabra-Shatilla."[32]

Yet, contrary to Chomsky's account, the army never encircled the city protecting rioters. For him, much like for Weizmann, the pogrom's details were part and parcel of common knowledge, an immediate reference point for the widest range of teachable moments.

Ari Shavit's 2013 best-seller, *My Promised Land: The Triumph and Tragedy of Israel,* places no less than the entire weight of the Zionist enterprise on the shoulders of the Kishinev pogrom, relating it to the story of the expulsion of the Arabs of Lydda (later Lod), the book's explosive epicenter. He tells of a Lydda that flourished in the Mandate period partly, as he sees it, because it was the site of a Jewish school established for the care of Kishinev pogrom orphans, trained there to become farmers. Once it failed, the school's buildings were occupied by a full-throated humanistic endeavor launched by a liberal Berlin Jew with a worldview shaped by Martin Buber and the anarchist Gustav Landauer. (The book's critics insist that the school was actually located in nearby Beit Shemesh, not Lydda.) A generation of displaced German Jewish youth was trained there, schooled in the need for peaceful coexistence with Arabs. At odd hours the students participated in military training as well.[33]

Then, with the onset of the Arab-Israeli War in 1948, those same students figured among the soldiers who, in July, expelled the nineteen thousand Lydda Arabs, who were forced to walk in suffocating heat, with not a few infants and elderly dying on the long road to the Jordanian border. Shavit writes: "Lydda is our black box. In it lies the dark secret of Zionism. The truth is that Zionism could bear Lydda."[34] Still, he feels contempt for "those bleeding-heart Israeli liberals . . . who condemn what they did in Lydda but enjoy the fruits of their deeds." Their politics is all the more absurd "[b]ecause I know that if it wasn't for [Lydda] the State of Israel would not have been born. If it wasn't for them, I would not have been born."[35] In his view the saga is all the more poignant because at its heart is Kishinev's pogrom:

> Forty-five years after it came into the Lydda Valley in the name of the Kishinev pogrom, Zionism instigated a human catastrophe in the Lydda Valley. Forty-five years after Zionism came into the valley in the name of the homeless, it sent out of the Lydda Valley a column of the homeless. In the heavy heat, through the haze, through the dry brown fields, I see the column marching east. So many years have passed, and yet the column is still marching east. For columns like the columns of Lydda never stop marching.[36]

Alexander Solzhenitsyn's late-life historical excursion into Russian Jewish history, *Dvesti let vmesti* (*Two Hundred Years Together*), devotes almost an entire chapter to Kishinev's deleterious impact—on Russians, not Jews. Solzhenitsyn's argument is that the blanket distrust it created of Russia in the international community and among Russia's own political moderates and intelligentsia rendered the regime incapable of withstanding the eventual Bolshevik onslaught. Much like Shavit, who draws a straight line from Kishinev to Lydda, Solzhenitsyn situates Kishinev no less emphatically as a station on the road to Bolshevism.[37]

The pogrom's durability, its ready slippage into today's politics, is also made explicit in Benjamin Netanyahu's frequent comparisons of the Jews of Israel and the massacred of Kishinev. In response to events as varied as the 2012 Toulouse school massacre and the murder of three Israeli teenagers in the West Bank (which was the prelude to the 2014 Gaza war), the Israeli prime minister has referenced Bialik's Kishinev poetry, long a mainstay of Israel's school curriculum. Always sidelining in these statements the poet's warnings of the corruptive impact of violence on all those singed by it, Netanyahu has cherry-picked from this work its apparent calls for reprisal. At the Toulouse memorial service, citing Bialik's "On the Slaughter"—"The vengeance for a small child's blood / Satan himself never dreamed"—he chose to overlook the words that come just before: "And cursed be he who cries: vengeance."[38]

Finally, comparable to the importance placed on the pogrom in Israel—while drastically different in its details—is its place in the raw, nascent politics of Transdniestria, or the Pridnestrovian Moldavian Republic, a separatist enclave with a population of five hundred thousand at Moldova's eastern edge. With its spotlessly clean streets (a sharp contrast to the hurly-burly and cracked sidewalks of today's Chişinău), sparse markets, and reigning ideology made of old-style Communism and Russian ethnic nationalism, Transdniestria has held on since the early 1990s with its economy in the hands of a clutch of megabillionaires.

History weighs heavily on this place, readily dismissed as one of the world's last Soviet-style anachronisms. In its effort to claim legitimacy, it holds high among its heroes Krushevan, whose stalwart Russian allegiance, prominence as a Moldavian intellectual, and commitment to what admirers call his "Christian socialism" offer a powerful alternative to the embrace of Western liberal globalism. So argues Transdniestria's now assistant foreign minister, Igor Petrovich Shornikov—son of one of Moldova's leading pro-Russian activists—who in 2011 completed the first sustained study of Krushevan's sociopolitical thought in more than a century.[39]

Written as a doctoral dissertation at the Shevchenko Transnistria State University, Shornikov's Russian-language study depicts a Krushevan who had nothing to do with the pogrom or the writing of *The Protocols*. Jews themselves, in the employ of the Russian secret police—which they assiduously infiltrated—produced the document that Krushevan was somehow persuaded to publish. The pogrom itself, Shornikov argues, was a minor affair blown out of all proportion by Jews who managed to claim far more money for their property than it was worth; the massacre was entirely justified by their economic stranglehold, their outsize political radicalism, and the understandable hatred of those oppressed by them.

All these claims are recycled from the arsenal of Russian conservative and right-wing accounts. Shornikov's insistence that it was the rapacity and the brashness of Kishinev's Jews that caused the pogrom cleanses Krushevan—and still more important, all Moldavians—of culpability. As portrayed by this young leader of a Russian-dominated rump state in one of Europe's most explosive corners, the Kishinev pogrom was a justified, even righteous exercise in self-defense. This is a tale long misconstrued—much like, indeed, the Pridnestrovian Moldavian Republic itself. Krushevan, long excoriated as a rabble-rouser, is thoroughly rehabilitated as a patriot, a lover of all things Russian—which, as Shornikov argues, is consistent with the staunchest Moldavian convictions. Krushe-van's anticapitalism (interlinked with a relentless hatred of Jews), his insistence on liberalism's incapacity to challenge either cultural decadence or economic oppression, and perhaps above all his ability to embrace a simultaneous allegiance to both Bessarabia and Russia have managed to transmute the long-forgotten reactionary into a bracingly contemporary influence.

■

Pogrom: Kishinev and the Tilt of History explores how history is made and remade, what is retained and elided, and why. I examine how one particular moment managed to so chisel itself onto contemporary Jewish history and beyond that it held meaning even for those who never heard of the town, know nothing of its details, and nonetheless draw lessons from it. It was a moment that cast a shadow so deep, wide, and variegated as to leave its imprint on Jews, on Jew-haters, and on wounds licked ever since. Studying Kishinev provides the opportunity to cut across standard barriers separating Russian and Jewish, European, Palestinian Jewish, and American Jewish history and to wade through the pogrom's residue in many different, oddly mismatched corners. Its gruesome stories would frequently outdistance the sufficiently gruesome events themselves. It took weeks for the press to disprove, for example, the widely reported rumor that the bellies of pregnant women had been cut open and stuffed with chicken feathers.[40]

From the start of my research for this work, it intrigued me that Kishinev's violence—the worst of it lasting some three to four hours in a cluster of intersecting streets—would come to epitomize this community to a far greater extent than any other moment in Russian Jewish life. These alleyways, especially Aziatskaia, or Asia Street, immortalized now in countless newspaper reports, would become the best known of all Russian Jewish locales, its humble dwellings soon the most telling of metaphors for the impoverishment and grim tenuousness of Jewish life under the tsars. The impact of these impressions, reinforced over the course of the past century, on Jewish perceptions of the world, the designs of gentiles, the exercise of Jewish power, and the immorality of what Netanyahu has derisively called "turning the other cheek" are among the questions that have kept me fixed on this moment and its resilience.[41]

This, then, is a microhistory as well as an international history of an event that was surely vile but less murderous and less catastrophic than so many others occurring soon afterward— that yet would overshadow nearly all. "The time and place are the only things I am certain of. . . . Beyond that is the haze of history and pain"; this is how Aleksandar Hemon begins his novel *The Lazarus Project*, built around a bizarre, widely reported 1908 incident in which nineteen-year-old Lazarus Averbuch was shot to death in the home of Chicago's police chief. Why Averbuch came to the house—he had never before met the policeman— and whether or not he actually threatened the chief's life, as was reported, remains unclear, but Averbuch's behavior was irrevocably linked at the time to his having been a witness to the Kishinev pogrom. Hemon writes: "Lazarus came to Chicago as a refugee, a pogrom survivor. He must have seen horrible things: he may have snapped. . . . He was fourteen in 1903, at the time of the pogrom. Did he remember it in Chicago? Was he a survivor who resurrected in America? Did he have nightmares about it?"[42]

My book, too, explores history's nightmares. And much like the Averbuch tale, it is a story of the uneasy interplay of truth and fiction—of fiction so unreservedly believed that it would become more potent than most truths. I revisit it in an effort to sort through it so as to better understand the tragedy itself

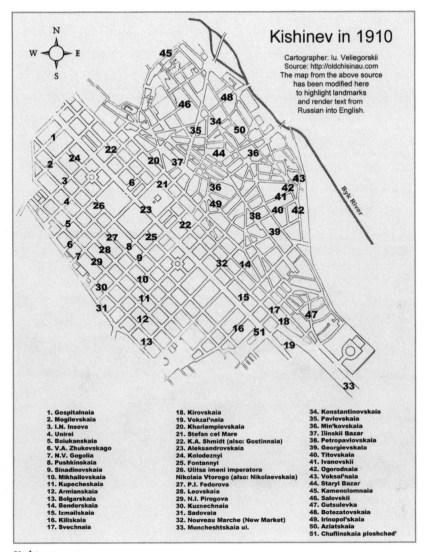

Kishinev map.

and what was made of it over the course of more than a century. Whether cited explicitly or not, the Kishinev pogrom continues to provide a well-thumbed, coherent road map, one that retains the imprimatur of history. Such accounts are bolstered by the use of evidence recalled endlessly, but such evidence is at best imperfect and—at its worst—not evidence at all.

Photograph of Lower Kishinev in the 1880s.

▪ 2 ▪

Town and Countryside

Most legends spring from facts.

—A. J. P. Taylor, introduction to
John Reed, *Ten Days That Shook the World*

Humdrum, rusticated, distant from anything world-important: Kishinev in the first years of the twentieth century—despite its handsome city center, a cluster of good schools, and a

healthy commercial life as Bessarabia's main agricultural depot—
continued to be thought of beyond its immediate region as the
dusty spot the young Alexander Pushkin had so savaged in the
early 1820s. Compelled to live there because of political indiscre-
tions, he captured it dourly:

> *Cursed town of Kishinev!*
> *My tongue will tire itself in abuse of you,*
> *Someday, of course, the sinful roofs*
> *Of your dirty houses*
> *Will be struck by thunder,*
> *And—I will not find a trace of you!*
> *They will fall and perish in flames,*
> *Both Varfolomey's motley house*
> *And the filthy Jewish booths.*[1]

After repeated pleading Pushkin was permitted to decamp to
Odessa, less than a hundred miles to the east. Comparisons
between the two cities were thus inevitable, nearly always to
Kishinev's detriment. Never could it match Odessa's inescap-
able vitality—nor, certainly, the storied pedigree of Kiev, some
three hundred miles away—with Odessa architects designing
Kishinev's best streets, the trees planted on them inspired by
Odessa's acacia-shaded boulevards, and nearly all of its banks
branches of Odessa firms. All this strengthened the belief that
Kishinev's urban qualities were only superficial and that it was
little more than a satellite of the larger, better, far more colorful Black Sea port. After all, at the century's turn, farms still
existed just around the corner from Kishinev's fancier streets.
Whereas Odessa's admirers, the Francophiles especially, liked to
compare their city—with a whimsical piety—to Paris, Kishinev's

Map of region showing proximity of Kishinev and Odessa.

reference point was Odessa, to which it seemed at best a third cousin. When Kishinev's longtime mayor, Karl Schmidt, spoke of his city's goals, the grandest yet most unattainable of all was to surpass Odessa.[2]

If Kishinev was susceptible to mythmaking, it was because so few facts were known about it. In contrast to Odessa, with its host of associations (Odessa's famously beautiful women were described in Yiddish, for instance, as "Odessa moons"), Kishinev was a blank slate. So much so that, in May 1903, the *New York Times* ran an article whose stated goal was to fill this gap: "So great has been the intent of the public in the recent massacre in Kishineff that little or no attention has been given to the physical characteristics of the place." The newspaper provided bits and pieces of institutional and cultural data, a portrait of a really rather inviting place—the reporter seemed surprised by what he had found—blessed with benign weather and surrounded by pleasant topography. If the city was similar to anywhere, the *Times* suggested that the most reliable comparison was sunny, temperate Southern California.[3]

The reporter's pleasant surprise was, of course, a by-product of the fact that Kishinev was now widely known as among the world's most hellish places. Still, even before then it had been undervalued. This was primarily because of its inaccessibility (there was not even a direct train route linking it to its sister city, Odessa, and the region's roads were among the worst in the empire), the rapidity of its very recent growth from an overgrown village into the empire's fifth most populous city (its population in 1903 was larger than Kiev's), and the sense, by now intractable, it seemed, that it was rather more akin to the California city of Fresno, sprawling perhaps, but a dusty, dull, cow town.

By the time the *New York Times* piece appeared, Kishinev was among the best known—and most infamous—of the world's cities, a place where, much like in the darkened scenes of a Frankenstein film, mobs with pitchforks and knives roamed its streets searching for victims. And the remains of those two days would soon define not only Kishinev but—for many both inside Russia and beyond it—the larger contours of Jewish life in Russia's Pale of Settlement.

■

Bessarabia came late to the Russian empire, with its eastern edge acquired from the Ottoman Empire in 1812, its southern region lost after the Crimean War in 1856, and Russian rule consolidated over the region wrested from Romania in 1878. It was a

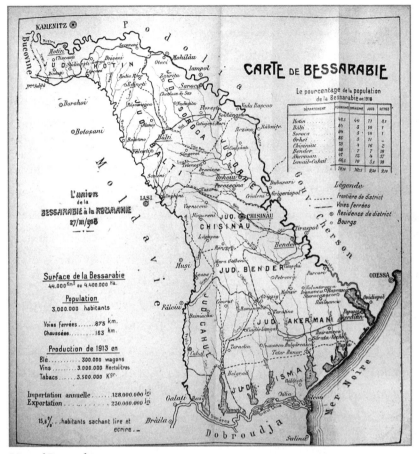

Map of Bessarabia.

mutt of sorts, little more than a sliver of land, less than six hundred miles long from its northern point on the Austro-Hungarian border to its southeastern tip nudging the Black Sea. Nearly all of it was landlocked, with no substantial port and with Kishinev at its geographic center.[4]

Bessarabia was the region with the highest infant mortality and illiteracy rates (barely 39 percent were literate at the turn of the century) in the empire, the fewest doctors, and the fewest paved roads—in 1914, a total of 144 miles. Yet it was blessed with balmy weather and known for the casualness of its mores, a lethargic peasantry, and a highly diverse mix of ethnic and religious groups—Russians, Germans, Swiss, Cossacks, Turks, Bulgarian-speakers, Serbs, and Old Believers (the Russian Orthodox sect that refused to accept seventeenth-century liturgical changes) as well as Moldavians and Jews. All these groups were said to live largely segregated but also amicably peaceful lives, with less-encumbered relations between them than elsewhere. A mark of the region's diversity, and the paucity of assimilatory pressure, was the persistence of Swiss wineries in Bessarabia's south and the German colonies at its north (named for Leipzig and Wittenberg), which remained largely ethnic enclaves even generations after their founding.[5]

On the surface Bessarabia seemed quite beautifully sylvan, a land of rolling hills and pastures full of grazing sheep, wooded in its north, with fewer trees in the south. Forests in northern parts consisted of beech, oak, and ash trees that provided the building materials for much of the construction in southern Russia. The Carpathian Mountains lay just across the Austro-Hungarian border, shielding Bessarabia from cold winter winds. Its weather in spring and summer was warm, often parched. (Just south of Kishinev, summer temperatures sometimes rose as high as 104 degrees Fahrenheit.) It was bounded on its east by Ukraine and the Dniester River, with the Prut and Danube Rivers on its western border with Romania. Its roads, especially those on its western rim, were poorly maintained; authorities likely resisted improvements to them and the railway system—despite the premium placed on the region's agricultural exports—out of the constant fear of a Romanian invasion.[6]

Such fears were not fanciful. Romania remained irate at having had to cede western Bessarabia after the Russo-Turkish War in 1878. Russia's hold on Bessarabia felt tenuous: Carved out only since 1812 by conquest, the countryside was overwhelmingly Moldavian, where the language was all but identical to Romanian. The Russianness of the region's towns felt almost fraudulent, like its desire to eclipse Odessa. Most of the people listed in its census reports as Russians in its officially designated urban centers (often little more than villages) were Jews, whose population had soared in the late nineteenth century, with newcomers arriving mostly from the nearby Black Sea region in search of economic opportunity. Provincial administration tended to be haphazard here; the northern boundary with Austro-Hungary was known to be especially porous, with smuggling all but openly conducted thanks to the ubiquity of bribery. Salaries of minor officials were astonishingly low, bribery barely frowned upon, and smuggling mostly in the hands of Jews.[7]

Despite being overwhelmingly poor, Bessarabia also happened to be extremely fertile—perhaps Russia's most potentially lucrative agricultural region. Its southern region had some of Russia's most prized pastureland, and hides were among its most lucrative exports. Staple crops included maize (more than 30 percent of Bessarabia's agricultural yield in 1910), spring wheat, barley, and grapes; more than 164,000 acres of vines crisscrossed the region. Large quantities of dried fruit and fish were also exported. Gardening was universal, with the province's large number of monasteries boasting particularly opulent gardens full of fruit trees. Industry was sparse; factories were mostly of modest size—nearly all with no more than thirty or forty employees—producing agricultural machinery as well as flour mills and sawmills. Bessarabia was also known for its skilled carpet makers who used rare dyes, the by-product of vegetable matter. However, no more than three thousand workers there made their living from industrial work at the turn of the twentieth century.[8]

Commerce was concentrated almost entirely in the disposal of agricultural goods—grains, flour, wine, brandy, and timber—with Jews owning most of these businesses. Jews, in fact, dominated nearly all its towns—Kishinev, Akkerman, Bendery—and the countryside, too, where they bought and sold much of Bessarabia's grains, manure, and wine. Thirty-two million gallons of wine were sold there at the turn of the century, with as much as half of it shipped to Odessa or Kiev. Bulgarian and German colonies bred livestock, pigs, and sheep; fishing was crucial to the economy of Bessarabia's seacoast and lagoons.[9]

Still, except for Kishinev, much of the region felt immutable, with little having changed since the mid-nineteenth century, when Kishinev, too, was no more than a ramshackle, haphazard cluster of villages. Bessarabia's population would double between the 1860s and the turn of the century, increasing to 2.4 million—a growth of six hundred thousand in the span of just four decades. Internal commerce languished because the bulk of the population was almost too poor to buy anything. In comparison with other parts of the tsarist empire, travel was cumbersome: Most of Bessarabia's roads were made of sand and thus impassable in winter. With a seventy-mile coastline intersected by waterways, Bessarabia had no real port, and Odessa dominated its commercial life as the region's seaport.[10]

Yet by the early twentieth century, Kishinev had grown into a prosperous commercial entrepôt, its vibrancy the product of the region's agricultural bounty, a lively black market, and a superb mayor who bludgeoned local businessmen to contribute to the city's improvement—he made them share, for instance, in the cost of the beautiful trees that continue to shade its main street to this day. Nevertheless, orchards stretched well into the edge of town, chickens could be seen walking its streets, and there was still no direct rail service between Kishinev and Kiev or Odessa; passengers had to change trains en route. Rafts continued to serve throughout the province as an indispensable mode of commercial transport, because barely 550 miles of train track—a paltry number and all single-track—covered its full expanse.[11]

Waterways would dominate the commerce of the region well into the first years of the twentieth century. River barges, rafts, ships, and boats—many the kind seen on the Mississippi in the early nineteenth century—transported Bessarabia's timber, wool and lambskins, sacks of wheat, barley, oats, corn, dried plums, honey, garden fruits, wine barrels, and nuts, mostly to Odessa. Shlomo Hillels, born in Soroki (some eighty-five miles north of Kishinev) in 1873, lovingly describes in his 1930 Hebrew novel *Har ha-keramim* (The Mountain of Vineyards) the home of his youth. He evokes a vast, bountiful land of burned wine (a local delicacy), a milieu crisscrossed by water, the rhythms of its economic life the by-product of sharply disparate seasons, huge casseroles, dockworkers dancing at night on sacks of wheat stacked on riverboats, harmonica music, and Gypsies.[12]

These goods were amassed in the spring by Jewish traders, each of whom had their own peasants to whom they had given money the previous winter as a down payment on their produce or hides. By the fall barns were full of provisions, ready for the heavy rains of winter, when roads became impassable and largely Jewish-owned wine and liquor bars were packed with porters, pimps, and seasonally employed artisans. Jews in Hillels's rather romanticized depiction were simple folk, with the social life of its men revolving around Sabbath afternoons in an empty lot in the town center, where they discussed the price of animals and

Jewish communal concerns, conversations that started peacefully and that slid, as often as not, into shouting and curses.[13]

■

"A dark-skinned race of middle height" is how a British Foreign Office memo in 1920 described Moldavians, who made up the bulk of Bessarabia's agrarian population. With increased migration in the region, their proportional size declined; census takers in 1897 tallied them at 48 percent, which may have been an underestimate. The countryside remained overwhelmingly Moldavian, though towns were packed with Jews who likely seemed more populous than their numbers alone might suggest because so many streets were lined with stores sporting Yiddish signage, and with Jews concentrated mostly in or near city centers. Unlike the many other Bessarabian ethnic groups that clustered in specific regions, Jews were found in large numbers throughout the province. In general the densest concentration of Moldavians was in the north, with Germans and Swiss in agricultural colonies near Akkerman, and Greeks in the Izmail region (now in Ukraine).[14]

Russian discomfort with the province's widely disparate ethnic mix was a matter of concern for decades. It was exacerbated in the late 1870s with the acquisition of southwest Bessarabia by Russia, a move that fanned apprehensions of Romanian meddling. Mandatory instruction in the Russian language was then introduced in the region's mostly church-sponsored schools, and eventually nearly every church school was shut. Prayer in Moldavian was outlawed in the 1870s, though this was impossible to enforce.[15]

Despite efforts at leveling differences, Bessarabia remained stalwart, a land of largely unassimilated groups. In 1897 no more than 4 percent of Moldavian women and 17 percent of men in the region were literate, as compared with 81 percent of German women and 83 percent of men there; literacy rates for Jews were 41 percent for women, 65 percent for men. Such vast differences, coupled with the fear of Romanian nationalism that trumpeted a reunited Bessarabia, nurtured an increasingly influential and xenophobic Russian nationalism. Several of its leading figures hailed from Moldavian, Serbian, or Polish backgrounds, often from the ranks of lesser or impoverished nobility who were all the more preoccupied with the prospect of social or economic slippage. Bessarabia was fertile ground for the recruitment of—often mutually recriminatory—far-right groups known as Black Hundreds. This inchoate conglomeration of the empire's most extreme and often most unprincipled defenders was feared by conservatives and leftists alike for their calls for violence against the empire's enemies. Here at Russia's edge, their belief in the insidious designs of Romanians, Austrians, Moldavians, and above all Jews provided an especially explosive focal point for mounting anxieties.[16]

Thus a cauldron of pressures simmered beneath the surface in this largely slow-paced wedge of Russia, with tensions between town and countryside, Romania's historic claims and the reality of Russian hegemony, and the overwhelmingly agrarian norms of a long-backward, fertile region and the increasingly vigorous pull of urban life. Turks and Romanians continued to see the area as historically their own, and Austria-Hungary butted up against its sparingly policed northern rim. Moldavians dominated much of the countryside, with Jews crowded ever more densely into its towns, especially Kishinev. By the turn of the twentieth century, the city's population was well over one-third Jewish—indeed, according to some polls, as high as 47 percent. The city had no particular Jewish neighborhood: Jews were concentrated closest to its largest markets as well as in large numbers in a neighborhood in Lower Kishinev near the river Byk, with the largest of Kishinev's synagogues a few miles away. Except for a few residential strips that housed almost exclusively Moldavians or poor Russians, Jews could be found throughout the city. Long having been viewed as a somnolent Turkish-like town, Kishinev was in the midst of rapid if also perhaps haphazard change, welcomed by some and loathed by others. The city's ever-expanding Jewish community was—as was true elsewhere, too—the most significant sign of these tumultuous changes.[17]

■

To understand the social forces that were converging to make Kishinev a tinderbox of sorts, one must delve deeper into its past. "A small market-town of slight importance," is how one writer described Kishinev, then known as Chişinău, in 1717, in one of the few, fleeting references to the place before the nineteenth century. Evidence of the city's origin is vague; the first mention of it gives a slightly different location in the early fifteenth century. Burned down by Russians during an invasion in 1748, it was rebuilt on land owned by a monastery. Well into the first decades of the nineteenth century, Kishinev remained under the control of a small group of noble families and one large, highly influential monastery. In a line drawing dating back to the century's start, it is pictured as clustered around narrow streets, numerous churches, and tiny shops, with a particularly generous sprinkling of church properties. Its streets bordered on fields of wild asparagus, Indian corn, and very large cucumbers. In the 1830s and 1840s, 20 percent of the city's inhabitants continued to make their living from agriculture or cattle.[18]

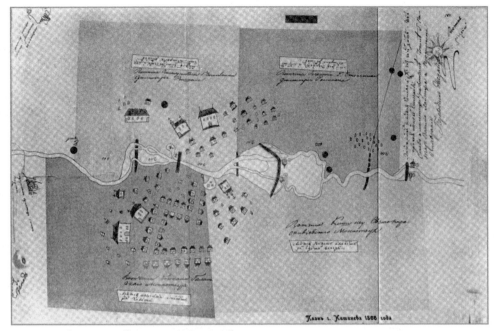

Early-nineteenth-century map of Kishinev.

From the outset, religious influences held sway in Kishinev; the church viewed the town as something of a parsonage. Soon after Russia's conquest in 1812, the patriarch of Jerusalem agreed to transfer ownership of the town and its surrounding villages from the control of local monasteries to the Russian emperor. The region's Russian metropolitan established his offices here, with a network of schools under his control that remained until late in the century the area's major source of primary school education. Already by the late eighteenth century, Kishinev boasted a seminary, and in 1818 the church established the city's first printing press, producing mostly educational materials for the area's Moldavian-language religious schools. Kishinev's religious seminary would continue to exert an overwhelming influence into the next century, with an impact well beyond the strictly religious sphere.[19]

Photograph of Lower Kishinev in the 1880s.

For decades, Kishinev remained a small town: built on a cluster of low hills, its growth would be sporadic, with much of its housing little more than patched-together huts that expanded over the years no less randomly. By 1812, according to varying accounts, between 7,000 and 12,000 people lived here, with some 2,100 houses and 448 stores. Already it had a glimmer, perhaps not much more, of urban amenities. Pushkin settled at first in a handsome if spare two-room cottage at the southern tip of Old Town; there he found decent if unexceptional restaurants, a society of convivial officers, moneyed civilians, and attractive mistresses.[20]

Built no more than a mile from the river Byk, Kishinev's city center would be dominated from the beginning by a neighborhood known as Alexandrov, itself dominated by Alexandrovskaia Street to the south of Lower Kishinev. Just beyond it, indeed around the corner, was a labyrinth of narrow, winding paths ris-

House dating to the early nineteenth century in Lower Kishinev. Photograph taken by author, September 2016.

ing and sloping along a hillside. There numerous small, multi-family houses were built around courtyards, often with stores or workshops and sometimes also synagogues tucked into the same buildings. It was an area muddy in the spring and dusty in the summer, with few trees or open spaces and none of the grand parks that dominated the center just a few blocks away. This "old town," with its "narrow, crooked streets, dirty bazaars, low shops, and small houses with tiled roofs . . . with many gardens planted with Lombardy poplars and white acacias," as Pushkin described it, looked colorful only to those from elsewhere. It was already an eyesore in the first years of the nineteenth century.[21]

Many of the city's poorest Jews lived, side by side with others, in this area, some in buildings dating back to the late eighteenth century, much of it still a gully of Ottoman-era ruins. Sewerage, street paving, and electricity were limited to the city's better areas, introduced even there only in the early twentieth century. Entering Old Town, or Lower Kishinev, required descending for blocks in the direction of the river Byk, which was little more than a marshy extension of the Dniester and a noisome stream for much of the year. Into the early twentieth century Kishinev (particularly in this neighborhood), with its large concentration of seasonal workers, most of them peasants seeking winter employment, retained the feel of a border town. The city's extremes of wealth and poverty were stark even by tsarist standards—hovels patched together so poorly that the mildest storm seemed capable of blowing them away existed around the corner from the grandest boulevards. And yet its enterprising mayor, Karl Schmidt, who in 1903 had been in office for twenty-five years, insisted that, if the city continued on its commercially vigorous course, it could soon overtake in importance its rival—and perpetual source of inspiration—Odessa.[22]

Photograph of a Kishinev street in the 1880s.

Its economic growth, despite the city's demographic surge in the second half of the nineteenth century, was agonizingly slow. Although its population would be larger than Kiev's—nearly 110,000 at the start of the twentieth century, the empire's fifth-largest city—Kishinev's infrastructure lagged far behind. Electric trams, introduced in Kiev in 1892, came to Kishinev only in 1913. A decision to launch a Kishinev electric utility was made in 1889, but it took until 1907 to start construction and two more years to put it into operation; Bessarabia's stultifying blend of lethargy and graft continued to flourish amid its quickening economy. The water supply remained inadequate though the Dniester was barely twenty-five miles to the east. Medical conditions, especially outside Kishinev, were among the worst in Russia: Only six doctors and twenty-five medical assistants serviced the entire Kishinev district in 1914, and nearly two-thirds of infants born at the time in Bessarabia died at birth.[23]

Alexandrovskaia Street, 1889.

Alongside all this gross inefficiency and civic indifference were the city's fine schools, a splendid ethnographic museum, opened in 1874, beautiful public parks, and lovely areas just south of Alexandrovskaia Street boasting rows of stunning homes. Bands regularly played in its largest park on Sundays, and reports from the 1903 pogrom noted that on the riot's first day, a Sunday, the sound of music could be heard wafting from the park as nearby shops were ransacked. "Rather pretty place," observed Michael Davitt, clearly surprised at this, in notes he took after his arrival in the city. "One or two very handsome boulevards planted with trees and many fine buildings built of a bright yellow stone. Streets wide & at right angles—like an American city. Pavement rough. Three or four small parks newly planted. A very handsomely built gymnasium for boys & one adjacent for girls."[24]

Despite its new trolley-car system, Kishinev was a place where nearly everyone walked, for it took about half an hour, less if one walked briskly, from the wide streets so admired by Davitt to the town's wretched northern rim on the banks of the Byk. Nearly the whole city was unpaved and pitch-dark at night; electricity serviced only its wealthier neighborhoods, which were by and large unscathed in the pogrom. Rioters had to trudge through mostly darkened streets on the massacre's first night—by its second the riot was almost completely quashed—in their quest for liquor, plunder, and women and girls.

Little known by even knowledgeable Russians, Kishinev did have a reputation—when it was noticed at all—of moral laxity, of a casualness with which strictures that inhibited elsewhere were blithely overlooked. Civility's constraints weighed less heavily here even in comparison with freewheeling Odessa. Governor General R. S. von Raaben, the city's chief administrator at the time of the pogrom, openly entertained guests side by side with a mistress registered as a prostitute. Smuggling was known to be more commonplace there than elsewhere, with bribery all but normalized. For this reason Kishinev was selected for the printing of the Social Democratic *Iskra* (Spark) the empire's most politically radical mouthpiece—the only place in European Russia where it was ever printed—for about a year, with the knowledge that there it could be safely printed and distributed.

Civility's constraints—like those of the wider world—weighed less heavily in this backwater. Set fees were allotted, essentially, to the various categories of graft: For example, the cost of operating as a prostitute without interference was one ruble per week.[25]

■

Why did the pogrom erupt here? According to a memo forwarded by Kishinev's Jewish communal leaders to Raaben soon after the attack, the reasons had nothing to do with long-standing enmity. The region's gentiles were "quiet and peaceful," the local economy healthy, and never in the past had an economic slump precipitated anti-Jewish disturbances. The document asserts that "the rich and fertile land of Bessarabia furnishes a certain existence to all kinds of labor," and highlights that there was little evidence beforehand of ferocious local Jewish hatred. (It notes how the city had barely been touched in the pogrom wave of 1881–82, following the assassination of Tsar Alexander II, despite eruptions barely more than a few dozen miles away.)

At the same time Mayor Schmidt spoke with what appeared to be true warmth of the role of Jews in the city's economic life, insisting that without them Kishinev and indeed Bessarabia's countryside would be economically bereft. The only new, toxic ingredient in this otherwise benign mix was, as the Jewish report argued, Pavel Krushevan's newspaper, *Bessarabets*. Purchasing it cheap—Krushevan spent much of his life desperately short of cash—he quickly turned it into one of the empire's most outspokenly anti-Jewish periodicals.[26]

Seen from Krushevan's vantage point, Kishinev had become a powder keg, a city fed up with Jewish exploitation and ready to explode. The same new economic trends that Schmidt so extolled terrified those like Krushevan, who deplored how the region was being destroyed, overtaken by the cacophonous savagery of Jews. He made a powerful case for protecting Bessarabia from the disruptions of the contemporary marketplace in 1903 in a lavishly illustrated oversize book—the first of its kind—celebrated in a letter of praise from Tsar Nicholas II himself, signed by the imperial clerk. The volume was a romantic evocation of Bessarabia's fecund fields, flowing hills, and attractive peasants; city life was portrayed as something of an afterthought, a presence to be noted but quickly passed over. Its portrait of Kishinev highlighted the handsome city center while also describing its marketplaces as being threatened by raven-like images—dark, alien,

Market Jews photograph in Krushevan's 1903 Bessarabia guide.

eerily thin—of Jews, their faces obscure, their designs on unsuspecting locals anything but clear.[27]

Bessarabia, not surprisingly, had the reputation of a place where it was easy to make money, where Moldavian peasants were more readily manipulated, more innocent, and known for their geniality and a tendency to accommodate. These qualities impressed even visitors to Kishinev's prisons, who found inmates—including those jailed for vile crimes during the pogrom—eager to share confidences and not infrequently oblivious, or so they claimed, as to why they were being held. This interplay between the reputed innocence of the local Moldavians and the cleverness of Jews may have exacerbated feelings here—but in ways that remain indeterminable.

The claim that day-to-day relations were amicable is likely on target; the insistence that peasants felt they were being exploited may well have been accurate too. Jewish exploitation of locals was often decried, and even those sympathetic to Jews acknowledged that there were some who engaged in particularly aggressive economic practices, leaving peasants with smaller profits than they might otherwise have earned. A steep fall in agricultural prices in the spring of 1903 also meant that there was less money to go around. Yet there is no evidence that Jews exploited the innocence or laziness of Bessarabia's peasants more than others did, and without the propaganda disseminated by Krushevan and those close to him in his newspaper in the months before the pogrom's outbreak, it is unlikely that Jews would have been the target for local frustration. Nonetheless local ideologues—including some of the most formidable and relentless antisemites in the empire—managed to pin such frustration onto something of a historical canvas, insisting that Jewish mistreatment of the region's gentiles had long existed and that Jewish ritual practice was not merely arcane or absurd but so irretrievably perverse that it included the killing of Christian children.

■

The great visibility of Jews in Kishinev was not just a figment of their enemies' imagination. Indeed, Jewish stores lined its streets, their stalls filled its marketplaces, and they were spread throughout the entire city in neighborhoods both poor and rich. Urussov recalls in his memoirs that—on the day of his arrival in June 1903 as Raaben's successor as governor general—the most animated by far in the crowds welcoming him were the Jews. Of course, they were in search of an authority that might protect them amid rumors of still more murderous attacks soon to come. Urussov made a point, after his tour of Alexandrovskaia Street, of going immediately to the area in Lower Kishinev most devastated by the pogrom:

> We passed through the more interesting parts of the city [and] descended to its lower portion, adjoining the bed of the Byk, where the poverty-stricken Jewish inhabitants had established themselves. On the Asia and adjoining streets I saw striking pictures of Jewish life. In the diminutive houses one could see the entire furnishings of the rooms through the open windows. There were sleeping children, adults preparing for sleep, a belated supper, the reading aloud of a book by an old Jew to the family around him, etc. Many of them slept on the verandas around the houses.[28]

The neighborhood's Jewish residents were mostly the working poor, employed in the local garment trade or as minor clerks, teamsters, coachmen, artisans, grape pressers, or har-

Jewish water carrier in Kishinev.

vesters. Because of the outsize ferocity of the attacks in this neighborhood, the information amassed about it—the occupations of its residents, the dimensions of its courtyards, the stock on the shelves of their looted stores, and their sparse domestic possessions—is more comprehensive and intimate in its concrete details about Jews than is available for anywhere else at the time in the Russian empire.[29]

Prior to 1903 the typical Jewish-owned shop in market squares or elsewhere was sparsely stocked. This was true throughout Bessarabia. (Urussov noted, "There are scores of watch-makers in small towns where the townsfolk, as a rule, own no watches.") And the burgeoning of the Jewish population was accompanied by an increased poverty: The number subsisting on charity doubled between 1895 and 1900. Most Jews engaged in buying and selling grains were poor, living from deal to deal. Boosters like Kishinev's Mayor Schmidt saw these agents as a positive force in local trade and commerce; others countered that the Jews, including the Jewish poor, were exploitative and an obstacle, that they blocked roads to town cajoling peasants hauling grain or hay to the city's markets to sell their goods on the spot at lower prices than they would yield if brought to market. Such critics loathed no less the region's itinerant salesmen—nearly all were Jews—who moved from village to village as peddlers, frequently doubling as moneylenders.[30]

Beginning in the 1880s, laws restricting Jewish residence in rural districts meant that an increasing number of Jews poured into Bessarabia's cities, especially Kishinev; by 1897, of the Kishinev district's 280,000 residents—encompassing a larger swath than just the city itself—54,910 were Jews. Rural residence for Jews was not impossible—the restrictions could be circumvented with the use of bribery or special arrangements with noblemen or others—but they were fraught with contradictions, and with ordinances permitting the temporary residence of Jews without, however, specifying what "temporary" meant. Thus, long after Jews had been expelled from villages, it was commonplace for them still to live there while leasing estates and then subleasing them to peasants. Such arrangements were all the more readily available in Bessarabia because of the prevalence of bribery and the eagerness of Jews, many of them recent arrivals, not to lose their newfound footing.[31]

With few buildings higher than four or five stories, many of Kishinev's Jews lived on village-like streets in apartments clustered around tiny courtyards surrounded by fruit trees; others resided in ornamented, handsome, one-story, Galician-inspired houses, many of which were near the New Market. Wealthier Jews lived in commodious homes and hired leading architects to design their businesses—pharmacies, print-shops, and the like—that were among the finest in the city. For example, the Kogen pharmacy was a city landmark, lavishly ornamented and filled with natural light because of its expansive windows; its wedding-cake-like structure was located prominently on one of the city's best streets.

Despite considerable economic growth at the turn of the century, Kishinev retained the feel of a smallish town, with its largest, shaded park adjacent to the city's Holy Gates and the Cathedral of Christ's Nativity, a spot where non-Jews and Jews sauntered side by side on Sundays and during festivals. A few blocks away, its first—and still its grandest—museum, dating back to the 1870s, the Museum of Ethnography and National History, which had been built in Moorish style and founded by one of the city's more distinguished figures (rumored to have been of Jewish descent), remained a favored destination. Pleasures were, on the whole, modest, and the local rich were rarely

Kogen pharmacy.

known to flaunt their wealth—in contrast, as it was often said in Kishinev, to those in Odessa.

Like elsewhere in Russia by the early twentieth century, in Kishinev too there was a small but visible cluster of Jewish professionals—doctors, pharmacists, lawyers, and notaries, few of them wealthy but several occupying prominent roles in Jewish communal life. Davitt was convinced, as he jotted in his notes, that nearly all the city's Jewish leaders were physicians. Kishinev's Jewish rich owned most of its factories, though nearly all of these were little more than workshops. By the turn of the century, of the thirty-nine workplaces in Kishinev listed as factories, all but ten were owned by Jews, and these included nearly all the largest ones. Five of them refined tobacco, four were print houses, and others were the city's largest grain mills, owned by a newcomer to Kishinev named Schartzberg, who had arrived within the previous ten years. (With few exceptions, all the city's most successful Jewish businessmen were newcomers.)[32]

Even those who acknowledged that they were antisemites admitted to Davitt that if Jews were to abandon the city in the pogrom's wake, it could well tumble into financial ruin. They spoke disparagingly of those who chose to leave—though they also derided the continued stranglehold of Jews who remained on Kishinev's economic life.

A glimpse at the confidence shared by the city's Jews on the cusp of the massacre was the handsome Yiddish-language commercial guide for 1901; it was a close facsimile of a much-touted publication that had long appeared in Odessa. Kishinev's version was in Yiddish, not Russian, designed as it was for merchants in particular, with a spotty knowledge of any language other than Yiddish, including those many newcomers to Kishinev from Romania and the southern belt of the Russian empire.

Doubling as a calendar—designed for use over the course of a ten-year period—and also a handy merchant's reference guide, it boasted advertisements for the city's impressive enterprises, large and small, in Jewish hands. Beautifully produced, it listed the dates of regional fairs and a glossary of commercially useful words—such as those for salt, cheese, wine, and fish, and some manufacturing terms, too—with translations into French, Turkish, Bulgarian, Romanian, Russian, and Hebrew. The calendar was packed with advertisements for Jewish-owned shops, many touting perfumes and expensive items. It was the document of a community on the rise, one whose story was just beginning.[33]

Known for its commercial opportunities, Kishinev drew few if any new occupants because of these Jewish cultural offerings. This was a region composed mostly of small-town Jews and of those recently in such places who now gravitated to the big city. None of Kishinev's rabbis—before the second decade of the twentieth century, at any rate—achieved more than local standing. Hasidism flourished in Bessarabia's towns, especially in the northern part near Austria-Hungary, but if this region appeared at all on the Jewish cultural map, it was because of the fabled gravestone cuttings, the most impressive of which were clustered to the north of Kishinev near Beltsy and Bostani. These intricate stone designs had been executed with rare skill, displaying flights of fancy, even whimsy.[34]

Most of the gravestones can be traced to the early eighteenth century, with the tradition dissipating over the next decades. But for nearly a hundred years, artisans from the region created many of the most original gravestones in the Jewish world. Today one can still see ornate Lions of Judah and Torah crowns, many tipped in gold and with the priestly four-fingered benediction, executed with breathtaking precision and drama. Particularly

Jewish gravestones in Bostani.

striking are representations of animals, many of them all but human in their features, which skirt the boundaries of traditional Jewish artistic expression while providing glimpses of the majesty and terror of death. Perhaps because of the region's isolation and the presence of one exceptionally talented family—nearly all are the products of this one clan over some 150 years—did the gravestones manage to enjoy such a long, fertile run.[35]

In Kishinev there was, of course, the standard array of Jewish religious and cultural institutions that existed in nearly all Russian Jewish communities: a large number of mostly quite small synagogues (the majority of these located in Lower Kishinev); two grand houses of worship; sixteen schools by the turn of the century, with a total of more than 2,100 students; many heders, or private Jewish religious elementary schools; and three yeshivas, or advanced rabbinic academies. None of these academies

Choral Synagogue, photographed 1930s.

exerted more than a local reach, however. In 1838 Kishinev had opened its first modern Jewish school with an innovative curriculum of secular and Jewish subjects—which was, like so much else in Kishinev, something of a satellite of a pioneering modern Jewish school in Odessa launched more than a decade before. A particularly innovative local Jewish school offered a full complement of courses in the Hebrew language, including classes in the sciences; in 1902 one of its teachers published a zoology textbook in Hebrew illustrated with beautiful drawings of animals from throughout the world and printed by a local Hebrew publishing house. Some seven hundred Jews also attended Kishinev's Russian schools. Various societies for the relief of the poor—which existed in nearly every Jewish community—could be found in Kishinev, as well, including a society for the assistance of Jewish clerks modeled on Odessa's far larger organization (with eight hundred members and a respectable library of fifteen hundred volumes).[36]

The spark, then, that set the pogrom into motion was once again a fictive charge widely believed to be true; it was cobbled together out of a host of intricate details and finely tuned over the centuries. By the late nineteenth century, its ingredients were these: Jews were obliged to utilize the blood of a young Christian for ritual purposes, and specifically before the Passover festival; this meant that they must murder their victims, drain their blood, and then blend it into their festive matzos.

The difficulty of refuting a practice that never existed proved time and again taxing. It often required, for example, that those defending Jews provide proof that the dead had not been drained of blood, leaving open the prospect that, had such drainage occurred, ritual murder might well have been the cause. This is just what had transpired in Dubossary, a slow-paced fortress town on the Dniester of some five thousand, with half its population Jewish; it sat in the shadow of nearby Tiraspol and Kishinev. Though numerous, its Jews were mostly simple folk employed as shopkeepers, wine pressers, and lumber and tobacco workers. There, in the months before Kishinev's pogrom, a drama unfolded that was at first macabre, eventually tragic.[37]

The episode in Dubossary started, as was so often the case, with the discovery of a dead Christian child, in this instance a fifteen-year-old boy. The orphan lived with his grandfather, who had designated him as his heir. Police soon investigated whether the killing was a ritual murder, prompted both by widespread rumors that this was the case (a local Jew was reportedly heard saying in Yiddish, "We already have the one we shall torment!") and by the many stab wounds on the boy's body. Their finding was that it could not have been a ritual murder because the body had not been drained of its blood. Still, the report's veracity was widely dismissed; many people and, most vocally, *Bessarabets* (which followed the tragedy with steady, bombastic attention) charged that authorities had been bribed by Jews. Even a second autopsy report failed to quell rumors that Jews were the killers, which was also believed by the murdered boy's grandfather.[38]

Rioting then broke out in the town, and those from neighboring towns and villages participated, as well. Reports sent to authorities on March 10, 1903, describe Jews beaten and a bazaar filled with Jewish stalls—most of them selling cheap manufactured items and food—plundered. Police attempted to arrest a rabble-rouser egging the crowd on; they jailed several local "village lads," and they ordered Jews to shut their stores. The episode ended with no one killed or badly injured but with riots elsewhere, too.[39]

Police investigation later revealed that the murderer was a cousin eager to inherit. A local man—unemployed, something of a drunk, and desperately in need of cash—testified that he was contacted by the killer to help with the deed. He explained that the killer outlined for him how he planned to do away with his relative, deflecting all attention onto Jews by simulating a ritual murder. (The practice's features were, apparently, well known.) This conversation took place as the two were sitting over glasses of wine at Jewish-owned "red-haired Yankel's liquor store." It was a tiny, spare spot, where they sat and plotted on one of its two wooden benches.[40]

Officials understood that, to test whether Jews were involved in the killing, it was necessary to determine if the body's blood had been drained—if so, this would constitute proof that a ritual murder had occurred. The belief that this was part and parcel of Jewish practice—perhaps not done by more than a select body, perhaps only by Hasidism, but nonetheless an aspect of mainstream Jewish activity—is why news of Dubossary's outrage could so readily inspire rioting there or elsewhere. Rarely did such suspicions erupt into violence, and that it did now was the work of Krushevan or his close associates fanning the flames. That such embers were ever ready to combust is incontestable. Those responsible for the pogrom in Kishinev were likely no less certain—without misgivings, pangs of conscience, or the sense of anything amiss—that ritual murder had been the practice of Jews since time immemorial.

From its start, their attack on Jews was justified as self-defense, a reasonable response to a pariah people, capable of any and all transgressions, whose toxic activities, as hoary as history itself, had to be put to an end.

Shredded Torah scrolls.

▪ 3 ▪

"Squalid Brawl in a Distant City"

This squalid brawl in a distant city is more important than it
might appear at first.

—GEORGE ORWELL, *Homage to Catalonia*

It began inconspicuously, as so many riots do. People jostled in a
sparsely policed public square lined with Jewish-owned shops.
Worshippers idled after Easter services at the nearby Ciuflea
Church, some drinking steadily once services ended, and teenagers as well as Jews—restless near the end of the long, eight-day
Passover festival—were all rubbing shoulders. The weather was
suddenly and blissfully temperate, dry after intermittent rain.

Soon it would be a commonplace to juxtapose the pogrom's
horrors and its benign springtime weather. Bialik, too, would do
much the same in "In the City of Killing," while also highlighting the buoyant expectations that surfaced for Jews at the start
of a fresh new century viewed against the obscenity of Kishinev's
butchery.[1]

Details of these terrible spring days, with their changes from moist to warm, would figure among the cascade of information, small and large, amassed by teams of reporters, Jewish activists, political radicals, well-known writers, philanthropists, lawyers, and civil servants in the months following the pogrom. The ubiquity of this knowledge had much to do with the city's location, the swiftness with which word of the massacre spread, and the belief that—in its wake—proof had finally surfaced of government complicity. An epoch of permanent pogroms was now predicted by some, making Kishinev into a sort of talisman, a glimpse of terrible things soon to come, which meant, in turn, that its contours provided immeasurably more than mere information about the recent past but an indispensable glimpse into the future as well.

■

Rumors of attacks surfaced nearly every year in Kishinev before the start of Easter. In 1903 they appeared to be especially threatening. Accusations of ritual murder in the newspaper *Bessarabets* remained shrill despite official repudiation; there was word of menacing anti-Jewish meetings held in the back room of a Kishinev tavern; and leaflets calling for the beating of Jews were discovered in bars, cheap restaurants, and flophouses. "Grant a zhid free reign [sic], and he will reign over our Holy Russia, will take things into his own paws," declared the leaflets. By then *Bessarabets* had launched a private club, a semisecret society that met regularly, it seems, with its goal being resistance to an imminent Jewish onslaught. All this, as Krushevan's colleague Georgi A. Pronin would later insist, was in response to news that Jews had held a secret meeting in Kishinev's largest synagogue, where they plotted to unleash horrible deeds.[2]

Against this backdrop, Jewish anxieties were heightened. Jewish shop owners admitted that, for the first time in recent memory, they took home bank records, receipts, and similar financial documents for safekeeping. Employees were informed that stores would likely stay shut for a day or two after the Passover festival—a precaution against Easter-day violence that was nearly always avoided since the long Passover festival already meant loss of profit. Such precautions were sporadic, however, with the risk of a particularly violent riot not taken all that seriously.[3]

Easter Sunday April 6 began with a chill in the air. Puddles from the downpour earlier that week still pockmarked the city's mostly unpaved neighborhoods. By late morning families dressed for Easter service sauntered in the cluttered streets near Chuflinskii Square at the city's eastern edge. Those at the Ciuflea Church spilled out onto the nearby square.[4]

By midday the square was packed. In previous years it had boasted a carousel, but officials seeking to dampen holiday revelry—which had sometimes gotten out of control—shut the ride down that year, stationing additional police at the square's edge. Some Jews had gravitated to the square, despite warnings issued at Kishinev's synagogues that morning that Jews should go directly home after services. With the Passover festival and its special foods and mandated conviviality nearly at their end, Jews overlooked the warnings to take advantage of temperate weather and the pleasures of the Christian festival.[5]

Around noon clusters of boys, few older than ten years old, started roughing up Jews. Police intervened, but the children ran away, and police caught only a handful. The taunting continued, but most people assumed it was no more than a harmless prank; Jews themselves took little notice. Children, some adults, too, started tossing rocks at the windows of Jewish stores—this in keeping with a well-trodden holiday tradition that was rarely more than annoying.[6]

By 2:00 p.m., the crowd had thickened, with some now much

drunker. Many witnesses later reported that in the square were students from the local Russian Orthodox seminary, some in uniform, inciting the crowd to turn on Jews. Trial witnesses insisted that the students were joined by dozens of men sporting the festive red shirts favored by workers. In the first reports appearing in Western newspapers, the riot was described as an attack by workers; testimony later given in court indicated that these "workers" were most likely rabble-rousers close to Krushevan's circle who were disguised so as to leave the impression that workingmen were turning on the Jews.[7]

In hindsight the questions are numerous: How many agitators were there in the first hours of the riot? How decisive were the provocations of seminary students spotted by so many at the riot's start, and of those in the *Bessarabets* circle? Was there really a close connection—widely believed at the time but not examined by the court or conclusively proved—between Krushevan's entourage and the massacre? Was this a linkage merely taken for granted because of his newspaper's persistent Jew-baiting? Cutting through the thicket of rumor and counter-rumor is difficult to be sure; many of the most reliable reports are the ones that surfaced early, before the massacre coalesced into the event it soon became. In nearly all of these, Krushevan's involvement, whether direct or somewhat less obvious but still critical, is prominently foregrounded.

Jewish-owned stores near Chuflinskii Square—today an ungainly parking lot just outside Chişinău's Academy of Sciences—were ransacked first. Liquor stores, given their tempting contents, were targeted immediately; by the riot's end, not a single Jewish-run liquor shop would be left unscathed, with many literally torn to pieces.[8]

Rioters later justified these attacks by saying that they had entered the stores merely to ask the Jewish proprietors for free drinks—and pillaged only once they were refused. Throughout the violence, similar explanations—with a roughly comparable interplay between seeming reasonableness and absurdity—circulated and were repeated at the subsequent trials. Rioters either drank all the liquor in these pillaged stores on the spot or poured what remained onto the street. Tobacco stores were ransacked next, with the remnants of their merchandise, too, scattered on streets now swimming in a mixture of rainwater and liquor. Arriving at the New Market, a mile and a half from the site where the riot had started and it, too, lined with Jewish stores, a shoe shop was emptied of its stock as those inside outfitted themselves with its goods. These forays, destructive as they were, involved only the theft of goods readily eaten, drunk, or worn.[9]

The riot spread westward through a cluster of a few streets, several of them quite large, where Jewish stores stood side by side with others owned by non-Jews—these were left unattacked; the mayhem stopped at the New Market, half a mile or so from the city center. Still no more than two or three dozen people were responsible for this rioting, and they could easily be written off as drunks or rowdy adolescents. However, by 4:00 p.m., the crowd had grown, with seminarians and others guiding the mob to Jewish homes, which they started to pelt with stones. Jews insisted that lists of Jewish addresses had been drawn up in advance, but no such lists ever surfaced.[10]

The first residence attacked was that of Herman Feldman, an opulent home just down the street from where Kishinev's mayor, Karl Schmidt, lived. It was also next door to the city's most exclusive brothel, whose employees had already been packed off elsewhere. Nearby, the office of *Bessarabets* had its windows stoned because a radical student misdirected the mob to it, claiming it was the property of Jews. Jews found on the street became objects of abuse: An elderly Jew, his wife, and grandchild found themselves threatened but managed to escape when a policeman intervened to protect them. Others beseeched the police for help but were told that the mob was now beyond their capacity to control.[11]

By 4:00 or 5:00 p.m., as the afternoon yielded to evening, cries of "Death to Jews!" and "Strike the Jews!" could be heard. Buildings with large numbers of Jews—much of Kishinev's housing had Jews and non-Jews living side by side—were surrounded and pelted with rocks. On the whole these buildings were attacked for no more than ten or fifteen minutes, the crowds then moving on to other targets. On rare occasions the mob stayed for hours, until outer doors were smashed and the building overrun. Jewish doctors seeking to respond to the needs of wounded Jews found themselves able to reach them only if they wore crosses. Christians scrawled crosses on the windows of their homes to protect themselves from attack; when Jews tried to do the same, it rarely worked—one more indication, as was widely believed, that rioters had been alerted in advance to where Jews lived. Jews managing to pass themselves off as gentiles were told that permission had been granted to attack Jews for the next few days because "they drink our blood." A Jewish saloon owner who watched as his inventory was subsumed by rioters or poured onto the street overheard the mob toasting Krushevan's health. A slab of meat found cooking in a shop owner's home adjacent to his wrecked store was waved over the heads of rioters with the announcement that it was the remains of a Christian child. The wife of the Jewish shopkeeper Yudel Fishman, whose building was broken into, managed to escape with her child in her arms, but she dropped the newborn as she fled to the train station, the baby crushed to death in the onslaught.[12]

David Doiben lived on Gostinaia Street, a boisterous street lined with three- and four-story buildings, many of them hotels, including the posh Swiss Hotel; it ran directly into the New Market and was the hardest hit on the riot's first day. Doiben described how he had obeyed the warning to stay inside until midafternoon, when he accompanied his wife and children to his brother's home a few blocks away. They spotted nothing at the time. Returning an hour and a half later, however, they ran into two non-Jewish acquaintances who warned them to go home immediately. Suddenly a group of rioters ran past them without stopping. Once they disappeared, Doiben and his family saw a Jew, his clothes ripped, who shouted, "They're beating us and tearing us apart!" Turning the corner to their apartment building, Doiben found it surrounded by a crowd of fifty boys (and a few girls), throwing rocks and smashing against its door. He managed to get into the building, hiding his family inside. After breaking the courtyard door, the rioters entered the building and demanded money, beating those who did not comply and stealing all they could carry.[13]

Reports on the first day were often contradictory. If, as seems clear, the riot stretched from Chuflinskii Square (where it started) to just beyond the New Market (where Feldman's home was located), this meant it covered an area of nearly two miles. Nonetheless, the Odessa-based British consul general described it as "a small sized crowd confined to three or four streets." Although this was technically accurate, it was also true that these streets were within striking distance of the city center. Some would claim that the first killings occurred that day, but this was almost certainly incorrect.[14]

Transportation across town under any circumstances was cumbersome—trolleys were few and far between, and not many

of the streets beyond the city center were lit at night—so rioters covering the area pillaged mostly by foot. Much of Lower
Kishinev, at its farthest edge little more than a mile from the center of the first day's violence, knew nothing of the mayhem until
the following morning. And except for the shattering of windows
here and there in Lower Kishinev—which commenced around
nine that night—not much spilled over into that densely Jewish
neighborhood until the next day. Attacks on women continued
elsewhere well into the night, stopping only at 11:00 p.m.[15]

It has been estimated that no more than two hundred rioters participated in the attacks that day. Rarely did they linger
in the way in which the mob did at Doiben's building. Mostly
they clustered in groups of twenty, sometimes as many as fifty,
spending no more than ten minutes at any address; youngsters
arrived first, followed by older and stronger rioters. Children
would rarely do more than throw rocks; the adults were more
intent on plunder. Already on the first day, those counted as
the fiercest were Moldavians—identified by the language they
used or their accents—many hailing, it seems, from the agrarian
edge of the city or adjacent villages. By the next day, many more
would arrive, often with wagons to carry away the contents of
Jewish homes.[16]

Violence continued to escalate that night. Yosef Aaron and
his brothers, merchants all, later described how they protected
themselves from attack at 10:00 p.m. by shooting bullets into the
air when rioters broke into their house. The mob immediately
fled. The merchants then gathered their neighbors together and
distributed iron bars and wooden clubs, with the decision made
that they would fight the next day but only if attacked by adults
and not children. Interestingly, even hours after the violence
erupted, it remained unclear whether or not this was merely the

work of adolescent pranksters. Nevertheless precautions were now taken by many of those with sufficient resources to flee to nearby hotels, or to board trains for Kiev or Odessa. Some even traveled nearly a thousand miles to Vienna.[17]

Warnings abounded—at least, as recalled once the massacre ended—of greater violence the next day. A gentile gatekeeper for a building near the New Market mockingly asked Jewish residents when he appeared for work, "What's happening here?" He added as he locked the courtyard for the night that it was well known that permission had been granted for three days of violence. Attacks on women that night were ferocious. In an apartment near the New Market on Nikolaevskii Street, one of the city's major boulevards, a woman was raped repeatedly for four consecutive hours by members of a mob that included seminarians, according to Davitt. At the same place another woman who beseeched police to stop this attack was told that Jews were getting just what they deserved.[18]

By now sixty rioters had been arrested; by the end of the next day, the number jailed would exceed nine hundred. Curiously, despite the day's horrors, many Jews—including communal leaders—remained convinced that the riot was not nearly as bad as had been feared, or that it had now been contained. Early on the morning of the second day, some 150 Jews converged on Governor General Raaben's offices. Only a small delegation was permitted to meet with him, and they were given the assurance that order would immediately be restored. Perhaps because the many rapes late the night before had not yet been reported or because the riot had been concentrated in only one slice of the city—albeit a highly visible and central part of it, with no one yet killed—this guarantee was believed. Such optimism would quickly vanish.[19]

It rained that night and was still raining at 5:00 a.m. Monday. The rain was light but persistent, with the likelihood of an overcast and wet day. "Perhaps the rain will be our deliverance," shopkeeper Yisrael Rossman recalls thinking early that morning. Soon the rain cleared, however, and the weather became balmy. As Bialik captured this moment in his poem "In the City of Killing": "The sun rose, rye blossomed, and the slaughterer slaughtered."[20]

Rossman hurried off soon after the rain ended to the New Market to check on the condition of his store. Footsteps could be heard all around him, he recalled, as he walked the still-wet, dark streets with many other Jews doing the same. On his way he spotted a policeman, whom he asked what to expect that day. The officer admitted he had no idea. Returning to his home a couple of hours later—it was now 8:00 a.m.—he found himself scrutinizing the faces of Christians passing by but saw no sign at all of antagonism. Yet once he reached his home, he found the building surrounded by an increasingly menacing mob. Hiding his family along with dozens of neighbors in a barn on the property—many in the building hid themselves in one or another of the outhouses—Rossman recalled that the mob sounded like "wild animals." The rioters concentrated now on demolishing the large wooden doors protecting the building's courtyard. Once these were shattered, marauders entered, calling out repeatedly, "Jews, right now!"[21]

Why the targeting of some buildings and not others? Probably a crucial factor, quite simply, was the condition of the external doors: Some were too sturdy to dislodge. In Rossman's building, with its mix of Jewish and non-Jewish tenants, it seems clear that much like elsewhere rioters found themselves able to readily identify Jews—including those without distinctively Jewish garb. There is little evidence of gentiles misconstrued during the massacre as Jews. Once the mob was inside, the loudest screams were nearly always those of women and girls, who were attacked first, with the men protecting them beaten. Rossman's brother first hid himself in an outhouse, abandoning it because, as he later insisted, he did not want to die in such a filthy place. As soon as he surfaced, he was beaten senseless. Soon afterward Rossman was also discovered, and he too was beaten and left for dead. He nonetheless managed to flee to the building's roof, where he found dead bodies lying about "much like slaughtered chickens." A neighbor, a Jewish convert to Russian Orthodoxy—he had saved himself by reciting for the mob passages from the Psalms—now arranged for wagons to transport wounded Jews to the hospital.[22]

Still, in the first few hours of Monday, the riot continued to be concentrated in the same area where it had broken out, mostly near the New Market. The neighborhood's stores continued to be ransacked: The newspaper *Odesskie Novosti* described how well-dressed women were seen eagerly participating, stealing clothes off the racks of Jewish shops and walking through the streets of the city with the goods. Unwanted merchandise was so plentiful that it was piled onto roads, often stopping all traffic including trams.[23]

A wealthy Jew named Sobelman, who prided himself on his close terms with local Russian officials, tried to return home that Monday morning from Raaben's offices but found his route blocked because the day's rioting had already begun. Managing finally to reach his building, he found it surrounded by children pelting it with stones. Joined by adults, the mob lingered for more than an hour, working hard at demolishing the front door. As soon as they entered, they started smashing tables on the heads of Jews while demanding that they pay for their lives. As little as a few kopecks—one woman discovered four kopecks in her pockets and gave it to the mob—could make all the difference. Sobelman found his family but was murdered while protecting them. A group of fifteen or so were overheard emerging from his building, calling out, "Sobelman is finished!"[24]

Some Jews were hit over their heads with tables as many as twenty times until they died. Hannah Bruvarman saved her own life, escaping with little more than a mild beating, when she handed over the three hundred rubles she had earned selling wood before Passover. Fleeing to her daughter's house nearby, which was also under attack, she had to barter once again for her life, handing over the three rubles that was all the money she had left.[25]

By late morning nearly the entire city, except for the far-western neighborhoods inhabited mostly by gentile workers and with few Jews, was enveloped. No less than two-thirds of Kishinev was affected by violence. Nonetheless its impact remained haphazard, with—as stated in a British consular report—"many streets within the affected area . . . comparatively (some wholly) untouched."[26]

Under the attacks, entire streets were all but leveled; an English reporter in Kishinev during the riot described the scene from his hotel window as one of utter devastation. And increasingly, the attacks were personal. Rossman watched as one assailant called out the name of his victim, asking him in Moldavian, "Are you Ben-Zion?" The Jew turned to him saying, "Why, children?" He was then hit with a pitchfork and killed. A gentile woman who offered to hide Jews in her apartment found pleasure nonetheless in taunting them, entering the hiding place every few minutes with news such as, "You no longer have any stove," or "You have no beds, no chairs, no table."[27]

In his notes Davitt described one Jewish victim caught up in Monday's violence: "Meyer Weissman. 3 children and a wife. His eye gouged out. He wanted them to kill him. Saw him in his bed. Fine type of poor man. Had a small grocery store." Wine seller Yisroel Hayyim Steinberg watched helplessly as a mob of fifty confronted his seventy-year-old father, demanding money. The terrified man found himself unable to utter more than a few stray sounds; the crowd responded in quasi-Yiddish, "*Gibbe gelt.*" When it was found that he had only half a kopeck in his pocket, he was beaten to death. As the son told Bialik, who spent much of his five weeks in Kishinev interviewing victims, "We were hiding the entire time watching all this hiding behind a fence. Four at the same time were hiding in the outhouse."[28]

■

It will never be known how many women and girls were raped over the course of the two days. Davitt counted forty, based on the testimony of a local rabbi, with others likely having failed to report for fear of losing husbands to divorce or, if unmarried, losing the opportunity to wed. (It was reported to Davitt by rabbis that they had indeed received requests for divorce from the husbands of raped women.)[29] In her apartment on Nikolaevskii Street, twenty-four-year-old Rivka Schiff, who had been married four years and was an immigrant from Romania, was the victim of serial rape. Her testimony to Bialik is by far the longest, most detailed, and most harrowing of all such accounts:

When the vile ones forced their way from the roof into the attic, they first attacked Zychick's daughter, hit her on the cheek with a tool, and surrounded her. She fell to the floor from the force of the blow. They lifted her dress, pushed her head down, and pulled her bottom up and started to slap her buttocks with their hands. Then they turned her around again, spread her legs, covered her eyes, and shut her mouth so that she couldn't scream. One took her from behind while the others crouched around her and waited their turn. They all did what they did in full view of the people in the attic. Others jumped on me and my husband. He tried to escape, and I followed him. They jumped on him. "Give us money!" Mitya Kresilchik sought to abuse me and asked for money. I pleaded for mercy. "Don't touch me, Mitya. You have known me for many years. I have no money." Others ripped open the back of my dress; one slapped me and said: "If you have no money, we will get pleasure from you in another way." I fell to the ground with Mitya on top of me, and he started to have his way with me. The other gang members surrounded me and waited. My husband saw this, as did the other Jews in the attic. My husband gave them his silver watch and chain. They thought the chain was gold, and as they were examining it, he jumped [out of the attic and] to the ground. There they beat him. The rest of the Jews jumped, too. Only Sima Zychick and I were left there. They were mocking and abusing me. "It seems like you haven't slept with a Gentile yet. Now you will know the taste of one." I don't know how many had their way with me, but there were at least five, and possibly seven. As they finished, they came down one by one. One Gentile . . . came up there and said: "Hide in the corner; soon a few other thugs will come up here. I will come soon with my wife and take you down." I sat in the corner (wearing my underwear and my coat); just at that moment,

Sima Zychick came and sat down next to me. We sat there silent and still. Immediately, one came up and started to call out his friends' names. He saw that none were there and left. Then four others came up, one after the other. One of them knelt down and pretended to sympathize with my sorrow. He saw my earrings, ripped them from my ears, and wanted once again to abuse me. But at that moment, the other Gentile, the righteous one mentioned before . . . came up and right in front of him, two had intercourse with me and two with Sima. He tried once again to convince them cunningly by saying: "You are Christians and are forbidden to take the women of Israel." But then they wanted to attack him as well, and he was afraid and only tried to save our lives: "Do whatever you want with them, but do not kill them." The four finished and the Gentile helped me to cover my head with my shawl, and Sima held my hand as we left there escorted by the Gentile to my mother's house. . . . There, too, all had

Nikolaevskii Street, soon after the pogrom.

been destroyed. I searched for my husband. I didn't know
where he was. [Was he] dead or alive? I was pulverized, and
crushed like a vessel filled with shame and filth. I returned
to my residential courtyard.[30]

■

That rape occurred was common knowledge in the city in the
pogrom's immediate aftermath. Still, the details of these attacks
remained obscure, rarely mentioned in post-pogrom trials. Bialik's transcript—the source of a wealth of information—was
withheld for reasons the poet never explained, left among his
unpublished material in the archives of Beit Bialik in Tel Aviv
until transcribed and released in print only in the 1990s. Davitt
also consigned his notes on rapes to his unpublished diary, leaving them out of his journalism and his subsequent book. (The
reason for these omissions on Davitt's part may have been the
strictures of the time—obeyed even by the sensationalist Hearst
press, for which he worked—on the reporting of outrages like
rapes.) In the diary he kept while in Kishinev, he describes in
great detail an atrocity that took place in a semirural part of the
city, probably the strip known as Muncheshtskii, or Manchester Way, composed largely of Moldavians "of the poorest & most
depraved kind. Their houses are wretched looking. . . . The few
Jews who live among them are equally poor." Davitt continues:

I found on entering a gateway that I was in the yard where
five Jews had been killed—one young girl violated & killed
& a Jew's wife held by fiends while others ravished her. . . .
She was cornered in there in the shed . . . and repeatedly
violated by several men & then killed. About a hundred feet
from this house is a long wooden shed used by the male Jews

in the yard as a carpenter's shop . . . the shed is some 40 feet long by some fifteen wide. . . . The young girl . . . by some accident of chance was left in her home, the house nearest the gateway entrance to the yard & she was caught & treated as above before she could escape. This was during the night of the first day's rioting. The 23 persons, men, women & children were inhabitants of the house in the yard. The shrieks of the girl were heard by the terrified crowd in the shed for a short time & then all was silent.[31]

As late as Monday morning little more than stray rumors of violence had reached Lower Kishinev. There had been some rock throwing the night before at the windows of Jewish houses and stores, and some of the neighborhood's Jews joined the self-defense in the wine courtyard. On the whole, however, the neighborhood had passed through that first night with many expecting that the worst was over.

The area, built on hills just above the Byk, was indented with tiny shops, synagogues, and houses built around courtyards packed with large Jewish families numbering sometimes as many as eight or even ten children. Here violence was concentrated on no more than six or seven intersecting streets, most of them little more than alleyways, packed with ramshackle structures some of which literally collapsed under the weight of attack.

In these cramped quarters Jews and non-Jews, mostly Moldavians, occupied apartments in the same building. The Russian short-story writer and essayist Vladimir Korolenko, in his stirring work "Dom nomer 13" ("The House at Number 13"), gave worldwide notoriety to the neighborhood and especially one of its modest dwellings at Aziatskaia, or Asia Street 13: "Stones, tiles,

Synagogue in Lower Kishinev.

and bricks and mortar choke the growth of trees. . . . The houses are small, and stone walls hide the entrances to the courtyards."[32]

Most of the dwellings in the area were flimsy, their belongings sparse; in the hot, humid months of spring and summer, residents spent much time outdoors in the courtyards or on the dusty unpaved streets. One Jewish home inventoried after the pogrom included only cabinets, beds, tables, and two photographs: one of the Anglo-Jewish grandee Moses Montefiore, which had been ripped into shreds, and the second of the late Tsar Alexander III and his family, which had been left alone. A Jewish woman living at Aziatskaia 13 would insist that, once the pogrom ended, all that remained of her possessions was a single pillow.[33]

With horror and puzzlement, Jews here would speak of the friendly, at least benign, relations between Jews and non-Jews that had existed prior to the violence; interactions, they said, had been more casual and less encumbered here than elsewhere in the city. In this neighborhood, with few pretensions and where workaday relationships—Jews often hired non-Jewish laborers as well as maids or artisans—were more likely to slide into friendships, it was more typical than elsewhere in Kishinev for gentile neighbors to take dangerous risks to save Jews. Hence it was not rare for Jews fleeing rioters to run into the courtyards or homes of non-Jewish neighbors, with the expectation of being hidden.[34]

Then again, it was also not uncommon for neighbors to slaughter or rape neighbors, and frequently with an astonishing indifference to suffering. This interplay between familiarity and ferocity was replicated in grim incident after incident. Victims of rape or beating were known to call out the names of their assailants. One raped woman spoke afterward of having held her rapist as a baby in her arms. The sons of a local shoemaker—the two boys hid behind a stove while their father was beaten and murdered—recognized the killer as a neighbor whose shoes they had recently repaired.[35]

Time and again familiar faces would come crashing into Jewish houses—this starting late Monday morning—often justifying their actions with the declaration that Jews had killed a local priest or demolished a church. The wine-shop owner Yeshaya Sirota described how the riot in the neighborhood had started, predictably enough, with children tossing rocks at the windows of his store and adjacent house; this was soon joined by older men, who began crashing against his front door. Once inside, they spent no less than an hour and a half ransacking his modest house, breaking nearly everything that they did not steal. Once all of Sirota's clothes and furniture were gone, the mob turned on his wine shop next door with at least sixty people— according to one report as many as four hundred—somehow squeezing themselves into this small space and stealing nearly all his stock until police finally intervened. No marauders were arrested; the police merely persuaded them to leave the building and move on. Sirota survived the onslaught, as he later told Bialik, because when rioters burst into his house and one was poised to kill him and his family, the assailant spotted his youngest child, five months old, and declared that only Turks slaughtered small children. Sirota then hid himself and his family—together with eight other families living in the same building—in the house of a neighboring non-Jew, a wagoner whom he described as a friend.[36]

The mob engulfing Lower Kishinev included villagers from outside the city, or peasants living at its edge; many brought wagons in which to pack stolen goods. Neighbors joined in along with, it seems, much of the same group of antisemites and seminary students spotted elsewhere. That morning one of the students encountered a Jew standing in front of his house with a terrified look on his face, and the student stopped to say, "Why weep? Tomorrow we'll murder all of you."[37]

Immediately after sacking Sirota's shop down the street, the mob converged on No. 13. It was a modest building wrapped around a courtyard with seven apartments housing eight families, all Jews. In one corner lived Naftoli Serebrenick, who ran a store located in the same small complex, selling candles, soap, matches, oil, calico, and sweets. The landlord lived elsewhere, in a better part of town, but his divorced daughter and family were in the building. The other residents included a bookkeeper, a glazier, a shop assistant, and a hospital orderly. Eight men were in the building when it was attacked by as many as a hundred rioters. Korolenko acknowledged that, under such circumstances, self-defense was inconceivable.[38]

The first casualty was the glazier, Mordecai Mottel Greenschopin, who was discovered hiding with his family in a shed and dragged by rioters—including at least one whose name he knew—to the roof of an outhouse, where he was beaten with poles until dead. Fearing a similar fate, Jews witnessing the attack made their way to an attic that was soon so crowded and intolerably hot that most found it impossible to remain. They were spotted and pursued while escaping, several fleeing to a roof within view, as later reported, of police on the street below. One after another, they were beaten to death, some smashed on the head with an enamel sink and others literally torn apart with crowbars. Their bodies were tossed onto the street, some covered—to further humiliate them—with chicken feathers. Corpses lay there for hours until the streets were cleared by the army late that afternoon; many lay in water puddles or were covered by the wine that had spilled from Sirota's store.[39]

Even two months later, when Urussov visited the street in late June—on his first day as governor general—"rough boards covered the broken windows and shattered doors of many houses. Here and there were damaged roofs and partly destroyed chimneys." Dried blood could be seen on some of the walls, and many residents in the neighborhood occupied houses that had no roofs or, in some instances, were in a state bordering on destruction.[40]

Nearly everything that would come to be associated with the pogrom was drawn from the events in Lower Kishinev on late Monday morning and early that afternoon.

The pogrom's lingering impact would also remain the most visible for locals, who were the least able to cover the cost of repairs. Not infrequently the violence in this neighborhood was the work of neighbors themselves living side by side with Jews in the same cluster of flats and sharing the same courtyard. The dense and deadly concentration of these attacks, the frequency with which they involved acquaintances, and the simple fact that the area remained in disrepair long after other parts of the city were rebuilt all contributed to making it the focal point for the pogrom's horrors. Perhaps the preponderance of traditional Jews in classic Jewish garb among its residents—and victims—also helped to consolidate Lower Kishinev as the pogrom's epicenter. Elsewhere in the city many Jews had by now abandoned Jewish dress, or at least modified it, with many here, as in Odessa, less fixated on the minutiae of Jewish practice.

Soon enough the best known of all faces linked to the tragedy would be Moshe Kigel, described as the devout sexton of one of Lower Kishinev's numerous, mostly tiny synagogues. He was said to have lost his life in an effort to save the Torah scrolls of his beloved house of worship from desecration at the hands of hoodlums. Kigel's martyrdom would soon constitute the most enduring of all portraits from the pogrom—indeed, arguably the most memorable of all moments of Jewish life in late-imperial Russia. Portraits of Kigel would be reprinted widely; prayers and poems devoted to him would be recited in synagogues, especially in the United States; and plays would be written in his honor. His martyrdom was made into a medieval-like tale, particularly once Ephraim Moses Lilien produced his evocative poem, "To the Martyrs of Kishinev," describing Kigel wrapped in a traditional tallith, wearing phylacteries, his arms outstretched in an effort to save the holy scrolls, his body enveloped by angelic wings.[41]

Kigel—bearded, age sixty, and pious—resided in a building around the corner from the synagogue whose Torah scrolls had been desecrated. Contrary to the later accounts, however, he was murdered right outside the door of his home, not in front of the house of worship. He was not a synagogue sexton (he owned a tiny shop adjacent to the synagogue), and there is no evidence that he attempted to protect its sacred objects. Nevertheless, once his body was found near shredded scrolls on the street, stories of his martyrdom quickly coalesced. His prominence deflected talk of Kishinev's rapes and the town's cowardly men. It focused attention on Kishinev's poor, thus reinforcing a theme pushed by the Jewish Socialist Labor Bund, especially in the weeks after the pogrom, namely that it was a catastrophe of the poor, not the rich, who abandoned Kishinev's most vulnerable while protecting themselves and their possessions.[42]

A similar interplay between intimacy—at least familiarity—and ferocious violence was evident in the slice of Kishinev's Muncheshtskii, or Manchester Way. There at the city's eastern edge the pogrom arrived late, much as in Lower Kishinev, and was all the more shocking because its Jews could recall years of peaceful coexistence. Technically a suburb, it was little better than a tumbledown row of houses, artisan shops, cattle slaughterers, and dealers in grains, hides, farm animals, and the like running alongside the railway tracks near the Byk, with the city's Botanical Gardens nearby. It was a neighborhood with perhaps a hundred Moldavian families and approximately thirty Jewish ones, mostly small peddlers. A Jewish-owned leather factory employed many locals, and the area's doctor was a converted Jew married to a Catholic.[43]

Muncheshtskii's Jews were so confident that they were safe, and so ignorant of what was transpiring only a few miles away, that the first reliable word of the pogrom came only because one of them—hoping to have his newborn circumcised on Monday morning—set off in a wagon for the city to pick up the mohel to perform the ritual circumcision, only to be informed that such travel was too dangerous. Soon afterward, outside a Jewish-owned grain store, a crowd gathered. Its young proprietor overheard talk in the crowd of the killing of a Christian child in a nearby town, and that it was the practice of Jews to use gentile blood for their rituals. Joining the mob were seminary students and others from outside the neighborhood, with the word now spreading that a Jewish house at the street's end had already been ransacked.[44]

Soon some two hundred people were outside the grain store, arguing about whether to attack Jewish homes and businesses; some of them tried to stop the riot before it erupted. Like elsewhere, however, violence took off when free drinks were demanded from the owner of a Jewish wine store, who, once he refused—at least he was rumored to have done so—was attacked. A large wagon now appeared outside the store, with the bulk of the Jew's stock loaded onto it. The grain-store owner was approached by a gentile acquaintance and offered the use of a cross to fool the crowd. He correctly figured it would do no good. The store was now ransacked together with all the Jewish houses

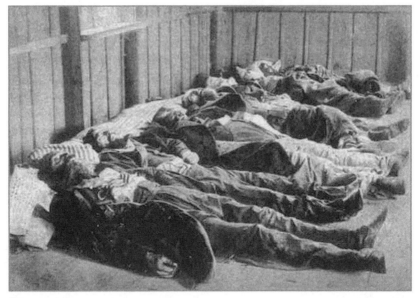

Pogrom victims.

on the street. Women were raped amid a fury inconceivable just an hour or two earlier.[45]

■

"Jews did not fight for their lives, but fled to wherever they could." This was in the testimony of Melekh Kaufman, as told to Bialik.[46]

Such accusations would soon be seen—and in no small measure because of how Bialik built the charge into the heart of his famous poem—as an assault on little less than thousands of years of Jewish history. Kishinev was said to have cut wide open a web of wretched, cowardly compromises stretching as far back as the last of the Maccabees, a welter of congealed terrors cleverly disguised that had over the centuries made Jews into who they now were: an overly cautious people who knew well how to negotiate but were incapable of fighting for their own lives or, for that matter, defending the honor of their kinfolk. The first stirrings of the Israeli army, the self-defense force known as the Haganah, launched in Palestine soon after the Kishinev pogrom, was the by-product of such shame. So were a multitude of other well-charted efforts at Jewish self-defense brandished as militant responses to Kishinev, with Jewish fighters in Gomel that September, for example, managing to leave more pogromists dead than Jews.[47]

Bialik's anguished cry had a particularly powerful impact on Jewish fighters once the poem was translated in 1904 into Russian and recited widely (and brilliantly) by the young, restless Vladimir Jabotinsky.[48] Bialik's work left little doubt that the response of Kishinev Jews to violence had been gutless. Curiously enough, however, Bialik recorded in the transcripts of the interviews he conducted during his Kishinev stay, often in copious detail, many efforts at Jewish self-defense, including one so notorious—in the minds of local antisemites and their sympathizers, at least—that they would credit it, not their own actions, as the main cause for Monday's violence.

When rioters broke into the shop of Mordecai ben Aaron Litvak, he and his family told them that they would be shot if they did not leave immediately, which they did. Jews elsewhere fought with kitchen knives and clubs until, as often as not, they were overwhelmed by the sheer number or physical strength of the attackers. Trying to protect his father in their house on that Monday morning, Mordecai Zvi Lis found himself pinned down by rioters who pushed against a door. Then, amid calls of "Christ has risen!" the mob jumped both father and son, beating both senseless. When fifty-seven-year-old Yehiel Kiserman fought off four attackers, throwing several of them to the ground, a rumor rapidly spread that a Jew had murdered Christians. This news further enraged the mobs, which now attacked with heightened fury. Elsewhere four Jewish teenagers—all of them employed as servants—tried unsuccessfully to stop the beating of a tailor threatened by a large and angry crowd by beating them first.[49]

Yehiel Pesker, the owner of a glass store at the New Market who, like Yisrael Rossman, went to inspect his shop early Monday for damage, encountered on the way home a large group of Jews—he recalled that they numbered at least two hundred—gathered in the wine courtyard, armed and prepared to fight. He saw the clubs in their arms; it turned out that several were carrying guns as well. Returning home inspired by what he had seen, Pesker set in motion plans to protect his building. He armed himself with a club, too, and instructed his neighbors to join him in battling the mob. This they did until they were overwhelmed. Fugitives from Kishinev arriving in Vienna and interviewed by the local press insisted that they, too, would have defended themselves had the authorities not intervened.[50]

Hence, after the pogrom's end, alongside talk of Jewish passivity were fierce denunciations of Jewish anti-Russian aggression. In arguments made by defense attorneys at the trials of pogrom-related crimes, Sunday's rioting was dismissed as a ruckus that would quickly have come to an end—much as the governor general assured the Jewish delegation on Monday morning—had Jews not overreacted. In this version it was the all-but-unprovoked aggression of Jews and subsequent rumors of attacks on a church and the killing of a priest that set in motion the unfortunate but, under the circumstances, understandable violence.[51]

The instance of Jewish militancy most frequently cited in descriptions inimical to Jews—yet sidelined in Jewish accounts—was the one whose start was witnessed by Pesker at the wine courtyard early Monday morning. Gathered were likely more than 250 Jews, armed with clubs, poles, and some guns. This crowd soon attacked a few dozen would-be rioters nearby, overwhelming them at first. Most of the Jews were laborers at the New Market, with a sprinkling also from Lower Kishinev—a medley of husky wagon drivers and others engaged in manual labor eager to fight back. One of the group gave Bialik a lengthy description:

> We decided to arm ourselves, not to be the first to start to fight. Many who had returned to their houses to hide their weapons, to fill the breaches, and to close the doors and shutters came back with poles and with some pistols. Chaim Kazioshner armed himself with an old rifle as a threat. At eight o'clock in the morning, gangs of gentiles arrived via the market. A battle broke out between the two groups, and we pushed back twice. On Bolgarskaia Street the Jews who did not have a chance to arm themselves fled, and the rest joined the Jews who were armed in the wine courtyard. As this was happening, the number of gentiles in the gang grew, and nearly a hundred of them attacked us—and there was no police or patrol in sight. We decided to strengthen our fortification so that not even one gentile could approach us, as other Jews joined our ranks—wine transporters, residents of the old settlement . . . who heard about the defensive war and came to help us so we numbered about 250 (others said that there were even more). Gentile passersby received light blows to scare them off. Some police came to the area and ordered Jews to put down their arms, but we did not heed their orders, and they returned to report this to the head-quarters. Immediately, patrols and police came to the yard from all directions. . . . In this manner, the gangs gathered and many stood behind the patrols and threw stones at us from there. We threw the very same stones [back] at them,

but the patrols that tolerated the gang's deeds acted against
the Jews.[52]

Before the outbreak of violence, preparations had been made to
store arms at the home of Jacob Bernstein-Kogan, whose apartment had for years been the main office of the Zionist movement's
correspondence bureau and was equipped with a telephone.
It was designated as a headquarters of sorts. But Bernstein-
Kogan and his family fled their residence on the first day of the
pogrom—soon afterward it was looted—and whether the arms
stored there were used or not is unclear. By and large self-defense
at the New Market and elsewhere seems to have been cobbled
together without assistance from the likes of Bernstein-Kogan. It
was apparently organized more or less on the spot, with little if
any coordination with Jewish political groups, whether socialist
or Zionist—perhaps a significant reason why instances of self-
defense were quickly erased from subsequent Jewish accounts.
With little if any institutional underpinning, they were an out-
growth of exasperation with the indifference or incapacity of
authorities, the density of able-bodied Jews accustomed to arduous labor, and simple fury.[53]

Ironically, then, those hostile to Jews would argue then and
later that the pogrom's outsize violence was the result of Jewish
aggression, while far more typical for Jews was an insistence on
Kishinev Jewry's passivity—indeed, its outright cowardice. This
would leave an indelible mark, especially since the latter charge
would come to be at the explosive center of Bialik's famous
Kishinev poem. But the belief congealed rapidly even before that
poem's appearance in late November/December 1903. With the
pogrom's outrages now overshadowed by the deportment of its
victims, just a few months later Jewish self-defense during the

Gomel pogrom in September 1903 would be touted as little less than redemption for the wretched behavior of Kishinev's Jews.

Soon a great deal of what had occurred—and had, at first at least, been reported in the weeks immediately after the massacre—all but disappeared amid the cascade of postpogrom journalism in the Jewish press and other media too. Rarely would Jewish self-defense be mentioned except by apologists for the government. The role played by seminary students would soon be downplayed as well. Krushevan would often be relegated to a surprisingly minor role as little more than a government-controlled puppet, a shadowy figure in an episode in which he played a bit part. With the government implicated as early as mid-May in having launched the miserable episode, nearly all the others held responsible before were relegated to the margins. And much of what had already been aired—but with its details all the more confounding because Kishinev's urban layout remained so little known—was reduced to a few discrete hours of particularly intense and murderous violence that erupted just hours before the pogrom was put to an end.

By the time the violence had reached Munchehtskii Street, order was being restored elsewhere in the city. This occurred once Raaben gave Lt. Gen. V. A. Bekman, head of the garrison in Kishinev, full authority to use the army to control the mob. Orders were issued in midafternoon of the second day of the pogrom, just after 4:00 p.m. The clearing of Kishinev's streets began in earnest about two hours later. Bekman divided the city into four sections and then rapidly removed the rioters. The majority of those arrested—about five hundred of the total nine hundred jailed—were brought in during this brief period. Before then Raaben had handled the troops on his own, dispatching them without clear orders and sending them to various locations with only the vaguest of ideas as to what tasks they should perform.[54]

Few countries, if any, at the time were widely believed to be as thoroughly regulated, as militarized as Russia. In *Principles of Sociology* in 1895, Herbert Spencer wrote: "Russia, as well as ancient Peru, Egypt, and Sparta, exemplify that owning of the individual by the state . . . for a social system adapted for war."[55] How, then, to explain the dreadful pandemonium on Kishinev's streets? Who set it in motion? How could it have occurred without government complicity at least on the local level, if not higher?

In reality Russia was far less militarized than then believed. The guidelines for the use of the military in civil disturbances were hopelessly complicated and designed largely for rural disturbances, not urban ones. The military typically resented being used for such purposes, and, more often than not, befuddlement or obtuseness were the main reasons why Russian officials like those in Kishinev so mishandled urban riots—which were increasingly common at the turn of the century, mostly in the form of ever-more-violent industrial disputes.[56]

All this had a decisive imprint on the muddled reactions of Raaben and others in his command to Kishinev's disaster. The governor general was an easygoing, bumbling man, not fervent in his dislike of Jews and probably sincere in his assurance that they would be protected. But he was lax about nearly everything—except his gambling and womanizing—and showed little interest in his administrative duties and no capacity to handle the crisis.[57]

It was not Raaben's ineptitude but news of government complicity at the highest levels that would soon fixate so much of the world's press on Kishinev. This would happen with the appearance in mid-May of the so-called Plehve letter. It was this letter that prompted the plethora of public meetings denouncing Kishinev's outrages, and that inspired Leo Tolstoy to speak out in defense of Jews for the first time. It was thought to signal the most resonant of all lessons to be learned from the massacre: namely that the government at the highest levels was directly responsible for it all, and that the government was intent on wreaking havoc on (perhaps on little less than the annihilation of) its Jews. This would become the most unassailable, the most canonic of all assumptions shared by Jews regarding the late-imperial regime. And the Plehve letter constituted the main body of evidence utilized by Jews and others in the effort—in the end quite successful—to block restrictions on Jewish immigration to the United States. Such restrictions were comparable to those under very serious consideration at the time in Britain and made into law with the 1905 Alien Act.

Vyacheslav Konstantinovich Plehve was the ideal bogeyman: mordant; haughtier than Tolstoy's Karenin. No photograph shows him with anything but a grimace. His loathing of Jews was deep, all the more so since, in contrast to most Russian antisemites, he had had sustained contact with them in the Warsaw courtyards of his youth. Rather obscure until the moment he became infamous, Plehve was barely known beyond St. Petersburg's bureaucratic circles before the Kishinev pogrom; he had been appointed minister of the interior only in 1902. Yet, when Theodor Herzl sped to Russia in Kishinev's wake, it was Plehve whom Herzl was most eager to see (once Nicholas II made it clear he would not meet with him), as Plehve was now widely viewed as the keeper of Russian Jewry's fate.[58]

He was a made-to-order villain: Recollections of him by government colleagues show someone ceaselessly conniving, end-

Vyacheslav Konstantinovich Plehve.

lessly self-important, too vile to be accused of mere corruption, a human cipher. Jews, Plehve said shortly after hearing news of the Kishinev pogrom, were "conceited" and deserved "to be taught a lesson." A year after the pogrom Plehve was assassinated by an agent of the Socialist Revolutionary Party—on orders to do so largely because of Plehve's responsibility for that tragedy.[59]

The single most damning piece of evidence implicating Plehve was a letter with his signature as minister of the interior, dated two weeks before the pogrom, outlining its basic details—in short, just the proof that for so long had been exasperatingly difficult to locate. It first appeared in the London *Times* a month after the pogrom and was then reprinted widely. The Russian government's immediate reaction was to expel the *Times* correspondent. It took eight days for the government to disavow the letter, and then it did so clumsily, with all sorts of reckless, insulting claims about Jews and their responsibility for the massacre. These disavowals only sharpened suspicions that the letter was authentic. By the time the regime decided to react, it was simply taken for granted—probably even by most of its allies— that Plehve had written it and that St. Petersburg's demurral was but a perfunctory one. The letter read in part as follows:

> It has come to my knowledge that in the region entrusted to you wide disturbances are being prepared against the Jews, who chiefly exploit the local population. In view of . . . the unquestionable undesirability of instilling, by too severe measures, anti-government feeling into the population . . . your Excellency will not fail to contribute to the immediate stopping of the disorders which may arise, by means of admonitions, without at all having recourse, however, to the use of arms.[60]

It was a shocking document, a green light to marauders whose only concern was that local authorities would not respond too severely and thus alienate the rioters. Not only did the letter offer no guide as to what ought to be done to stop the massacre, but it helped to explain why the government's response turned out to be so ineffective.

There is no doubt that Plehve greatly disliked and distrusted Jews. He made these feelings amply known: He saw Jews as a disruptive force, economically untrustworthy, politically subversive, and alien to the natural rhythms of Russian life. He hated them because too many of them were radicals, and he suspected that most of them were insufficiently loyal to the regime. There is little doubt that he would not have minded if there were far fewer of them in the empire.

Nevertheless, claims that Plehve's long career was an unrelentingly anti-Jewish one are exaggerated and mostly untrue. Aleksei Lopukhin, who served under Plehve as police director, published remarkably candid memoirs after the 1917 Revolution, in which he stated that Plehve had nothing at all to do with fomenting the Kishinev pogrom. When Plehve's papers were opened to scholars after the fall of the Romanov regime, researchers scoured the materials for evidence of the infamous Kishinev letter and any other signs of Plehve's responsibility for the pogrom, but nothing was found—despite the fact that they discovered a great deal of highly embarrassing data on a wide range of other sensitive matters.[61]

Later, in the regime's final years on the eve of World War I, when it seemed to be teetering out of control, the government did include some officials—most prominently those who had engineered the cynical campaign to prosecute Mendel Beilis on the charge of using the blood of Christian children for Jewish ritual purposes—who were prepared to sacrifice the stability of Romanov Russia for a radical, right-wing agenda. It was antisemitic men of this sort, albeit not any in the employ of the central government in St. Petersburg, who, as we will soon see, likely set the Kishinev pogrom in motion. Plehve was not one of them, however. He could easily have lived without Jews; no doubt he would have much preferred to do so, but he would never have done anything—certainly not bring disorder to Russia's streets—to do away with them.[62]

It is all but certain that the letter was a forgery; its origins remain obscure and perhaps always will. Still, there is good reason to believe that whoever wrote it believed it to be essentially accurate. This is because it was widely presumed at the time that an explosion like the Kishinev pogrom simply could not occur in autocratic Russia without governmental sanction, and that such permission could only have been issued by Plehve. And self-evident as this presumption was, it was, unfortunately, unlikely that it could ever be proved to be true. So, although those responsible for the letter knew that the exact words it attributed to Plehve were inaccurate, the sentiments the letter conveyed were as good a stab at reality as anyone was likely to muster.

The belief that the riot must have been coordinated, whether by St. Petersburg or by local authorities, carried weight if only because it appeared to be so well organized. The pinpointing of Jewish properties by the mob, the collaboration of the seminarians—many in school uniform—all seemed to confirm the workings of a plot. Of course the insistence—no doubt overstated—by Jews and others once smoke cleared that interethnic relationships had been uniformly peaceful until the massacre's outbreak reinforced the belief that outsiders *had* to have set it in motion. Then again, it is difficult to sort out how much of what seemed to have been coordinated was instead the by-product of rumor amid the confusion and the terrors of the attack.

The question of whether the violence was coordinated was never taken up in the court proceedings against those charged with pogrom-related violence conducted in Odessa that fall and winter, and attempts to raise the issue were quashed. But sufficient evidence exists to point to a clutch of local activists—not the imperial government—closely linked to *Bessarabets*; it was they who, with the help of right-wing student radicals, likely managed to stir up the riot's start amid the barrage of newspaper articles charging Jews with the Dubossary killing. In the lead-up to the massacre, those activists are credited with having distributed leaflets to bars and flophouses, accusing Jews of the ritual murder. *Bessarabets* had formed a benevolent society with meetings in the back room of a local bar. The builder Georgi Pronin admitted to circulating antisemitic literature before the pogrom later defending such activity in court as a weapon against Jewish plans—concocted in the city's largest synagogue—to attack gentiles. The owner of a Kishinev tavern testified that he saw the circulars distributed at his bar. It was later claimed that, the night before the riot's start, axes, iron bars, and clubs were distributed for use against Jews and that the first rioters were clothed in the festive red shirts of workingmen so as to persuade onlookers that the attack was a spontaneous uprising of laborers against Jewish exploiters.[63]

■

At the helm of the pogrom were almost certainly Krushevan's closest associates: Pronin, a local activist named Popov, an examining magistrate named Dawidowitch, a semiliterate worker named Stepanov, and a few doctors. They seem to have been the backbone of this conspiracy. Pronin was seen as sufficiently dangerous that he was expelled by Urussov for a year's time. There may well have been no more than six or seven members of this fraternity, with the key inspiration being the longtime *Bessarabets* editor, Krushevan. True, he was in St. Petersburg during the riot, and he had sold the newspaper before his move. But his correspondence with the new editor demonstrates that he managed to maintain control over the paper; the shadow he cast over the pogrom was, by all accounts, considerable. His name was cited repeatedly during the massacre, with rioters drinking to his health during their attacks, justifying their violence by citing him as an authority, and calling out his name as they attacked Jews. Davitt names him as the riot's prime culprit on the authority of Kishinev's stalwart, eminently trustworthy mayor, Karl Schmidt.[64]

Krushevan's devotion to his native Bessarabia was profound and undoubtedly sincere. His travelogue of the region, published shortly before the riot, was the finest evocation to date of its underappreciated charms. He was a charismatic man who inspired intense devotion as well as loathing. He managed to put out several newspapers simultaneously, often writing much of

Georgi Pronin's home.

their copy. He was a public figure who was keenly, even obsessively, secretive, in his younger years a liberal who turned for reasons never aired to far-right politics; he would become, soon after Kishinev's pogrom, the publisher—and almost certainly among the authors—of the first version of *The Protocols of the Elders of Zion*. None of the effects of the Kishinev massacre would prove nearly so consequential as this bizarre and spectacularly influential forgery.

Devastated Kishinev market.

▪ 4 ▪

Burdens of Truth

again some writer
runs howling to his art.

—W. H. Auden, "Journey to Iceland"

The same streets in Lower Kishinev that Sergei Urussov would find so shocking at his first glimpse as Bessarabia's new governor general had already been anticipated in a 1903 play performed before sellout crowds on three consecutive nights at New York's Chinese Theater. Kishinev had struck a nerve with Chinese American leaders, perennial strangers in their new land, who immediately threw themselves into its relief effort. Located on Doyers Street, the theater was the only hall in Chinatown with a capacity (five hundred) large enough to seat the crowd wishing to attend. The *New York Times* reported that this was "almost certainly the first time in history that the Chinese people had come forward in the defense of Jews."[1]

The event was spearheaded by the community activist Joseph Singleton, who was born Chew Mon Sing in China. His

Kishinev-related efforts, however, did not end there. The debut was capped off with a banquet at Mon Lay Won, a Pell Street eatery that billed itself as the Chinese Delmonico: a reference to the famed New York steak house. The restaurant, packed with a mixed crowd of Jews, Chinese, and a host of city dignitaries, heard a veritable multitude of speeches, including a breathtakingly lengthy oration delivered by a local rabbi in Yiddish—a language familiar only to a sprinkling of the audience. Singleton himself spoke about how his people, much like the Jews, had been the victims of Russian tyranny. The actors donated their wages to Kishinev relief, and the enterprise yielded the handsome sum of $280, worth around $8,000 today.[2]

The Pell Street restaurant was on New York's Lower East Side, where the U.S. government's 1902 confirmation of restrictive immigration policy toward the Chinese made the prospect

Pell Street restaurant, Chinese Delmonico.

of linking their cause with that of their Jewish neighbors particularly compelling. The Kishinev tragedy continued to dominate newspaper headlines, with crowds gathering daily outside the offices of William Randolph Hearst's *New York American*—which had, with Michael Davitt's reporting, made itself into a central address for news of the pogrom—and other newspapers as well, seeking information about the fate of relatives: "The American people in this matter are not being led by the press; the press is being led by the people."[3]

By now, just weeks after the pogrom's end, it was commonplace to liken Kishinev to the worst of Jewish history's catastrophes, including the destruction of the temples of Jerusalem. Special liturgies highlighting the tragedy were introduced into American synagogues. (Elsewhere, in France and England, for instance, synagogue ritual was more centrally controlled.) The poem "Have Pity," by Shimen Frug, which appeared soon after the pogrom, was immediately set to music and recited at Yom Kippur services that fall: "Brothers, sisters, please have mercy!/Great and awful is the need/Bread is needed for the living/Shrouds are needed for the dead." The Yiddish writer Sholem Asch produced a *yizkor*, or memorial for the dead, that also would be widely integrated into religious ritual life. The ersatz Yiddish poet Yisroel ben Yehudah Fein, a Baltimore clothier, captured attention for a time with snippets of his unseasoned, ferocious work, much of it built around reverent evocations of Moshe Kigel; it was recited at communal gatherings throughout the United States.[4]

The impetus for nearly all of this was the Jews of New York City's Lower East Side. As the historian Jonathan Frankel writes: "This was the time that the new immigrant community in the United States (more than half a million Jews had arrived from the Russian empire since 1881) found itself observing from afar a major crisis in the mother community, in *der heym*."⁵ The socialist leadership of the Jewish Lower East Side—particularly *Forverts*—was able to stand at the forefront of a massive, community-wide campaign with its emphasis on relief, not politics. (Rumors that they had collected as much as five hundred thousand dollars even in the first few weeks may well be accurate.) They found themselves able to galvanize the initially quiescent established American Jewish leadership—hailing from the German Jewish immigration of the mid-nineteenth century—into action, and found a ready ally in the Hearst press. Within two or three weeks of the news reaching the United States, a previously reticent *New York Times* started reporting regularly on the pogrom as well. By May 16 the *Times* admitted that the Lower East Side was completely "wrought up" amid the steady stream of dreadful news still coming from Kishinev.⁶

Hugely popular were plays celebrating the heroism of the Jewish Socialist Labor Bund. Frequently knocked off in a matter of days, they were performed—much like the spectacle at the Chinese Theater—to create communal solidarity and especially to help with relief support. A vocalist performing "The Song of the Suffering Jews" in a Bowery theater so excited the audience that, as the *New York Times* reported, "they threw $500 in coins and bills on the stage during her performance."⁷

Far more elaborate was the production written for the resplendent New Star Theater (why it was never staged remains unclear): The play *Kishineff* features as its protagonist the swashbuckling Dave Michels, a naive and good-hearted journalist from the United States, whose courage is all the more impressive since he is one-handed. The villain is a powerful, lustful local nobleman—modeled, it seems, either on the Kishinev-based secret-police official Baron L. M. Levandal or Plehve himself; the character is relentlessly antisemitic, and his infatuation with a beautiful, innocent Jewish girl inspires him to foment the pogrom. Michels manages to save the city's Jews—he is particularly attentive to the fate of its maidens—and the play ends with the brother of the beauty so coveted by the nobleman declaring that Michels is without doubt "the truest, dearest friend our people ever had."[8] Similar in its theme was the production by M. Horowitz of *The Story of Kishineff: A Tragedy in Five Acts*, which was performed at the Bowery's Windsor Theater for weeks. In this play Bessarabia's governor general falls madly in love with a Jewess whom he rashly pursues. She is killed in the pogrom, and a Jewish youth also in love with her commits suicide on her grave.[9]

Jewish audiences required no prompting to recognize that Dave Michels was modeled on Michael Davitt, whose articles from Kishinev in the *New York American* had so mesmerized readers. One-handed (because of a childhood accident) and Irish (not American), he was responsible for the most harrowing— certainly the most widely read—accounts of the Kishinev pogrom, all of which were sympathetic to the Jewish victims, which catapulted him to meteoric fame. He was the inspiration for several other plays, too, as well as Yiddish poetry. His untimely death in 1906 would be treated much like the death of a holy martyr, marked by Jewish commemorative events attended by huge appreciative crowds.[10]

Davitt riveted such large audiences both because of his widely reprinted articles and because they were followed almost immediately by his book, *Within the Pale: The True Story of Anti-Semitic Persecution in Russia*. The volume, culled largely from his newspaper pieces, would set the standard for the next decade for almost all treatments in the United States of Jewish life in Russia. Its enthusiastic reception was unsurprising: It

Michael Davitt.

was a firsthand account by a seasoned and trusted non-Jewish journalist—and celebrated Irish radical—who, after a ten-day stay in Kishinev, agreed with nearly everything Jews and their sympathizers already believed about the pogrom, its origins, and its dire long-term implications.

The book's popularity was instantaneous. "It is an unfortunate thing that this book cannot be in the home of every Jewish family in this country," declared the *Independent Order*, a periodical sponsored by the Jewish Masonic Lodge of the Free Sons of Israel; "It is likewise unfortunate that it cannot be in the home of every non-Jewish family." The Jewish Publication Society of

America soon reissued it under its own imprint, releasing several thousand additional copies of the book (produced originally by the publishing house A. S. Barnes) and arranging for copies to be sent to the president, vice president, members of Congress, and justices of the Supreme Court. So inspired was the society's board, which boasted a rich array of American Jewry's grandees, that despite the book's support for Zionism—which upset many of them—it announced a plan to launch an entire series of new books built on the basis of Davitt's spotlighting the terrible fate of Russia's Jews. This effort would culminate with Simon Dubnow's magisterial three-volume *History of the Jews of Russia and Poland*, published by the Jewish Publication Society of America between 1916 and 1920, still the most widely consulted work on the subject.[11]

To the extent that any other work on Kishinev could capture a readership equal to Davitt's, it was Bialik's "In the City of Killing," still seen as the finest—certainly the most influential—Jewish poem written since medieval times. A writer celebrated earlier in the smallish hothouse of Hebrew literature as its "national poet," the thirty-year-old Bialik's reputation soared with the appearance of "In the City of Killing." Davitt's book portrayed a community of many millions, surrounded by hatred and in need of instant repatriation, with a return to ancient Zion the only credible solution. In contrast Bialik offered an unforgiving portrait of the weight of age-old persecution having recurred time and again, now in full view on Kishinev's streets and causing irreparable harm to the bodies and souls of contemporary Jews.

"In the City of Killing" almost immediately swept aside nearly all other literary works on Kishinev, including Frug's ubiquitous—if also transparently maudlin—"Have Pity." Entire schools of Jewish poetics would define themselves in relation to

Bialik's work, with some insisting that it was not poetry at all but, at best, a mere journalistic compendium. Others excoriated it for its lack of accuracy and the cruelty of its unwarranted attack. On and off, Jewish educators in Palestine and later in Israel would debate whether it benefited or harmed the Israeli school curriculum (where it would long occupy pride of place). Debate over the public role given his poetry remains robust: Israel's most prominent literary critic, Dan Miron, recently insisted that the noxious influence of Bialik's pogrom poetry on schoolchildren—particularly because of its jaundiced view of Diaspora Jewish life—was sufficient reason for it to have been removed from Israel's school reading lists.[12]

With its biblical cadence and the authority of a witness—Bialik had spent five weeks in Kishinev soon after the pogrom—it sounded much like a call from the grave: "Rise and go to the city of killings. . . ."

Joseph Klausner, a leading Odessa-based Hebrew critic of the day, said that, when first reading the poem, he read and reread it over three consecutive days, fearing at times that he was on the verge of going mad. Later he wrote Bialik that he was convinced it was a greater achievement than Ecclesiastes. Bialik's Hebrew combined declarative biblical cadence with a delicately individual poetic voice; its capacity to capture—through the eyes of a witness of sorts—the most jarring of all Jewish horrors of the time gave the work a role comparable in its day to that of Elie Wiesel's *Night* half a century later.

Different as it was from Davitt's reportage, Bialik's poem, too, was the product of meticulous and prolonged examination of Kishinev's tragedy. It was this that prompted critics, including several of the very first responses to the poem, to argue that its detailed evocation was not poetry at all but little more than a newspaper account. Its first reviewer in the Hebrew press, Shmuel Perlman, went so far as to insist that he found it lacking any semblance of imagination. Bialik's five weeks in Kishinev overlapped with Davitt's stay, and they shared the same assistant, a local Jewish schoolteacher. But, it seems, the two men never met, coming as they did from such vastly different backgrounds and with, quite literally, no common language. Bialik's poem has, indeed, something of the feel of a reporter's notebook: Miron has astutely suggested that it bears a resemblance to the wartime reportage of Stephen Crane, widely celebrated in the Jewish press, with its reliance on an interplay between copious detail and sensationalism similar to that displayed in Yiddish journalism in the United States and elsewhere.[13]

Both Davitt and Bialik had been dispatched to Kishinev to amass data; Bialik's decision to scuttle the task and write his poem would come somewhat later. Both managed to distill the catastrophe in ways all the more enduring because their accounts were so precise and concrete. And both would come away, as it happens, with the same sense of what they were certain was the event's single most disturbing feature—namely the cowardice of Kishinev's Jewish males. Both writers saw this as what most decisively defined the tragedy. Davitt excised all mention of it in his published work. Bialik situated it at the heart of his poem.

■

Even before the pogrom Bialik, born in 1873 in the village of Radi, near Zhitomir, was lauded as one of Jewish literature's most promising writers. The prophet-like figure he would soon become in the Jewish imagination—echoing, no doubt intentionally, in his Kishinev poem features of Alexander Pushkin's brief and powerful "The Prophet" ("Tormented by a spiritual thirst/I stumbled through a gloomy waste")—differed drastically from the convivial, somewhat coarse, mostly self-taught man his literary friends knew well. The essayist and rabbinic scholar Chaim Tchernowitz, a close friend, wrote in his memoirs that the Bialik whose reputation so soared in these years bore little resemblance to the rough-and-tumble fellow with whom he spent so much time once he settled in Odessa. A farm boy ever concerned about his rusticated manners and the tenuousness of his intellect in contrast to the more rigorously disciplined figures around him, Tchernowitz's Bialik little resembles the genius whose lines would soon be memorized by generations of Jewish readers. A good example, Tchernowitz suggested, of the chasm between his reputation and reality was the notion that Bialik was a veritable Talmud master (a *matmid*, a prodigious devotee), which was the title of one of his most beloved poems. Tchernowitz insisted that this was inconceivable if only because Bialik was so hungry for company that rarely would he permit himself to be alone long enough to achieve true mastery of rabbinic Judaism's voluminous library.[14]

Bialik moved from Volozhin, near Vilna, where he studied in its famed yeshiva, to Odessa in 1891, eager to fall in with its celebrated Jewish intellectuals. He worked hard to gain their approval, to rub shoulders with the group's luminaries, and to publish his poetry in their journals. Most important, as he saw it, was to put himself at the disposal of its dominant figure, the Hebrew essayist Ahad Ha'am (the pen name of Asher Ginzberg), who had been embraced by the small but ambitious Odessa-based group of Hebrew-inflected intellectuals as indispensable to the redefinition of Judaism: He was seen by them as the most original and subtle of all living Jewish thinkers.[15]

Ahad Ha'am's writings were mostly in the form of brisk, tightly constructed essays melding classical Jewish and worldly erudition. Authoritative in their prescriptions—such authority was greatly valued by readers, often barely more than a few steps removed from the traditional Jewish study house—they were rendered in a limpid, elegant Hebrew. Broadly speaking Zionist in its convictions—with his goal, much like Theodor Herzl's, the creation of a Jewish political entity in the land of Israel—Ahad Ha'am's writing about the movement was bitingly critical. He attacked its capacity to translate goals into reality, its vaunted realpolitik (which he scored as childishly naive), and its professed pragmatism (which he loathed because of its inattention to morality).[16]

Zionism's goals, he insisted, must be both less and more ambitious than Herzl proclaimed. Its belief that it was capable of immediately transporting large numbers of Jews to Palestine was not merely unrealistic but undesirable: The local economy could not absorb them, the Arab population would resist the encroachment, and the national entity born of a haphazard, ill-conceived exodus of this sort would be a dreadful embarrassment. What could be achieved by Zionism was still grander; however, this was achievable only in Palestine and, unless confronted immediately, was certain to slip out of Jewry's hands.[17]

This goal amounted to little less than the salvaging of Jewish civilization. No comparable challenge had faced Jews since the temple's destruction in the first century; this moment was no less momentous. And, much as in the distant past, the tools essential for such work were cultural, not political—a marshaling of Jewry's spiritual timber with far-reaching influence on all aspects of Jewish life and profound impact on the rhythm of Jewish life in Palestine. The errors of Herzl's Zionism were not in its focus on Palestine but in its mindless aping of European nationalism.[18]

Hence the moment at hand, as Ahad Ha'am saw it, was no less convulsive—also potentially redemptive—than the crucible following the destruction of the second temple in Jerusalem. Then Judaism had been confronted by its implosion as a cultic faith in the first century. Now Jewry's entry into a larger cultural world no longer demarcated by religious differences meant that—unless new, credible boundaries were constructed to define the contours of Judaism that were receptive to larger currents but also true to Jewish cultural qualities—these qualities could well recede into oblivion. Such a delicate mix was conceivable only if its epicenter was in the land of Israel, where the inexorable pressures elsewhere to assimilate would be mediated in a Jewish milieu and where modernity could be embraced without risk.[19]

Ahad Ha'am offered men like Bialik—nearly all in his Odessa circle were males steeped in Jewish tradition and eager to blend past beliefs into the present—an indispensable road map. The symbiosis he promised could be realized only if Jews built a new home in their old land with a suitable cultural infrastructure. Only there would the interplay between isolation and cultural immersion permit Jews to live free from ethnocentrism and yet be unreservedly Jewish. It was England that provided Ahad Ha'am with his most palpable model of how this might work: It was the mightiest empire of the age with a singularly cohesive culture, as he saw it, secular yet in tune with its unobtrusive religious rhythms. No more intrusive than England's fog or rain, these rhythms offered Jews a model for the future.[20]

In its own way Odessa was no less an influence. Boisterous, multinational, and relatively young (the city was founded in 1794), Odessa had long been a major commercial port and had a rich array of cultural institutions—with its lavish opera house and its schools and libraries—all of which were a major

S. Raskin

A Palestinian Gallery

WE REPRODUCE on this page four sketches prepared specially for The New Palestine by Mr. Saul Raskin, the well-known Jewish artist, who is now in Palestine. These are the first of a series which Mr. Raskin has undertaken for us and which will be reproduced in forthcoming issues. The comments to the sketches are supplied by Mr. Raskin.

ACHAD HAAM

Quiet, retired, infinitely modest—this is Achad Haam, the father of spiritual Zionism, one of the most distinguished men of this generation. You may see him at every meeting in Tel Aviv, withdrawn somewhere in a corner, smoking his eternal Russian cigarette. He comes to listen, and not to speak. He is watching others develop the dream to which he gave the earliest inspiration, and he does not interfere. But on the rare occasion when he does take part in a debate or discussion, he has the breathless attention of the entire audience, and his words are greeted like manna from heaven.

CHAIM NACHMAN BIALIK

Bialik is, in one sense, a new-comer to Palestine; but in the real sense of the word, he is one who has never been outside of Palestine. He is a part of Palestine wherever he is, and carries the country with him. But he came to Palestine with a difference — he has removed his sparse Russian moustache. He has something of the American in his appearance, and sometimes, in certain lights, and in profile, he awakes distant memories of Woodrow Wilson. I made the above sketch while he was addressing the assembly of school-children who had turned out to bring him greetings. For a new-comer Bialik speaks good Hebrew.

MAYOR DIEZENGOFF

Mayor Meyer Diezengoff, of Tel Aviv, who became mayor and remains mayor without being a politician—certainly the most popular man in Tel Aviv, and one of the most popular men in Palestine. He built a city and became mayor of it—and he is still adding to it. Always busy—without a chance to recuperate in Palm Beach, eternally concerned with all the details of his administration, following with loving care even the most trifling developments in the city. And withal a charming personality, as American Jewry can now attest.

M. GOLINKIN

M. Golinkin is the Director of the Palestinian Hebrew Opera. Directing Hebrew Opera in Palestine is not merely a matter of music: to a love and understanding of music the pioneer of Hebrew Opera must add an iron will and unquenchable faith. Mr. Golinkin has all of these. He has brought opera of the highest standard into Palestine. His conductor's baton is a kind of magic wand, which inspires the young men and women of Palestine to an understanding of music, and, stranger still, to the ability to sing.

Ahad Ha'Am, Bialik, and their circle.

influence on the tenor of its Jewish life. Jews constituted a third of its population—albeit with the same swollen army of Jewish laborers and poor as elsewhere. But here too lived a large, highly visible slice of professionals (half of the city's doctors were Jews), most of whom were liberal in their cultural and political convictions, and many were second-generation Russian-speakers, often distant from the patterns, linguistic as well as religious, of Jewish life. Odessa's Russian schools, despite quotas, were packed with Jews. Vladimir Jabotinsky, born in Odessa, in his early twenties was already a successful journalist for the city's Russian-language liberal press and fluent in Italian long before he mastered either Hebrew or Yiddish.[21]

So it was that, unlike smaller towns in the Pale of Settlement, in this highly acculturated Jewish milieu neither Ahad Ha'am nor Bialik were viewed as particularly relevant. In the minds of local progressive youth, to the extent that Ahad Ha'am and Bialik were known at all, they were seen as musty conservatives obsessed with the perils of assimilation, speaking a homegrown, awkward (at least accented) Russian, and were proponents of curious endeavors like the revival of literary Hebrew. Hence the preoccupation of Ahad Ha'am's circle with first-century Judaism that had managed, as they saw it, in the shadow of the temple's destruction, to rebuild a vibrant Jewish life. The first meeting between Ahad Ha'am and Simon Dubnow (then still little known but soon the leading chronicler of Russian Jewry) found the two lost in a spirited talk about first-century Judaism, a topic jarringly pertinent for both.[22]

Bialik's Jewish nationalism was especially fierce, stitched out of wounds—above all the scars of an awful childhood (the early death of his father and his mother's abandonment) that he would come to see as a correlative of exile's terrors. Thus, in his Kishinev masterpiece, he managed to conflate—more powerfully than ever before or since in Hebrew—nationalist aspiration with personal anguish. Its narrator is the messenger of God, an irreparably flawed divinity that is, as Miron aptly put it, "irrational, moody, arbitrary, capricious, and at certain moments half-demented."[23]

Bialik arrived in Kishinev armed with patronizingly detailed instructions drawn up by Dubnow, who was head of a historical commission—as he himself rather grandly characterized it—cobbled together in the wake of the Kishinev pogrom. Dubnow, a decade older than Bialik and with a touch of pedantry, immediately identified Kishinev's massacre as a historical turning point that demanded just the sort of politically engaged scholarship he and others of this milieu had long championed. He hoped to amass detailed, accurate information regarding the tragedy and to use these data to strengthen the cause of Jewish nationalism. His was a liberal nationalism fixed on Jewish continuity in the Diaspora, not in Palestine, and he saw a healthy Jewish life in the immediate future sustained by Jewish autonomy in a multinational, liberalizing world.[24]

Nonetheless, like Ahad Ha'am, Dubnow was intent on the reconstruction of Judaism as uncompromisingly modern, secular, and authentic. Lessons culled from Kishinev's tragedy—of self-sufficiency, national honor, and resistance to tyranny—could now, as he saw it, prove to be crucial building blocks in this larger project. His intent was to use the raw data culled by Bialik for historical reconstruction that would help instruct Jews as to how best to respond to horrors in the future. In Kishinev's wake, Dubnow was convinced that such eruptions were certain to recur time and again.[25]

Shy, essentially unschooled, Bialik was an odd choice for the assignment; most likely he agreed because he was desperately short of money. Greatly respected in the small circle of devotees of Hebrew poetry, he was little known beyond it. He brought with him to Kishinev his list of interview questions for eyewitnesses and had already written an initial, poetic response, "Al Ha-Shehitah" ("On the Slaughter"). The poem was rather conventional in structure and theme: "Vengeance for the little children/ The devil has not framed." He now devoted himself to the meticulous recording of witness testimony. His weeks in Kishinev, listening day after day to victims, drove him, as he later admitted, "half-mad."[26]

Drawing out witnesses with a rare delicacy—an assistant later described Bialik's singular power of empathy—he and his associates filled five notebooks with the testimonies, translated from their original Yiddish into Hebrew. Once this labor was finished, Bialik left Kishinev for his father-in-law's summerhouse several hundred miles away, in the countryside between Kiev and Zhitomir. There he set his notebooks aside, never touching them again, and worked instead on his Kishinev poem, which he had already started during his sojourn in the pogrom-afflicted city.[27]

There is every reason to believe that Bialik set out to do just what he had been asked to, but then, of course, he did the opposite. Or so it might appear. Yet this would not be how Dubnow saw it: He was greatly pleased with Bialik's poem, and he recognized that it had a far greater impact than any work of history could. Curiously, as Dubnow seemed to see it, no substantive difference existed in this instance between the tasks of a chronicler and those of a poet; the lines separating history from journalism or poetry blurred in the pogrom's wake. With victim relief as well as the moral education of the Jewish people at stake, poetry seemed a far more valuable—perhaps an even more accurate—vehicle than the historical narrative Dubnow had first envisioned.[28]

In part this was because (as Dubnow's Odessa circle saw it) there was little new information to be learned, since the substance of Kishinev's story was already known. Immediately on hearing of the massacre, that circle of writers had formulated— and circulated widely—their sense of what transpired; this occurred well before Bialik was dispatched on his mission. Kishinev's tragedy was amply visible to all around them: Odessa's hotels were packed with refugees, the Odessa railway station was inundated, and rumors of still another pogrom were rife. Based on little more than what might be gleaned from those fleeing Kishinev for Odessa and points west, as well as the reports of the Kishinev schoolteacher Pesach Averbach—an eyewitness, soon one of Bialik's Kishinev assistants, whose accounts were already appearing in the St. Petersburg Hebrew daily *Ha-Zeman*—a declamation was issued within days of the riot. This statement prejudged not only the pogrom's cause but also its long-term implications. It was written largely by Ahad Ha'am and declared that, without doubt, Kishinev's massacre was only the first of many such tragedies, that Russian authorities were culpable (this was written weeks before the surfacing of the Plehve letter), and that the most troubling aspect by far was not the violence perpetrated by gentiles but the cowardice of the Jews.[29]

Supported by Bialik together with others in the Odessa Jewish literary orbit, and circulated throughout Russia's Jewish community, the declamation insisted that the lamentable shortcomings of Jews were Kishinev's most shocking feature. When asked a week or so after the disaster to contribute to a volume whose earnings would be donated to victim relief, Ahad Ha'am wrote in a letter: "This isn't, in my view, a run-of-the-mill misfortune for which it is appropriate to provide succor with the use of regular solutions of this sort." No one doubted the usefulness of such efforts, he admitted, but they failed to address the fundamental dilemma so vividly revealed by the pogrom, namely the "inner poverty" of Jewish life now apparent for all to see. It was because of such wretched inadequacy that Jews responded in Kishinev like "slaves" undergoing humiliations that healthy human beings would never have tolerated. The only credible response now was the "raising of a new flag . . . a flag of inner freedom, a flag of individual honor."[30]

As soon as he heard news of the massacre, Ahad Ha'am said it "filled his heart," making it "impossible to do anything else." It so shattered and overwhelmed him that his deep-set inclination toward moderation—such caution being among his most pronounced characteristics—and his politics, so often assailed as hopelessly bourgeois, were now decisively cast aside. So thoroughly were these renounced that he insisted that the Odessa document call for Jews to defend themselves by taking up arms and that all its signatories list their names despite the risk of imprisonment. Calmer heads prevailed, and, once the text was issued, its authorship was attributed to the (nonexistent) "Association of Hebrew Writers." (Learning of this decision after it was already on record, Ahad Ha'am's response was bitter and uncompromising.)[31]

The thrust of the statement, however, was just as he wrote it. It condemned the terrible actions of the mob and the inaction of the Russian government as inexcusable. But these comments were almost an afterthought. Its target was Jewish passivity— a passivity so noxious that such behavior was itself a possible source of gentile hatred.

Not since the massacres of the seventeenth and eighteenth centuries—more or less in the same region—had Jews undergone anything comparable with the Kishinev pogrom that was not the doing of rank criminals, as Russian officials claimed. Such behavior would have been inconceivable had Jews enjoyed equal protection under the law and not been subjected to the whims of the mob. "A human being for whom there exists no obligation to treat with justice" possessed no true rights. In the absence of such protection, the belief prevailed that beating—even killing—Jews was justified. No decree, no commission, no jail time could dislodge such assumptions, reinforced daily by government hostility.[32]

This was all sufficiently dreadful. But far worse—and here the document reached fever pitch—was the wretchedness of a people numbering some five million who saw as their only recourse to throw themselves on the mercy of others, indeed to do so without so much as trying to protect themselves or their loved ones from attack. "Who knows if such disgraceful behavior isn't the fundamental cause for the hatred felt for us by the masses?" Had it been known that Jews would not tolerate such treatment, the pogrom never would have erupted.[33]

"Brothers, the blood of Kishinev cries out to you," the document exclaimed, as much cri de coeur as reproof. What must be launched, it urged, was a "perpetual organization" with its goal being ever-vigilant preparation for armed resistance. The document never spelled out explicitly its call for the arming of Jews; indeed, it acknowledged that the precise details of what Jews were to do must not be spelled out. But its militant message was sufficiently clear—so clear, in fact, that many of its readers were shocked at its brazenness. Though issued without a listing of the names of those responsible for it, this soon became an open secret among Jews. Bialik, a chubby, nondescript man, arrived in Kishinev with its bitter words ringing in his ears.[34]

■

Davitt came to Kishinev with altogether different baggage. Long a fixture in the Irish struggle against England—a point of identification that helped shape his sympathies—he was widely regarded as a figure of stalwart principle. (He broke with Irish Parliamentary Party leader Charles Stewart Parnell after the latter's divorce.) An ailing, middle-aged man of strong independent views, Davitt exerted significant political influence for a time. His early advocacy of working-class solidarity across English and Irish lines was a major force in the creation of the British Labour Party. Tireless in his insistence on the linkage between landownership and political freedom, he was a powerful inspiration for the young Mohandas Gandhi. James Joyce, an admirer, would draw on him in *The Portrait of the Artist as a Young Man.* Self-made, born into a poor family, Davitt endured long terms in British jails as the result of his political activity; these stints, curiously enough, were interspersed with his election to Parliament. For years he eked out his living from journalism and public speaking.[35]

Contacted by the London editor of Hearst's *New York American*—then a scandal-splattered tabloid with sparse international coverage—Davitt was invited during an age of great muckraking (Upton Sinclair's *The Jungle*, for instance, was published in 1906) to travel to Kishinev to cover the pogrom's aftermath. Front-page notices declared him the paper's "emissary" to devastated Kishinev. The trip was an arduous one: It required connections in Paris and then Constantinople, with transport to Odessa before, finally, arrival in Kishinev. Despite precarious health— Davitt died three years later, at the age of sixty—he threw himself into the task.[36]

As it happens, Davitt's views on Jews were complex, born of sympathy yet based on unassailable beliefs regarding inbred racial characteristics that presumably led Jews to exploit the weak, ignorant, or naive. In a bloated six-hundred-page tome published in 1902, *The Boer War for Freedom*, he singled out as prime exploiters of the beleaguered South African region no fewer than forty "Anglicized and German Jews" who, alongside Cecil Rhodes, were "the capitalist kings" most responsible for oppression of the Boers. Davitt never entirely turned his back on such notions: In the preface to his Kishinev book, written the following year, he states: "Where anti-Semitism stands in fair political combat . . . or against the engineers of a sordid war as in South Africa . . . I am resolutely in line with its spirit and programme."[37]

It seems that Davitt endorsed not-dissimilar views even while on his way to Kishinev. By coincidence he found himself traveling on a sleeping car in a seat across from the British businessman and Marxist politician (the author of the first introduction to Marx in the English language) Henry Hyndman. Hyndman knew Davitt because of his activity in Irish causes, and he relates in his memoirs how surprised he was on entering the car and noticing on the opposite seat the name "M. Davitt." Once Davitt entered, Hyndman writes, "Our fellow travelers were astonished to see two elderly and apparently sane travelers suddenly set to work to dance a fandango of jubilation in the corridor of the sleeping-car." The first words out of Davitt's mouth were: "There is not a police bureau in Europe [that] would believe this was an accidental meeting."[38]

They talked about the boon of small landownership (by far Davitt's greatest preoccupation as an Irish nationalist), about the beauty of the Bavarian and Austrian countryside, about socialism, and about Jews. Hyndman would remain in touch with Davitt after his Kishinev stay. The gist of what Hyndman took away regarding Davitt's views of Jews was that, while he felt great antipathy for those responsible for the massacre, he saw Jews as fanning discontent or worse. "Undoubtedly, Davitt in private while not excusing the Russian authorities felt that Russia would be much better off if she had no Jews at all in her boundaries." (Hyndman might have exaggerated Davitt's antagonism to Jews in light of his own jaundiced opinions: "Anglo-Hebraic empire in Africa" was how he referred to South Africa.) Sitting together on the train, Hyndman related to Davitt the story of one ragged Jew who, within a few months of stumbling into a Russian village, had "to use Marx's phrase, . . . eaten up the pores of this simple society. All now was his with the peasants and their families little better than his slaves." Hyndman was left with the impression that Davitt agreed that the story captured something essential, if also tragic, about the economic activity of Jews.[39]

True, upon returning to Ireland, Davitt defended Jews in the wake of the Limerick riot and boycott of 1904, widely described at the time as a pogrom—no more than two thousand Jews then lived there—where he criticized anti-Jewish attackers in print while also visiting the homes of victims. However, he continued to share a set of staunch views regarding the intractable characteristics of the races: English motivations he would forever distrust; African "savages" he sidelined in his book on South Africa; and the responsibility of Moldavians for most of Kishinev's violence could be traced to their ancestry as Roman slaves. And then there were the Jews—harmless where gentiles were clever, such as in the United States, but justly feared in backward Russia. He never did rationalize their oppression, but it was a sufficient argument for Jewish mass migration elsewhere—preferably, as Davitt would come to see it, to Palestine.[40]

Davitt reached Odessa on May 2 amid fear of new anti-Jewish attacks and was greeted straightaway by the local Jewish leader Meir Dizengoff, who served as Davitt's translator during his first day or two in Russia. (A few years later, in Palestine, Dizengoff would emerge as the founding—and long-standing—mayor of Tel Aviv.) Davitt quickly summoned Kishinev's Jewish communal leader Jacob Bernstein-Kogan, just back from St. Petersburg, where he had gone to report on the pogrom, to his Odessa hotel room. (Davitt had arrived in Odessa eager to speak with Bernstein-Kogan since, when first hired by the Hearst press in London, he had been given a list of local contacts, with Bernstein-Kogan's name at the top.) In that hotel room he related details of the massacre for seven or eight hours. Davitt spent the next two days speaking with a cluster of Russian officials and merchants and also an English merchant or two residing in the city. All condemned Kishinev's violence while also singling out the rapacity of Jews as its essential cause. As one Russian official put it, the Jews "exploited the Christians in a hundred unscrupulous ways, to their own aggrandizement."[41]

Once Davitt arrived in Kishinev some five weeks after the pogrom's end—during the Russian Orthodox festivities of the Feast of Ascension and Holy Trinity and persistent rumors of new riots—his hotel room was swamped by Jews beseeching his help to immigrate to the United States, though he was unlikely to have much influence on this score. He communicated with the help of two translators, Averbach (who would also work with Bialik) as well as a retired Hungarian Jewish officer, both of whom were fluent in Yiddish.[42]

A meticulous journalist, Davitt spent his few days in Kishinev collecting impressions, speaking with Mayor Schmidt and others, and even seeking out Krushevan and—once it was clear that the latter had left months earlier—his closest coworkers. Almost immediately Davitt was browbeaten by his London editor for articles and warned that, if he did not come up with something soon, he would have to abandon Kishinev for an interview with Tolstoy. Davitt resisted the pressure, insisting on gathering with care the many disparate details of the massacre. Thus, as he would acknowledge in his book, "to discover the truth amidst a mass of conflicting evidence would be a formidable task; to arrive at definite conclusions as to the immediate and the contributory causes of the sanguinary outrages perpetrated upon the Jews of Kishineff on the 19th and 20th of April, was a tedious and painful process, beset with innumerable difficulties."[43]

It is no exaggeration that the five weeks Bialik spent in Kishinev irrevocably changed the rest of his life. Entering ransacked homes, day after day, he sat with victims and bystanders, prompting them with rare gentleness to air the most gruesome experiences. Not infrequently he spent hours at a time with a single victim.

During the same period Bialik was urged by the literary critic Klausner, a close friend and editor of *Ha-Shiloach*, the journal most closely linked to Ahad Ha'am, who had now stepped down from the editorship, to write an autobiography of sorts. Klausner planned to draw on it for a biographical essay, the first to appear, on Bialik. The poet threw himself into this task too, producing a document in the form of a letter many dozens of pages long. In it he dwelled, much as Klausner had urged him to do, on his earliest years. At the same time, of course, he also started work on his Kishinev poem. The meshing of childhood recollections—some of them achingly painful as he listened, day after day, to stories of the rampage on Kishinev's streets, including the rape of its young girls and women—served to strengthen his belief in the perversions of exile. This contagion, as he now felt more strongly than ever before, could only be rectified once Jews finally removed themselves from the Diaspora's dark, terrible shadow.[44]

Quite how intimately Bialik conflated his personal anguish with that of Kishinev's defiled females has been explored by the literary scholar Michael Gluzman, who unearthed how Bialik expropriated the language of Rivka Schiff without quoting her—whose rape testimony was the lengthiest and most detailed that Bialik recorded—in an early draft of his autobiographical letter. Schiff had described to Bialik how, once she finally stood up after the multiple rapes that she endured, "I was pulverized and crushed, like a vessel filled with shame and filth." So overwhelmed was Bialik by the phrase that he expropriated it, introducing the same words into the first version of his letter to Klausner. He did this in a description of a childhood humiliation that he now admitted had haunted him ever since; it involved the repeated beating of his buttocks in an outhouse by an older cousin, who was probably mentally unstable, soon after the death of young Bialik's father. The phrase would also appear in the original Yiddish version of the autobiography—though this manuscript remained unpublished—but was eventually dropped once the Hebrew version adapted by Bialik appeared in print.[45]

Gluzman believed that Bialik's inner turmoil at the time was composed of a fierce condemnation of weakness directed simultaneously inward and at the Jews of Kishinev. The raw recollections of the rape victims he now heard, sometimes daily, recalled for him a long-suppressed, dreadful memory when he too found himself intimidated, powerless, and shamed. What Bialik would do with this humiliation was to recast it, replacing it with rage directed at the beaten Jews of Kishinev. "This rage," argued Gluzman, ". . . leads him to construct the Jews of Kishinev as abject, and in the process to reshape and reconstruct his own identity."[46]

Amid this turmoil—intimate, political, and literary—Bialik fell in love, quite how deeply remains unclear. The object of this love was a married woman four years his senior who had a child. The interplay between shame and silence figured prominently in his poetry, with this episode an unspoken but nonetheless open secret in Palestinian-Jewish and Israeli literary circles that was revealed publicly only after the death of his widow, Manya, some forty years after Bialik's passing in 1934.

The woman with whom he fell in love was the painter Esfir Yeselevich, known later by the pseudonym Ira Jan. A friend of Ahad Ha'am's daughter, Jan grew up in a Russian-speaking acculturated Jewish home in Kishinev with no knowledge of Hebrew and probably little Yiddish. She was married to a physician with close ties to the Social Revolutionary Party, and her father, a lawyer assisting Jewish pogrom victims at the time, hosted one of Kishinev's most-sought-after intellectual salons. He had opened his home to Bialik so that he might write in peace during his Kishinev stay, and Bialik spent a good deal of time sitting on their veranda in the temperate spring weather. It was there that the romance blossomed. His wife, Manya, whom he had married young, was unschooled, rough-hewn, and intensely loyal, and she went to her death unaware of Bialik's affair—or, at least, of its intensity.[47]

Jan's letters to Bialik are passionate; his to her have disappeared. Soon after his departure she announced that she was leaving her husband and child. She began studying Hebrew; she translated Bialik's poems; and she drew the portrait that appeared in the second volume of his collected work. Jan continued to collaborate with him until she eventually left for Jerusalem with her daughter; in 1907 she joined the newly opened Bezalel Art Academy, where she was Palestine's first female Jewish artist. Soon

Esfir Yeselevich, known as Ira Jan.

after meeting her, Bialik announced that he too would soon leave for Palestine, where he agreed to take up a teaching position at a new school planned for orphans of the Kishinev pogrom. He went so far as to negotiate his starting salary as well as a teaching schedule, and his plans to emigrate were aired in the Jewish press. However, he changed his mind, and he never publicly explained why.[48]

Her love for him persisted; whether or not his did remains ambiguous (he was known at times to speak of her disparagingly to friends). He may have continued to meet her in Odessa and Warsaw, perhaps also in Palestine. Whether or not she still hoped he would join her is also uncertain. She remained in Palestine until World War I, then was forced to move to Egypt when wartime Russian Jews came under suspicion from Ottoman authorities. While she was there, most of her paintings disappeared. Her return to Palestine was disastrous: She contracted a fatal illness and died just after the war's end.

Bialik's love poetry was fiercely erotic; the most powerful of the love poems were almost certainly written with Jan in mind, but they also contain a palpable revulsion at sexual passion or, better said, the act of sex. This attitude could well have intruded on their relationship, which was one of his very few passionate romances.[49]

Stepping out of this cauldron—something of an idyll, too— and spending the summer at the home of his father-in-law in the countryside just beyond Zhitomir, Bialik was now slated to produce his summary of the Kishinev massacre transcripts. There is little mention of this work in his letters of this period; nearly all his correspondence about his writing focused on the progress of the pogrom poem.[50]

How the witness accounts Bialik absorbed during his five weeks in Kishinev informed his poem has long bedeviled his readers. Was its half-mad narrator God himself or a hapless emissary? Either way, the government censor responsible for approving it for publication—he was a Lubavitch Hasid and also a Russian Orthodox convert who reverted to Hasidism during annual visits to his family abroad—would permit its appearance only after the removal of lines he deemed offensive to Jewish tradition.[51] Its lacerating portrait of the bestiality of gentiles and the passivity of Jews would contribute to its sanctification in Israeli culture but also to repeated calls for its removal from the school curriculum because of its distorted portrait of exile.

Yet despite such controversy, it retains an authority akin to that of an amalgam of Samuel Taylor Coleridge with Walt Whitman and the Book of Job:

> *Rise up and go to the town of the killing and you'll come*
>   *to the yards*
> *and with your eyes and your own hand feel the fence*
> *and on the trees and on the stones and plaster of the walls*
> *the congealed blood and hardened brains of the dead.*[52]

His narrator moves from neighborhood to neighborhood, often building on the massacre's chronology. He uses imagery drawn from Bialik's interviews as well as newspaper reports. Hence the poem opens with feathers filling the city's streets from the ripped bedding of ransacked Jewish houses on the riot's first day. Bialik invokes the interplay between Kishinev's sudden temperate weather on the first morning of the pogrom and the pogrom's eruption; critics have suggested that one reason he does this is to juxtapose early-twentieth-century springlike expectations with the backdrop of the massacre's terrible reality.[53] The city's courtyards, attics, and outhouses, sites of many of the worst outrages, are described with details drawn from the newspaper accounts—like the disemboweling of pregnant women—that were eventually dismissed as inaccurate:

> *The case of a disemboweled chest filled with feathers,*
> *the case of nostrils and nine-inch nails with skulls*
>   *and hammers,*
> *the case of slaughtered human beings hung up from beams*
>   *like fish.*[54]

Bialik introduces the worst of the outrages in Lower Kishinev as the narrator descends physically as well as psychologically:

> *And you will go down the hill of the city and find a vegetable*
>   *garden. . . .*
> *And like a camp of giant owls and terrible bats*
> *fears sprawl over the corpses drunk with blood and tired.*[55]

Although holy martyrdom in the Jewish past was once enacted in the name of fealty to the divine, such faith is now in tatters. God is no longer a palpable presence in the lives—or the deaths—of Jews. Such killings are thus now meaningless, with God himself but a shadow, a veritable beggar:

> *Forgive me beggars of the world, your God is as poor as you,*
> *poor he is in your living and so much more in your deaths*
> *and if you come tomorrow for your due and knock*
>   *on my doors—*
> *I'll open for you: come and look! I've gone down in*
>   *the world!*[56]

Bialik's prophecy looks, wrote Miron, "as if it came not to revive the people but to put it to death. . . . God sends the poet-prophet on a difficult and frustrating mission. He must go to the city of slaughter, scour all its corners, penetrate its basements and attics, its gardens and stables and, in each place where there transpired during the pogrom a deed of murder or rape . . . the impressions will accumulate in a painful mass, but God forbids him to give them expression of any kind."[57]

Still, the incendiary core of the poem was its devastating laceration of Jewish male cowardice. Amid the din of accusations and counteraccusations following the pogrom—with many Jews, most vocally the Jewish Socialist Labor Bund, denouncing the wealthy for caring only to protect themselves and their property—was the charge that Jewish men hid themselves while doing nothing to stop the rapes. These accusations would eventually capture a greater visibility than the horrors experienced by the city's females, drawing on the stereotypes of feminized Jewish males hopelessly softened by the humiliations of the Diaspora (as argued by Zionists) or the superstitions of a blandly passive religiosity (as argued by Jewish socialists and others).[58]

By the time Bialik's poem appeared in late November, the public had seen a steady spate of newspaper coverage of Kishinev's massacre that featured photographs of devastated synagogues, shredded Torah scrolls, down feathers blanketing the city streets, and, of course, rows of shrouded dead bodies awaiting burial. But now, with the appearance of Bialik's poem, the moral failings of Kishinev's men would overshadow all else; it soon became shorthand for the utter vulnerability of the Jewish people, their devastation of soul and body alike.

Bialik's taunts are relentless:

The descendants of the Maccabees, the great grandchildren of
  lions . . .
They fled the fight . . . and like tics
Died like dogs where they were found.[59]

With these are his best-remembered, most horrifying lines:

And see, oh see: in the shade of that same corner
under the bench and behind the barrel
lay husbands, fiancés, brothers, peeping out of holes,

at the flutter of holy bodies under the flesh of donkeys
choking in their corruption and gagging on their own
   throat's blood
as like slices of meat a loathsome gentile spread their flesh—
they lay in their shame and saw—and didn't move and
   didn't budge,
and they didn't pluck out their eyes or go out of their heads—
and perhaps each in his soul then prayed in his heart:
master of the universe, make a miracle—and let me not
   be harmed.[60]

There is no mention in the poem of Jewish self-defense—not even the most concerted of all such efforts, the Jewish attack early in the pogrom's second day—which Bialik himself recorded in considerable detail in his Kishinev transcripts. Contemporary critics found this elision all the odder since the fight was given considerable prominence in the trials of pogromists by their defense attorneys—the trials were closed to the public but news of their proceedings invariably leaked where the case was repeatedly made that the defendants were the true victims of Jewish aggression. Moreover, Bialik knew well the wide range of Jewish responses during the massacre. For instance, when recording the gut-wrenching account of Rivka Schiff, the most painfully candid of all those who gave rape testimonies, his transcribed notes made clear that not only did she exonerate her husband from all blame but, as soon as her rape ended, she went searching for him, fearing that his vigorous resistance to the attack on her might well have led to his death.[61]

Bialik's decision to shunt this aside in the poem has mostly been explained in terms of his inclination to merge nationalist conviction with individual despair. Literary historian David

Roskies saw this as evidence of Jewish culture's preference for memory over history—the discrepancy between lived reality and the incomparable power of received wisdom—with long-reigning beliefs overshadowing all else. This is consistent with Bialik's constant gesturing in his poem toward the prophets (Isa. 8:9: "Make an uproar, O you peoples and you shall be broken! . . . Gird yourselves and you shall be broken") as well as his desire to produce a modern-day literature of lamentation that, despite his work's many concrete details, was intended as commemoration rather than history. David Roskies also argued that "it is never the public record, however, that tells the story. Having come to expect the subjective reality to set the norm and give rise to new responses, we should look to Bialik's creative effort before and after the visit to see how one man writing at a critical moment in Jewish history was able to provoke action by transforming the poetics of violence."[62]

To be sure, Ahad Ha'am had reached the same conclusions even before Bialik's arrival in Kishinev, distilling them into his statement on the pogrom on which Bialik signed off. It should not come as a surprise that Bialik held firmly to them despite evidence to the contrary; not only was this consistent with his cultural and political predilections, but it was also in line with his belief that the massacre's overarching lesson—namely, its searing spotlight on the degradations of Jewish exile—was far more crucial than the riot's many conflicting details.

Yet Davitt, too, recorded the same impressions of male cowardice. In contrast to Bialik, however, he chose not to publish them and left them in his notes. Davitt was a meticulous note taker. Over the course of his Kishinev stay he recorded lengthy lists of issues he planned to clarify, the summaries of books on Jews he read, and statistics on Jewish and non-Jewish occupations:

"Visit Cemetery, Hospital, Prison. Investigate alleged mutilation of women & children. Ascertain if there is any trans Carpathian propaganda from Roumania working with anti-semitic feeling in Bessarabia. . . . No. of Moldavians & Wallachs in Kishineff. Workingmen? Or Merchants, shopkeepers. Jealousy?"[63]

Arriving in Kishinev, he described in detail the city center, which impressed him as more imposing than he had expected. He toured the "Jewish quarter," which was his designation for the Old Town, or Lower Kishinev, finding it "in no way repulsive" though its residents still had "frightened & hunted looks particularly in the localities where people were killed." He recorded the continued misery weeks after the pogrom's end at the Jewish hospital: "Saw two girls—one very beautiful in the female ward. Perfect type of Jewish beauty. Head battered with iron bludgeon. Her father killed but she does not yet know it." Based on numerous interviews, Davitt sought to ferret out the number of rioters. Told at first that there had been no more than three hundred—an underestimate, he soon learned—with the bulk of them "imported thugs," he jotted: "What were the 30,000 Jews doing?" He identified weapons used by the attackers (mostly clubs) and how they occupied themselves at night ("violating women"). He quantified the number of the city's liquor stores as well as the brothels owned by Jews, calculated how many Jewish prostitutes worked in Kishinev, asked if there were disproportionate numbers of masons amid the pogromists, and wondered how many women participated in the attacks alongside men. He sought to discover whether the rumor that a five-year-old girl had been raped was true; after interviewing no fewer than ten doctors at the Jewish hospital and two more at the Russian institution, he found himself unable to confirm the report. He learned that the youngest pogrom victim, just a year old, died when the mother dropped the infant while in flight.[64]

Davitt counted the fresh graves at the Jewish cemetery, interviewed rabbis to learn how many husbands had divorced their wives because they were raped (eleven is the number he recorded, but he suspected there were more), and confirmed that in at least one instance nails were, as rumored, driven into the head of a Jewish victim. After much effort he managed to acquire a list with the names of thirteen girls and women between the ages of seventeen and forty-eight who were raped, with another six unnamed but identified, and he speculated that there were at least forty rapes. The Russian doctors with whom he spoke admitted that the press reports of the pogrom's outsize violence were not exaggerated. He noted that "some of the Jewish ladies told me that scores of girls who were engaged to be married are now disregarded by their promised husbands."[65]

No Jewish saloon, he said, remained intact, whereas not a single non-Jewish bar or store was damaged. In one instance the mob labored no fewer than four hours to break into the safe of a Jewish-owned liquor store—and all the while police were "actually looking on while the robbery was being done." Still, the story that surfaced in his notes, and soon afterward in his articles and book, was nuanced, filled with often-conflicting details regarding the riot and, in particular, the responses of local non-Jews. He discovered, in fact, considerable sympathy for the victims in nearly all the intellectuals he met, and many of the nobles vociferously deplored the violence. He also spoke with some of the city's wealthier merchants, who repeated the charge that Jews were all "pro-socialists and enemies of the Govt." Davitt's analysis of the pogrom's origin (he saw Krushevan as its crucial influence) emphasized the acute tensions in Bessarabia between town and country, the interplay between the mob's culpability, its savagery, and hunger for booty and drunken distraction. Much of his account aligns with the better, more persuasive historical literature written about the riot. In short, Davitt's account holds up, on the whole, as first-rate journalism and reliable history.[66]

On his return to Ireland, Davitt admitted that "in [its] naked horror" what he learned surpassed "almost anything which the imagination could invent." Invention was something he assiduously avoided—his notes are studded with lists of "facts," many laboriously extracted. Known in Irish nationalist circles as stalwart, principled, and rather stubborn, his resistance to the forwarding of articles before he felt them to be ready obviously exasperated his London editor. The sheer quantity of interviews he conducted during his ten days in Kishinev was testimony both to his industry and to his commitment to precision. Davitt also claimed that no fewer than a hundred Jews sought him out in his hotel room, with many of them sharing dreadful tales that may have been linked to attempts to persuade him to help with their emigration, since their lives and those of their families had been rendered unbearable. In this context he then added the following:

> Note: Jewish men appear, except in rare instances, to have acted as contemptible cowards. In no instance have I heard from women of any courageous stand being made either by their husbands or sons. . . . Several of these miserable poltroons came to my hotel to recount their marvelous escapes but no one had a story of courage or of counter attack to relate.[67]

Davitt knew, of course, of efforts of Jews to resist; he described the fight waged by those in the wine courtyard. Yet nowhere in his dispatches or his book did he mention the confessions made by Jewish men in his hotel room. The nearest he came is the observation in the book of how striking it was that the mayhem was caused by rioters numbering no more than two thousand—his initial estimate was revised considerably after further research—in a city with tens of thousands of Jews. "Ninety percent of [the Jews] hid themselves or fled to safer parts in and out of the city for refuge." He then let the statement stand without further comment.[68]

It seems likely that both Davitt and Bialik recorded what was then common knowledge and also just the sort of indelicacy that tends to fall between the cracks, especially when a beleaguered people like Jews are its target. Davitt's decision, apparently, was to excise or at least disguise mention of it, whereas Bialik built the accusation into the very core of his poem. Like Davitt, so Dubnow, too: Neither in his memoirs, in which he devotes considerable attention to the pogrom, nor in his historical work on the subject does he allude to this charge despite a lengthy description of his collaboration with Bialik and his great admiration for "In the City of Killing."

Bialik may well have felt that introducing this accusation— part and parcel of talk among Jews at the time—into an imaginative work was an act less overtly provocative than including it in a journalistic or historical account. Bialik understood that his poem would be read alongside the cascade of pogrom reportage still being produced at the time of the poem's appearance, since trials of the accused continued well into December 1903. But already by then an essentially canonized version of the massacre had consolidated for Jews across the political spectrum, the bulk of liberals and radicals in Russia, and their sympathizers abroad. In such accounts, news of Kishinev's wealthy Jews and their rush to safety or, for that matter, the role played either by Krushevan or by local seminarians in fanning the pogrom's flames was sidelined or entirely dismissed. This was consistent with the certainty that the massacre was, first and foremost, the work of the government.

The appropriation by Bialik of some details of the pogrom and not others, and his decision to sideline resistance, were tinged, no doubt, by his own deeply felt cultural Zionist convictions. Still, the choice to concentrate so much of his poem on the most cowed of Kishinev's Jewish males was likely part and parcel of his effort to piece together the pogrom's raw data, his culling of unmediated reportage devoid of contextualization or countervailing evidence that was nevertheless not inaccurate. Like so much else in Bialik's poem, traversing in astonishing detail every quarter of the city and its suburbs, this too can be said to have been done with the intention of telling the truth—an expression of the poet's desire to capture the pogrom's terrors as meaningfully as he could.

Bialik's poem was designed to coexist with the onslaught of press reports, ideological tracts, instantly crafted synagogue liturgy, protest meetings, and the like inspired by Kishinev's tragedy—to complement it while also superseding it. (Never was Bialik more ambitious or more fertile than at this point in his life.) In this respect at least, his prophetic-like eruption can be seen as more transparent than Davitt's journalism. Perhaps it felt to Bialik less of a cruel confrontation to inject into a work of poetry the reference to the failings of Kishinev's men than it did to journalist Davitt, scrupulously honest as he was but also attentive to the overriding message he hoped to deliver—namely that the likely fate facing the Jews of Russia was catastrophic and that their exit from the empire was essential. Here as elsewhere in his writing, journalism was hitched to an overriding moral or political lesson.

Indeed, Bialik's anguished poem—long seen by critics, literary scholars, and historians as brilliant in its imaginative power but a distortion of the historical record—deserves to be reassessed. At its core is a kernel of historical truth that is painful to acknowledge, aired widely at the time and then, like so many other details, deemed shameful and therefore sidelined. This is an indication of how the most lavishly remembered event of the Russian Jewish past is also among the most assiduously edited, with many of its details treated like unnecessary baggage for an already overburdened people.

Bialik sought to piece together the pogrom with the intention of capturing its terrors as tellingly as he knew how. And it seems likely that he felt better equipped to include all that he did because his was a poem detailed much like journalism but of course *not* journalism. Criticized then and later for all that he excluded, he nonetheless managed to reveal in it uncomfortable details that those writing about Kishinev in newspapers or elsewhere felt less equipped to acknowledge.

Avraham Kariv, among Bialik's most enthusiastic Israeli boosters in the 1950s and 1960s, commented often on how surprising it was that, sixty years after the appearance of "In the City of Killing," it still inspired such vigorous debate. Bialik had long since passed from the scene, dead since 1934. Yet despite the many upheavals in Palestine, later Israel—political, demographic, and cultural—he retained a presence unlike any other writer. Even after his death, Bialik would be referenced in discussions of the full range of contemporary affairs—above all, the European Jewish catastrophe. The titles of his Kishinev poems remained household words: For example, the memoir in a Tel Aviv weekly in May 1940 about the escape of a Jew from Vienna to Lublin with the heading "In the City of Killing" needed no elaboration. Despite his secularism, he would be cited on religious conundrums, as well. When the religious Zionist newspaper *Ha-Tsofeh* reflected in 1947 on theodicy during the Nazi horrors, the writer thought it natural to query what Bialik might have said.[69]

Amid the turbulence of prestate Palestine and the rise of Israel, such veneration served to intensify the antagonism of some. Bialik's poetic romanticism, his skittishness with regard to the use of sexual imagery in his poetry, his insistence that Jewish tradition must somehow animate his people's future, and even his bourgeois lifestyle—as a publisher, public figure, and eventually also as the owner of one of Tel Aviv's grander homes—made him into a natural target for those who found such characteristics repelling. Joseph Klausner had marveled, in his turn-of-the-century sketch of Bialik, at his capacity to capture the attention (not infrequently, the ire) of readers across the generations. This would remain true later in the century, too. Bialik was that rare figure who bridged the otherwise mostly unbridgeable chasms of early Israeli society. Bialik had long been praised by right-wing Zionism's Vladimir Jabotinsky, one of his best translators, and by Israel's first prime minister, David Ben-Gurion, an avid reader since his teens. But for those exasperated with the new state's wariness of individualism, its insistence on sacrifice, and its disdain for the Diaspora past, the ideal foil was Bialik.[70]

His Kishinev poetry was offered pride of place—alongside some of his other writings—in Israel's school curriculum; this was set in motion in the early 1950s under the aegis of Minister of Education Ben-Zion Dinur. A superb historian and devoted nationalist, his admiration for Bialik was boundless, and he knew the poet from his days in Odessa. His curriculum sought to infuse the next generation of Israelis with a sense of shared destiny as well as a ready-made literary canon. This seemed all the more critical because half of the state's school-age population came from outside the European orbit. Bialik would come to occupy a prominent role in this endeavor; his poetry slotted into the widest of rubrics.

Bialik's poems—annotated with requisite lessons to be learned from them—became a fixture of Israeli textbooks in the first few decades of the state's existence. They were said to teach, for example, that absolutely nothing new happened in Kishinev that had not already long been an aspect of Jewish fate. The value of prayer was now for Jews a thing of the past, since it was, as Bialik wrote, "all dried up." So large would the poet loom that one seventh-grade text from the 1950s included no fewer than three sections featuring him: "the ways of torah," or sacred knowledge; "Jewish childhood"; and "festivals."[71]

Once this curriculum found itself undergoing a thorough review in the mid-1960s—similar efforts were then under way in the United States and Great Britain—Bialik's prestige became subject to particular scrutiny. High on the list of criticisms was his portrait of Diaspora Jews as cowards. Whether or not critics of his portrait of Jews cowering in the face of aggression were inspired by Adolf Eichmann's 1961 trial in Jerusalem and its constant talk of Europe's Jews going "like sheep to the slaughter" is unclear. But Prime Minister Ben-Gurion's use of the trial as a vast schoolroom—an effort also at the core of Hannah Arendt's lacerating attack in *Eichmann in Jerusalem: A Report on the Banality of Evil*—likely provided the backdrop to the discussion among Israel's educators about Bialik's value in the classroom.[72]

The idea that Bialik's Kishinev poems, because of their disparaging talk about Jewish passivity, were a corrosive influence was spearheaded by the Haifa-based educator and poet Noah

Peniel. A graduate of Vilna's Tarbut, or Hebrew school system, and a wartime refugee, he greatly admired Bialik, and over the years he had produced a spate of textbooks that prominently featured him. But Peniel now argued that Bialik's works, especially his Kishinev poems, brilliant as they were, caused irreparable harm and planted—more authoritatively than anything else—in the hearts of schoolchildren a loathing for Diaspora Jewry. Amid the torrent of recent references to pathetic Jews going abjectly to their deaths, a generation had been left with no sense of what it meant to live alongside gentiles.[73]

Peniel's campaign met with little success—so little in fact that, in a 1977 book on the role of literary study in Israel's school curriculum, he offered a systematic evaluation of responses to Bialik's poetry in Israel's university-qualifying exams, or *bagrut*. He admitted it was inconceivable to imagine a high-school literature curriculum stripped of Bialik, but still insisted that the heavy reliance on him left a deep scar on Israel's collective psyche. As proof he cited repeated mention in *bagrut* answers to questions about "In the City of Killing" of the cowardice of European Jews, of shock at their unwillingness to save their own lives, and of their succumbing to death much like a beaten pack of dogs.[74]

Whether Bialik's portrait of Kishinev's Jews was historically accurate remains a source of controversy, but, even if it was, Peniel doubted the value of teaching contempt for Jews of the past, whose attitudes toward military matters were completely different from that of the new generation of Israeli schoolchildren. When teaching "In the City of Killing," he described how he sought to soften its blow with a fuller portrait of Jewish life in the past. Short of this and unless—as he continued to insist—the poem was not sidelined in all of Israel's schools, there remained the risk of rendering the country's youth incapable of under-standing anything about their immediate past. The poem had long left a pernicious residue, Peniel said, with its portrait of the intractability of gentile hatred and, above all, its targeting of Jewry's exilic origins, the dreadful clay out of which Israel inex-plicably emerged.

"True Russian Heroes." Postcard with satirical drawing of Krushevan (left) alongside extreme nationalists V. Gringmut and V. Purishkevich.

▪ 5 ▪

Sages of Zion, Pavel Krushevan, and the Shadow of Kishinev

Have you forgotten that, luckily, there are still anti-Semites?
And, thank God, that there are still pogroms from time to
time? However much you're assimilated in a hundred years,
you'll be set back ten times as much by a single day's pogrom.
And then the poor ghetto will be ready to take you back in.

—MIHAIL SEBASTIAN, *For Two Thousand Years*

No one would be held more responsible for Kishinev's riot—
in the weeks just after its eruption, that is—than Pavel
Krushevan. Newspaper headlines in Europe and the United
States flaunted this Moldavian-born publisher, novelist, and
short-story writer without need for identification. The cascade of
accusations leveled in the months preceding the pogrom in his
Kishinev newspaper, *Bessarabets*, including the charge of Jewish ritual murder, singled it out as Russia's most notorious hate
sheet. For years after the Kishinev pogrom, Vladimir Lenin still
referred to arch-reactionaries as Krushevans; Yiddish songs orig-

inating in World War II cited him alongside the latest, most murderous oppressors of the Jews.[1]

Krushevan had so hungered for just such notoriety—infamy, he readily admitted, was far superior to anonymity—acknowledging already in adolescence that he cared for nothing so much as for his name to be widely known. Yet once his moment passed, the most consequential of his accomplishments would soon be overlooked or, at best, only fleetingly acknowledged. His role as Kishinev's Svengali was sidelined when in mid-May 1903 the Plehve letter surfaced, with Krushevan now largely dismissed as a government stooge, as a hoodlum shielding true criminals in the upper reaches of officialdom. More surprisingly, his role as publisher of the first version of *The Protocols of the Elders of Zion* has also tended to be overlooked. Rarely is he more than mentioned in passing in the huge body of literature on the infamous text, arguably the most influential antisemitic one ever produced. And considerable evidence has surfaced indicating that Krushevan's contribution to the document was still more critical: He was almost certainly its author or coauthor, writing it in response to the unseemly, destructive hubbub in the wake of the Kishinev pogrom.

Released by Krushevan in nine consecutive installments in late August and early September 1903 in his St. Petersburg newspaper *Znamia*—with an introduction and afterword clearly written by him—this inaugural version fell into obscurity while the text itself, albeit revised somewhat, was reissued in book form six times over the course of the next five years. One indication of the curious inconspicuousness of Krushevan's version is that Herman Bernstein's pioneering study of the text, *The History of a Lie*, published in 1921, made no reference to it at all, and he seems to have been unaware of its existence. Norman Cohn's influential

1967 book, *Warrant for Genocide: The World Jewish Conspiracy and The Protocols of the Elders of Zion*, dismissed Krushevan as "a typical pogromshchik."[2]

"Peter Krushevan," declared the *American Hebrew and Jewish Tribune* (misstating his first name) in June 1934. "That black name is not easily forgotten." Contrary to the newspaper's claim, he mostly was. Momentarily he was then revived in the mid-30s because of the mention of Krushevan's *Znamia* version in the 1934–35 Bern trial when Swiss Jews brought the publishers of *The Protocols* to court seeking to stop its publication. Rarely was it cited later. The authorship of *The Protocols* would be widely attributed to the tsarist secret police, the Okhrana, with the likes of Krushevan viewed as marginal, as rabble-rousers on the fringe of the Russian right. The many book-length versions of *The Protocols*, soon translated into numerous languages, entirely overshadowed Krushevan's serialized text, published in a tough-to-acquire newspaper and available at the time only by subscription.[3]

Krushevan's death from cancer at the age of forty-nine in 1909—after releasing his version he never spoke again of the text—also contributed to its obscurity. Though a public figure in both St. Petersburg and Kishinev, at the helm of the best-oiled branch of the Soiuz Russkogo Naroda, the Union of Russian Peoples (the Black Hundreds), and elected to the Second Duma in 1907, Krushevan nonetheless spent his life mostly behind the scenes at his writing desk or his printing presses. (At the time of his death he owned two, which took up nearly all the space in a sparsely furnished St. Petersburg apartment.) His reclusiveness was, if anything, only reinforced by a botched assassination attempt on him on a crowded St. Petersburg street in June 1903.[4]

For someone so hungry for recognition, such self-protectiveness was counterproductive and no doubt contributed to the excision of his name from nearly all accounts of *The Protocols*, among the most influential works of contemporary life. Certainly no other antisemitic work would come to enjoy the document's endurance. In contrast, say, to Hitler's *Mein Kampf* or the turn-of-the-twentieth-century best-seller William Houston Chamberlain's *The Foundations of the Nineteenth Century*—these relegated either to the back shelves or the domain of misfits and cultists—*The Protocols* continues to draw widespread attention. In recent years a well-publicized Egyptian television series was built around it. Countless websites in a host of languages foreground its teachings, with the document given visibility in the presidential campaign of Donald Trump and its talk—peppered lavishly with Semitic names—of the mysterious cabal in control of the world's finances.[5]

Only recently have its origins been traced to the impact of the Kishinev pogrom, with Krushevan identified as its sole or collaborating author. The evidence is persuasive, and this heightened attention has occurred, coincidentally, as he has captured great prominence as a pioneer of pro-Russian, anti-Western sentiment in Moldova and the surrounding post-Soviet region. He is now touted as an early, singularly incisive exponent of "Christian socialism," which is seen as a healthy antidote to liberalism's anonymity, its soullessness, and its susceptibility to the machinations of Jews.[6]

Krushevan's vision is now embraced, at least in its broad strokes, in large swaths of Moldova and elsewhere nearby as a reasonable response both to late-imperial Russia's mounting ills and to the region's current malaise as well. Apologists claim that Jews contributed significantly toward making these ills intolerable because of their large numbers, malevolent financial aptitude, and insistence on operating as a monolith—a veritable kingdom with their own selfish interests. Jewry's dangerous insularity, it is argued, would have been challenged by any healthy state: It should have been challenged, as Krushevan urged, in the last years of the Romanovs—and must be now.

With regard to Kishinev's 1903 massacre, such accounts see it as a scuffle born of great economic frustrations that soon got out of hand if only because of the aggressive response of Jews. Refusing to acknowledge responsibility, Jews immediately took advantage of it, pumping the world's press with grossly exaggerated, one-sided accounts overlooking their own culpability, cashing in on relief funds. Amid all this they did so much damage to Russia's reputation that it was defenseless by the time the Bolsheviks sought to take control.[7]

This recent spate of apologetic work now exists alongside new scholarship by the German historian Michael Hagemeister, the Italian Slavic specialist Cesare G. De Michelis, the linguist Henryk Baran, and others who have reassessed Krushevan's contribution to *The Protocols* saga. He was a central figure in a small group hailing from Bessarabia and nearby regions smarting from—and intent on retaliation for—the pogrom's slings and arrows, which they blamed on the Jews. The actual words they produced in their text they knew, of course, to be inaccurate, but its message they were certain was nonetheless true. And they were equally certain that they had just seen its insidious impact right up close in Kishinev: a Jewry so committed to conquest, so effective that it willingly sacrificed its own in the planning of the pogrom, and capable of transmuting all this into a tale of anti-Jewish persecution.[8]

Ever since embarking on this book, I have found myself keenly intrigued by Krushevan. Capable of producing the vilest, most contemptible trash, Krushevan also wrote work of distinction, even beauty. He was rightly depicted during his lifetime as a sensitive, yielding man and a hysteric; a rank pogrom monger and yet also Bessarabia's most distinguished intellectual. His evocation of Bessarabia's landscape in a full-length book on the region—the first of its kind and released shortly before the Kishinev pogrom in 1903—is skillfully executed, a moving depiction of the quiet, undramatic wonders of the province's meadows, rivers, and woods. The most celebrated of his novels—he wrote several—*Delo Artabanova*, a psychological crime thriller, was recently reissued in a handsome Russian edition. A Russian-language novel picturing him as *The Protocols*' author appeared in the late 1980s. Umberto Eco's villain in his 2010 novel, *The Prague Cemetery*, built around the writing of *The Protocols*, is undoubtedly modeled on him. ("And who are the capitalists? The Jews, the rulers of our time," Eco has his character muse. ". . . I shall write a book about it. Who are the Jews? They're all those who suck the blood out of the defenseless, the people. They're Protestants, Freemasons. And of course, the people of Judah.") An oversize edition of a substantial part of Krushevan's extensive, long-neglected nonfiction, accompanied by a book-length introduction in which charges of antisemitism are blithely dismissed, appeared in Moscow in 2015. Here and elsewhere in recent Russian-language descriptions he is identified as a seminal pro-Russian intellectual whose reputation was unfairly savaged by those, particularly Jews, unsympathetic to Russia and its destiny. "I have heard so many diverse views of him," wrote Sergei Urussov in his memoirs, "that his moral physiognomy is not clear in my mind."[9]

Just months before completing this book, I found it possible to clarify at least some of these mysteries. This is because of my discovery of a cache of Krushevan's personal papers, including a startlingly frank adolescent diary, brought from Moldova years ago by the journalist Mikhail Khazin and kept since the mid-1990s on a shelf in his Brookline, Massachusetts, apartment a few blocks from Fenway Park. When I asked Khazin—a handsome, earnest, gentle man of eighty-five—whether he had ever visited Fenway, he looked at me with some surprise.

Khazin was also a remarkably trusting man: After I spent a few hours with him and his wife, Luda, Khazin suggested that I take the papers with me—they were bunched together in an oversize white folder—and seek to find them a suitable archival home. On my way the next evening to Chişinău, I was soon faced with the need to estimate the value of the personal papers of the likely author of *The Protocols of the Elders of Zion* at a FedEx shop, where I packed them up for shipping back to California.

How Khazin was given these papers is part and parcel of the stormy story, the mayhem of the last years of Soviet rule. Born in Soroki near Krushevan's birthplace, he had long been fascinated by the man. (It was common practice among Jews during his childhood, Khazin told me, to call dogs "Krushevany.") Writing in the 1980s about the history of a psychiatric hospital just outside Chişinău, where he lived most of his adult life, he discovered that among the inmates was the nephew of Krushevan, described as suffering from hereditary insanity. On the nephew's death, the director of the sanitarium offered the documents to Khazin, who then brought them with him to the United States when he left Chişinău—along with most of the region's Jews—in the 1990s.

Stuffed into the folder was a mass of documents among which were several singularly embarrassing ones. How the nephew came to have them remains unclear, but it seems plausible that as a trusted relative—the orphaned nephew idolized Krushevan,

Portrait of Mikhail Khazin.

something of a surrogate parent who died when he was fifteen—
his uncle gave him these items for safekeeping once he knew that
he was nearing his end. Included was correspondence as to why
he had so resisted marriage, a diary with startling confessions
that would likely have caused considerable discomfort if made
public, and proof of financial chicanery, serial bankruptcy, and
the like. Alongside this mass of documents detailing near-fiscal
ruin and sexual secrets was an ornate letter of commendation
from the tsar's clerk complimenting Krushevan on the publication of his 1903 Bessarabia volume.

Drawing on this rich, previously unknown material, the recent scholarship of De Michelis and Hagemeister, and little-used sources in Hebrew and Yiddish, we can now open up Krushevan's career on the road to Kishinev and its immediate aftermath in ways impossible before. It is now clearer why his shadow would loom so large in the pogrom's immediate wake, and how intimate a link there was between composition of *The Protocols*, in which he played a central role, and the 1903 massacre. Even as the details of Krushevan's culpability for the Kishinev pogrom or *The Protocols* fell into obscurity, his name retained its capacity to elicit the greatest contempt.

Hence when Sholem Aleichem sought in 1905 to capture the quintessence of antisemitic fanaticism, it was Krushevan and his infamous newspaper *Bessarabets* that he used as the most obvious and extreme examples. His short story "Two Anti-Semites" is built around the machinations of an all-too-clever Jewish traveling salesman with an undeniably Jewish face who has so tired of the intrusions of other Jewish train passengers that he hits on the idea of hiding himself behind *Bessarabets*. He finds a copy of the paper and then drapes it across his face as a sure way of keeping all, Jews as well as Russians, from talking to him. Sholem Aleichem reminds his readers that this newspaper is the handiwork of "a certain ugly anti-semite named Krushevan . . . a man who never rests nor sleeps in his tireless search for new ways to warn the world against the dreaded disease Judaism—and who is loathed by nearly everyone." The ploy works at first until, unsurprisingly, the paper slips off the sleeping man's face, revealing the Jew beneath it.[10]

In the privacy of his diary at the age of seventeen, written in a florid hand (he would always pride himself on his splendid pen-

manship), Krushevan acknowledged having overpowering obses-
sions: despair over his poverty; envy of the rich; nightmares of
crabs devouring humans. At that time, he was living with relatives in Odessa, having dropped out of school, and was eyeing the
local rich with a mixture of disdain and intense envy.[11]

He wished, according to his diary, that he had been "born
a lady." He was passionately in love with a Cossack whom he
described as his *krasavitsa* (the beautiful one).[12] On these pages
he alternated between despair little short of manic—and dreams
of grandeur. Fame, he declared, he desperately needed yet feared
it would always be beyond his reach:

> *Suffering souls, unfortunate desires*
> *And the relentless swarm of heavy, black doom. . . .*
> *When I die—I will die—I will die completely without a*
> *trace. . . .*
> *In my coffin with a nasal voice I will be reproached for a*
> *worthless life.*[13]

Krushevan was born in 1860 to an impoverished nobleman in
the village of Gindeshty, near the town of Soroki in northwest-
ern Bessarabia on the Dniester River—the same rustic, remote
region described so poignantly by a contemporary of Krushevan's,
Shlomo Hillels, in his Hebrew novel. Urussov wrote: "I know of
no town in Russia to be compared with Soroki. . . . The varying
shades of light, and the picturesque indentations in the gradually
ascending river-bank." With little if any formal education until
his adolescence, Krushevan mastered French and read widely,
embarking at the age of fourteen on a "literary journal"—as
he titled it on its cover—a notebook that included a sampling
of his unfinished essays and fiction. Leo Tolstoy was his earli-

est inspiration—literary as well as political—whom he eventually rejected as he moved rightward: His politics well into his twenties were conventionally liberal, his cultural inclinations unremarkable.[14]

From the start, however, his favored themes were financial decline, family humiliation, and above all the terrible, mysterious forces that undermine the best of intentions. He was essentially self-taught, tutored in his childhood, it seems, but with the bulk of his learning picked up on his own. By the time that he started gymnasium in Kishinev, he showed little capacity for patience; schoolmates would remember him as a "maniac." (One of them was Jacob Bernstein-Kogan, whom Krushevan would later identify as a key figure in that most nefarious of plots, the Jewish design to overthrow the world.) At sixteen or seventeen Krushevan left school, moving to Odessa (he would later insist that the city, despite its multiethnic reputation, was unambiguously Russian) and returning to Kishinev a few years later. There he worked as clerk for the city duma, or council.[15]

In his writings he described his early home life only fleetingly. His father seems to have been a distant figure, and his mother died when he was still quite young. He treasured his memory of her and was raised by a stepmother, along with a younger stepsister named Anastasia. In an unfinished memoir written in old age by his nephew, it is mentioned—though this appears nowhere else in work on Krushevan—that his stepmother was Jewish.[16]

The nephew, Pavel Epiminovdovich Krushevan, who was fifteen at the time of his uncle's death, remained deeply devoted to him, continuing to see Krushevan as a model and a hero. His memoir was designed as no less an exculpation of Krushevan's legacy than a tale of the nephew's life under Romanian and Soviet rule. (He served in the Romanian army, worked later as an engineer, and loathed the Soviets.) It seems inconceivable that he would include information about Krushevan's intimate Jewish links if it was untrue. Yet no one else familiar with Krushevan, including the Jews acquainted with him at his Kishinev gymnasium who later wrote about him so disparagingly, ever mentioned his father's remarriage to a Jewish woman. It is not unlikely that they never knew of it, and that although he often aired details of his unhappy childhood, he excluded all mention of this odd, discordant detail.[17]

There is no doubt, however, that Krushevan spent his life well into his twenties surrounded by Jews. Soroki at the time of his youth was 60 percent Jewish, with nearly all its retail stores in Jewish hands and many of them sporting Yiddish signs. The region's larger commercial concerns too were intimately linked with those of Odessa; many Jews traveled between the two towns, negotiating the purchase of local produce and arranging for its transport. Soroki's liquor shops and taverns (much like those in Kishinev) were nearly all owned by Jews and packed with peasants and laborers during the long winter months.[18]

Later, too, once Krushevan set out to work as a journalist (after leaving the clerkship at Kishinev's city duma), he was hired by newspapers—at most of them doing hack jobs such as reporting on crime and local scandals—in Vilna and Minsk, two of the most densely populated Jewish towns in the Pale of Settlement. True, at the time Krushevan's political views were progressive, and he did much to seek the attention of Russia's leading liberal-leaning journals. His stepsister, Anastasia, would later insist that Krushevan's hatred of Jews only started after he was jilted by a Jewish girl—though this seems unlikely in view of his passionate declaration of love for the Odessa Cossack. Others ascribed his

Krushevan in his twenties.

antisemitism to utilitarianism, the desire to prevail as a newspaperman once he gained control of *Bessarabets*.[19]

Neither argument, however, explained the ferocity and overall toxicity of his antisemitism. Krushevan's turn in the early 1890s or so was in line with a general embrace of Russian conservatism on the part of many intellectuals who would also show a new antipathy for Jews, appalled as they were by Jewish radicalism's excesses. Many now expressed fear of the empire spiraling into anarchy and the doubt that Jews, so numerous among its fiercest radical opponents, would ever be capable of true integration.[20]

Still, Krushevan's loathing of Jews stood out as his most singularly defining belief. Perhaps his stepmother's origins were a cause. His sister's marriage saga—this, too, overlooked in treatments of Krushevan—may well have reinforced these convictions: Anastasia, eventually renamed Sarah, would marry a Jewish student in Kishinev and run away with him to the United States.

The story of his sister's marriage was first mentioned briefly in an American Russian-language newspaper in 1934, revealing that she was living in Baltimore as a Jew. Soon *Forverts* followed up with a fuller—perhaps also rather embellished—version. There it was described how Anastasia met a Jew named Efim (or Efraim) Borenstein at a Kishinev student ball, soon fell in love, and fled to the United States, settling in Baltimore. She was pictured with her head covered in the traditional mode of a religious Jewish woman, smiling broadly, and describing thirty years of marital bliss. Why she decided to tell her story at that point, she did not say. Perhaps it had to do with the Bern trial at much the same time, during which Krushevan's name was suddenly, and after so many years, frequently cited.[21]

The Jewish press accounts were packed with readily disprovable details, however. It was claimed that she was born into wealth and that Krushevan's father had divorced his first wife. Once Anastasia fell in love, according to *Forverts*, she escaped with her beloved, hiding in a forest. The family insisted that Jews had kidnapped her for ransom, and Krushevan placed a notice in the press, threatening to murder her Jewish kidnappers. This reportedly was what persuaded the young couple to escape abroad. Settling first in New York, they finally married. The husband worked running a synagogue as a sexton (despite the couple having lived together out of wedlock in the forest). Fearful of Anastasia being recognized as Krushevan's sister, they decided to move to a mixed neighborhood in Baltimore with few Jews, where they had lived ever since.[22]

∎

After Krushevan returned to Kishinev in 1897 to take control of the struggling daily *Bessarabets*—eight pages in length, produced at first in his apartment—he would enjoy the most productive period of his life. Though nearly always in debt and often unable to pay his paper suppliers, he managed to put out the multipage daily, sprinkled generously with articles written by himself under various pen names, and a weekly literary magazine also full of his own writings.[23]

By the time he took charge of *Bessarabets*, Krushevan had published in 1896–97 the most ambitious of his books, *Chto takoe Rossiia?* (What Is Russia?). Traveling by train and reporting on conversations with other passengers, he sought to capture the full expanse of western Russia's social and cultural landscape on the cusp of the new century, with special attention to the region's many Jews. Krushevan's antisemitism was here in full view. At the heart of the book's many lengthy disquisitions about Jews was the message that the Jewish march toward world hegemony clashed with Russia's existence and must be stopped. This battle was nothing less than a struggle for Russia's survival—a viewpoint all but identical to the one espoused in *The Protocols*.[24]

The book's unnamed narrator—clearly Krushevan himself—is affable, a touch naive, and prone to sudden outbursts that disarm and never alienate. He is a man of strongly held beliefs, eager to draw people into conversation and candid on all topics, and especially his feelings about Jews. And he manages to sway most of those he meets, including Jews, with the most objectionable of his opinions.

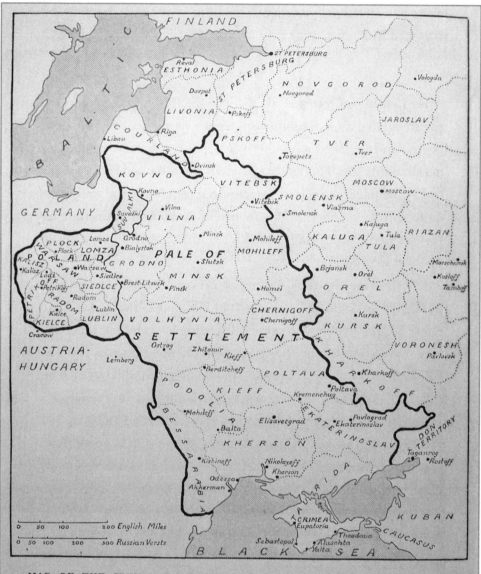

MAP OF THE JEWISH PALE OF SETTLEMENT AND RUSSIAN POLAND

Practically all the Jews in Russia—95 per cent. or even more—are confined to the fifteen governments of the Pale and the ten governments of Poland, which altogether constitute only one twenty-third part of the Russian Empire. The vast majority of them are still further restricted to the towns and townlets of the Pale, an area forming a two-thousandth fraction of Russian territory, although in point of actual numbers the ratio of the Jewish population of the Empire is to the Russian as one is to twenty-four.

Map of western provinces.

His travels take him across Russia's western provinces, criss-crossing by train the Pale of Settlement. He takes these journeys reluctantly, he admits, and always feels an alien, eager to leave the region as quickly as possible to rejoin "his own." Musing as the train nears the Pripet Marshes outside Pinsk, he finds himself in conversation with a landowner, and the talk turns to whether either Jews or Poles might ever fit into Russia. As they speak the narrator revels in the glorious countryside in an area nonetheless swarming with Jews. The contrast between nature's overwhelming beauty and its relentless pollution by Jews is stark: "On the west, an entire lake spills out, decorated with a purple sunset. On the north, lapping at the distant shores, the Dnieper reflects this purple with scarlet shimmers. The boundless steppe, shrouded in rose-colored fog, sinks into the approaching twilight of autumn evening."[25]

Others are soon drawn into the exchange, including an artilleryman and two Jewish businessmen from Gomel. The traveler expresses pleasure that the other passengers are willing to speak about these matters candidly, since the press has either been bought off by Jews to hide their misdeeds or has decided to ignore the issue entirely out of despair that it could ever be aired honestly. Truthfulness about Jews tends to be avoided, he says, because it is so often criticized as "savage" or "disgusting," but such conversation is more necessary now than ever before.[26]

The narrator continues, insisting that energy and resources have been expended on resolving the Jewish question with no concrete results. Russia has sought so hard to address it honestly, but Jews and their sympathizers have done all in their power to obstruct such efforts. The fact, he says, that this issue continues to loom large—indeed, that it remains intractable—sickens Russians, since all that is required for the problem to be resolved is for the Jews to allow themselves to be absorbed into Russia. Their *sliianie*, or assimilation, would settle the issue for all time. Had Russia employed (as it could have) the fullest and most vigorous range of options, he argues, the dilemma would have been solved long ago. But Russians are peaceful and refuse to resort to brutal methods even when justified. This may well now need to be reassessed, because Jews constitute the empire's only sizable group that insists on separation from all others.[27]

One of the Gomel businessmen, the owner of a large pharmaceutical concern, interrupts. He admits that he is the beneficiary of the ready access to higher education Russia provides to Jews. Speaking with a "solid, rich baritone, nearly without an accent," he makes the case for lifting restrictions on Jews, including those limiting their ability to purchase land. Only then, when they are given the opportunity to "utilize the land [on] which they stand and the air that others are permitted to breathe freely," can they be expected to embrace Russia without reservation.[28]

The traveler reacts angrily. It is precisely these privileges, he retorts, that had already been granted to Jews, who then squandered them, taking advantage of the freedom bestowed on them and using it to manipulate Russia's economic well-being. True, he admits, Russians also engage in questionable economic practices, but in contrast to Jews they continue nonetheless to remain loyal to the nation. This is not true of Jews, who remain loyal only to their own. These traits, coupled with an unnaturally keen commercial ability sharpened over the generations, make Jews better able to exploit others while protecting their narrow parochial interests. Over time, he argues, they have lost all capacity to work the land or to live in the way that healthy people readily do.[29]

Moreover, the narrator continues, never have Jews sought to remedy this dreadful situation. Instead they dream of a "Jewish

stardom," always thinking of themselves while dismissing everyone else. Never are they willing to admit that there is anything
of value in the Christian world, and their obstinacy is something
extraordinary to behold. They persist in their isolation from the
larger world despite the humiliations they have suffered since
the time of Titus, and the hatred leveled against them everywhere they have lived: "Just think! Can there be a greater curse
or a greater punishment" than the loss of all links to the land, all
love of it, and being completely stripped of any connection to the
rest of humanity? Yet all their energy has been concentrated on
commerce, shutting themselves off from all except their own. Is it
any wonder that they are the target of "hostility and pogroms"?[30]

Yet, he says, there is nothing new to Jewry's self-imposed
alienation: Jews have inspired hatred as far back as Kiev in 1092.
Nothing has changed since then: "Remember Darwin's idea . . .
that by the laws of heredity, with time humankind will lose its
left hand which is increasingly atrophied? Jews are the left hand
of the organism of humanity."[31]

As the Jewish population expands, with some five million of
these "aliens" wedged up against Russia's western border, per-
ilously close to Russia's enemies, it is imperative that the problem finally be resolved. The narrator argues that if Russia is to
avoid the use of draconian measures, then the only alternative
is for the Jewish intelligentsia to see to the thorough reedu-
cation of their own people. They are the only ones capable of
teaching Jews to shift their priorities toward useful, decent
labor. It is their responsibility to press Jews to abandon their
isolation, to recognize that the interests of Russians are the
same as their own. The old, tired methods used by Jews for so
long, he says, whereby they pay for good press, hide the truth,
and spread hatred and lies, will only serve to deepen antipa-

thy. The traveler feels no hatred, only pity, toward Jews, but he certainly understands why so many despise them: "Russia has poured too much blood into its unification and can't tolerate a foreign element hindering its move toward full strength within its very core."[32]

Jews sitting near the traveler are all but persuaded. One student admits that nearly everything the traveler has said is accurate, countering only that Jewry's bad traits are the by-product of age-old "isolation from the human family." The Gomel businessman is left utterly confounded. He acknowledges that if Jews cannot extricate themselves from the miserable residue of their history, then it is clear that Russia has no alternative but to turn its back on all constraint and to go after them with all the might and power at its disposal.[33]

Later, Krushevan's *Bessarabets* would print still worse accounts of Jews, though it sought to be a newspaper that covered a full range of national and international affairs. The front page of one issue (picked up by Michael Davitt during his Kishinev stay), dated May 12, 1903, featured reports on Austria-Hungary, the United States, and the two-hundredth anniversary of the founding of St. Petersburg. A chronicle of local government notices, a regular feature, appeared on page 2. Essays on the arts and literature were printed side by side with local news, much of it sober, straightforward, and dull.[34]

By that time Krushevan had relinquished day-to-day control of the paper. In the pogrom's aftermath, the government tightened its hold and imposed greater control on media content. Even before the massacre, *Bessarabets* had covered the larger political and cultural scene, but its focus on Jews was relentless: "Zhidy think about how best to rob the honor, the conscience, the truth of peasants" (March 17, 1903). "What is the source of the success of the Jews? It is their unification under one single corruption and their capacity to act collectively, all for one and one for all. And we can mirror them united into one guild, one brotherhood" (March 4, 1903). "Everywhere Jews live they figure among the bulk of deviants, counterfeiters, handlers of illegal documents, goods, food, wine, medical supplies, delicacies" (March 23, 1903). It was furthermore claimed that Jews had invented a way of producing wine without grapes, and that Jewish doctors were part of a secret syndicate designed to swindle innocent patients.[35]

■

With the outbreak of the pogrom, the fame Krushevan had sought since his youth was finally his. In many quarters, of course, this was actually infamy, since Krushevan was now lambasted in Russia and abroad as being among Jewry's most powerful enemies. His lavishly illustrated guide to Bessarabia had elicited a commendation from the tsar. That volume was deemed so impressive that the new governor general, Urussov, regarded it as his main source of information about the province before his arrival. Krushevan had also recently received a handsome subsidy of five thousand rubles for the publication of *Znamia*. These expressions of sympathy reinforced the impression that Krushevan lived something of a charmed life and was supported generously by officialdom.[36]

Yet barely three weeks after Krushevan received the tsar's laudatory letter, his debts were deemed so crushingly heavy that he was served with a bailiff's letter inventorying his belongings for auction. The list was strikingly meager: bits and pieces of furniture, including one chair, one table, a few bookcases, and two printing presses, all stuffed into a modest flat on Gogol Street. He had sold *Bessarabets*, taking payment for the newspaper but managing nonetheless not to deliver it to its new owner; subscription payments were still in his hands. As a result legal proceedings were now initiated against him. In an undated letter Krushevan admitted to having incurred more than 11,400 rubles in debt. In compensation he offered the proceeds from the sale of his personal library.[37]

Quite how he recovered, if at all, remains unclear. He would continue—even though he had sold *Bessarabets* when launching his new St. Petersburg daily—to serve as editor of the Kishinev paper. His new St. Petersburg publication was a four-page, large-size weekly available only by subscription because censors feared

Krushevan in 1900.

its explosive content, especially its antisemitism. They had good reason to do so. It was there that Krushevan published serially a text attributed to the "World Union of Freemasons and Sages of Zion," under the banner headline "The Program of World Conquest by Jews." This, as he acknowledged in the document's foreword, was his own description of what the text contained.[38]

Known universally, albeit read sparingly, with its essential message a commonplace, *The Protocols of the Elders of Zion*, as the document would soon be called, was translated into German, English, Swedish, Danish, Bulgarian, Finnish, Hungarian, Lithuanian, Italian, Greek, and Arabic. In recent years it has become a mainstay of popular culture as the immediate backdrop to the wildly popular *Da Vinci Code* books and movies. *The Protocols'* belief in dark, hidden forces that have long controlled the destiny of humanity remains among the cardinal assumptions of conspiracy theorists throughout the world.[39]

Why this continuing allure? In part, no doubt, it is the byproduct of the document's anonymity as well as its insistence that it was an authentic transcript. The authors never came forward to acknowledge it as their creation: Its authorship was attributed variously by its devotees to a member of King Solomon's entourage, Theodor Herzl, Ahad Ha'am, or the chief rabbi of Stockholm. The fact that it purported to be the real and uncensored words uttered by an elder of the Jews gave it a rare immediacy. Its repetitiveness, which for some was a source of annoyance, was also a boon, because no more than a few pages were required for readers to absorb its message. This meant that even the illiterate or semiliterate could be readily acquainted with it if others read them just a page or two. And though it was written and first published in 1903, the text would rise to prominence only once Russia was in the grasp of the Bolsheviks and their explosive message was getting a receptive hearing across Europe. As an accessible, readily digestible text with a tantalizingly mysterious authorship, *The Protocols*' horrifying message was tested amid the convulsions of war and revolution.[40]

It has, of course, long been recognized as a forgery. Almost from the moment of its first widespread circulation, it was clear that it was lifted from an obscure anti-Napoleon III political satire: Maurice Joly's 1864 *Dialogue aux enfers entre Machiavelli et Montesquieu*. In 1921 the London *Times* published a three-part series featuring side-by-side passages from *The Protocols* and Joly's work, revealing that nearly 70 percent of its words—still more, as it happens, in the 1903 version published by Krushevan—were drawn verbatim from Joly. The fact that the *Times* saw the value in this exercise is a good indication of the credibility that the document had already achieved.[41]

The first mention of such a text had appeared in print a year before Krushevan's version. Mikhail Osipovich Menshikov, a well-known antisemite and journalist, described how in 1902 a "mysterious lady" came to him with it, saying she had managed to acquire the document—apparently stealing it—in Nice and had translated it from its original French into Russian. Menshikov said that he doubted its authenticity and refused to have anything to do with it.[42]

Questions regarding its credibility were raised, as we will see, even by Krushevan. Why was it discovered in French? Why would the Jewish elder, whose voice is its centerpiece, admit to all the dastardly things he acknowledges in it? What relation were these protocols meant to have with the protocols of the Zionist movement published in German, not French? These and many other issues—aside, of course, from the verifiable fact that nearly the entire document was lifted from a book that had nothing at all to do with Jews—have bedeviled the text's credibility from nearly the moment it first surfaced in the public arena. But for many people these questions were overshadowed by its rhetorical power, the prospect it provided for eavesdropping on the most horrible of Jewish voices—one who was willing to acknowledge his contempt for all, including the Jews, his plans for world conquest, and his map for the restoration of the Davidic kingdom.

Such enormous ambiguities have also done little to dampen the allegiance of the text's adherents, some of whom insist, contrary to all evidence, that Joly himself was Jewish—as if that were a test of its accuracy. And the secrecy surrounding its authorship—those who produced it were committed, of course, to sustaining its anonymity—helped to perpetuate the notion that the voice captured in the document contained the actual words of a vaulted Jewish leader: It is a text whose greatest thrill is in the purported access to the unvarnished talk of humanity's greatest foe.

Until recently it was widely assumed—beyond, that is, its most loyal devotees—that *The Protocols* had been stitched together by the Paris-based Okhrana chief Pyotr Rachkovsky and right-wing journalist Matvei Golovinskii, and that it was produced either at the time of the First Zionist Congress in 1897 or a year or two before then. Evidence supporting the claim, solidified in the wake of testimony at the Bern trial of 1934–35, in which Swiss publishers of the tract were accused by leaders of the Jewish community of plagiarism and forgery, has subsequently been upended by conclusive linguistic and historical evidence. Especially because of its reference to events occurring after its reputed composition in the mid-1890s, it is clear that neither Rachkovsky nor Golovinskii was its author.[43]

Amid the welter of tales surrounding the document's origins, there has never been any doubt that its first version was in Krushevan's newspaper. This remained, however, the most obscure of all its Russian-language versions, all but forgotten until it appeared in several editions in book form in 1905–6. Krushevan himself would never mention the document again, despite its many subsequent editions and his continued prominence on Russia's Right. Benjamin Segel, the author of one of the earliest exposés of the text—*Die Protokolle der Weisen von Zion*, published in 1924—did not even know of the existence of Krushevan's version. In the tale of the origins of *The Protocols* as told in right-wing circles by a Russian princess of Polish origin, Catherine Radziwill, it was an agent of the foreign branch of the Okhrana, the Russian secret police, Golovinskii, who visited her Paris apartment in 1904 or 1905 (on Rachkovsky's orders) and handed her the first version, in French, of *The Protocols*. "Radziwill," writes Michael Hagemeister, "gave an exact description of the manuscript: different handwritings, yellow paper, and a big spot of blue ink on the first page." Radziwill also showed no awareness that *The Protocols* had already been published in Russia a year or two earlier.[44]

Evidence that Krushevan was its author, or at least its coauthor, is convincing. The Italian linguist Cesare G. De Michelis has identified crucial markers in the document itself that he likens to fingerprints in his annotated translation of the first version, *The Non-Existent Manuscript: A Study of the Protocols of the Sages of Zion*. To unearth the document's author, he considers "the sole element that cannot lie: the text itself, its linguistic nature, its construction and the modalities of its tradition . . . an operation as obvious and banal as it has been systematically overlooked."[45]

It was revealed by these textual markers that the text was produced in the eastern Ukraine or Bessarabia. There, for example, the preposition *u* was standard rather than the Russian *v*, and it is the Ukrainian variant that is utilized throughout the first version. Prolific in all versions was the word for "gentile," which in *Znamia*'s account was Ukrainian *goyevskii*, not the Russian *goyskii*. These and other examples of Ukrainian usage were then corrected or excised from subsequent book-length editions of *The Protocols*, together with the many redundancies and misprints scattered throughout the original text.[46]

The first variant, copied almost straight from Joly, also leaves the clear impression of a hurriedly produced text. Curiously Krushevan himself would acknowledge this sloppiness in his foreword, as we will see. Evidence that it was the product of very recent work—done no earlier than 1901 or 1902—abounds: for example, references to the Boxer Rebellion in China in 1900 and to the killing of President William McKinley in Buffalo in 1901. No less persuasively, the fact that the ferociously anti-Jewish compendium *Talmud i evrei* (Talmud and Jews), which contains every conceivable antisemitic text appearing in Russia at the time, includes Krushevan's variant—publishing the first of its sections in full—only in its third edition, which was released in 1903, dates its composition explicitly to 1902–3.[47]

Krushevan and his close friend G. Butmi from the same region (Butmi was born in Yampol in central Ukraine), both fluent in French, were likely the first authors of the document. Butmi would publish his own version in 1906, titling it *The Enemies of the Human Race: Protocols Extracted from the Archives of the Central Chancellery of Zion (where the root is of the present disorder in Europe in general and of Russia in particular)*. He was then a widely translated if idiosyncratic economic theorist, but he had fallen into obscurity by the early 1920s when *The Protocols* first captured widespread attention. By then Krushevan had long been dismissed as little more than a crass rabble-rouser. Both had been leaders of the Union of Russian Peoples, which— except in the rarefied confines of the far Right—had by then been wholly discredited after the White Army's outright bigotry and slaughter in its battle with Bolshevism. Of course no one on the Right had a vested interest in identifying the authors of *The Protocols*. Both Butmi and Krushevan were therefore overlooked or sidelined in the vast body of literature generated by partisans and critics of the infamous work.[48]

■

The only comments Krushevan would ever make about the *Znamia* text that he published were in its foreword and afterword. These were disjointed, uncharacteristically meandering pieces, replete with excuses and equivocations. In them Krushevan apologizes for the document's imperfections—though what they are he does not say—and how drastically it differs from the original—though he does not indicate where the original copy might be found or what it contains. He also points out that the document is incomplete, and—though he rejects the idea that it is a hoax—he leaves open the possibility that it could be, as he puts it, "apocryphal."[49]

In the foreword Krushevan describes how he received the minutes of the "World Union of Freemasons and Elders of Zion" after they were stolen in France and brought to St. Petersburg. Why the document was written in French, who the courier was, and how it was acquired are all left unasked. Yet time and again he dwells on its "authenticity," sometimes insisting that proof of its Jewish authorship is in its "cynical logic" and coldness of heart, so intrinsic to Jews. But he backtracks, too, allowing for the possibility that it is not what it purports to be—which, he insists, does not minimize its significance, since it is clear that, no matter who wrote it, the author is a "profound observer" of the Jewish people.[50]

Its author understood well, according to Krushevan, the intention of Jews to "take over the world and create a 'super-state.'" Consequently, whether the actual words of the text are apocryphal or not, its importance is undeniable, especially since Jews have now put their plans into motion through the channels of the Zionist movement, which "calls for all Jews in the world to unify into a union more cohesive and dangerous than the Jesuit order."[51]

In the afterword Krushevan continues recycling much the same medley of unprompted apologies. He says that he feels awful about making so many cuts to the document, but he insists again that, despite the text's imperfections, it offers "a fairly accurate idea of the program of world conquest by Jews." This is the terrible, fervent dream shared by all Jews. How is it possible for anyone but a Jew to describe the workings of such a mind, its contempt for all the Christian countries of the world? This is sufficient proof that the document is neither apocryphal nor, as Krushevan puts it, the workings of a diseased mind. Only a "cruel Jewish mind" would be able to sum up the catastrophic contours of a world in which Jews enslave everyone else. There is little time to stop the clock. Resistance to the disastrous scenario now nearing its culmination can succeed only if action is taken immediately.[52] What he says here is startling: First he insists on the document's authenticity though no one had questioned it, and his answers are curiously thin. He appears to acknowledge this inadequacy: The most conclusive proof he is able to muster in this regard is that the incomparable coldness of the Jewish mind is something no non-Jew could ever replicate. Moreover, he admits that the document was rushed into press—why, he does not explain—with all sorts of errors strewn throughout. He is willing to acknowledge such errors—indeed, even the text's possible fraudulence—while trumpeting how revealingly it airs the terrible intentions of the Jewish people.

Chapter 10 of the document opens, for example, with a proclamation of the Jewish obligation to wipe all other faiths off the face of the earth. This devastation admittedly might result in the rise of several generations of atheists, but it is certain that they will eventually be won over to the religion of Moses. The key to Jewry's strength, according to the text, is in its unalloyed confidence, its certainty of its own indomitable power that will ultimately result in the subjugation of all under the weight of its kingdom: "We will not tolerate any kind of religion espousing one God except our own . . . since we are the chosen people, and we have been fated to rule."[53]

The document sees the slow, steady march to Jewish power that began in antiquity and is now nearly successful. And, though Jewry's stated goal is the restoration of the Davidic kingdom, it is obvious that a more pressing issue is the capitulation of Christianity—which is, arguably, a euphemism for the annihilation of Judaism's foes.

■

Why were these heinous "admissions" made in the form of a word-for-word transcript? Who transcribed it, and why? None of this would be explained. However, the reason why the present moment was so dire is made clear: The sudden rise of Zionism was proof that Jewry's goals were nearing success. Zionism had openly acknowledged that it was ready to take control of Christianity's most sacred sites in the Holy Land and that this was merely the opening sortie in Jewry's march toward universal mastery.

Krushevan—and others close to him on Russia's far Right—had long seen Zionism as among the most destructive of all Jewish efforts at world dominion. The right-wing journalist Menshikov summed up these fears in the wake of the Fifth Zionist Congress in December 1901. The movement, he argued, constituted the starkest shift in Jewish history since the destruction of the Second Temple. Since then Jews had been absent from history—"historically defunct" is how he put it—plotting their return, no doubt, but constrained by the heavy yoke of "the Talmud and the Kahal."* This meant that Jews had been no more than a "desolate and gray" presence on the world stage, a condition that was now over because of Zionism's alarming capacity to revitalize Jewish political life. Clearly this perilous situation had to be carefully monitored, though mere monitoring could not go nearly far enough.[54]

Krushevan, according to his nephew, had never hated Jews, only Zionists. Krushevan's own words contradict the claim, of course, but the nephew could have remembered accurately that Theodor Herzl's movement filled him with special terror.[55]

Why this preoccupation with Zionists? Jewish radicals were justly obsessed, now more than ever, but why was fear focused on Zionists, who had their sights set on a faraway land and had a comparatively mild, even conservative constituency drawn largely from the ranks of shopkeepers and synagogue attendees? Their leader, Herzl, sported formal wear at its congresses and reassured every world leader willing to meet with him—including Plehve, in meetings held in St. Petersburg soon after the Kishinev pogrom—of his disdain for revolutionaries. The most compelling of all Russian Zionism's ideological mentors, Ahad Ha'am, was

---

* "Kahal" means both the Jewish community as a whole and the administrative body of a Jewish community.

an intense, reclusive former businessman who was now an editor and essayist. Far from being a firebrand, his two-hour oration delivered in a monotone at the movement's first officially authorized conference in Russia in September 1902 had thoroughly bored most in the Minsk hall. Judged by any realistic standard, this was not a movement intent on taking Russia by storm.[56]

Nonetheless the Zionist movement was by the turn of the twentieth century, more so than ever before, the object of the greatest scrutiny in Russia's right-wing circles. This interest was prompted by Zionism's stated intention to purchase the Holy Land. "Most legends spring from facts," as the historian A. J. P. Taylor once observed, and there was sufficient evidence available to make the case for a Jewish plot—as outlined in the Zionist movement's own protocols—whose goal was world domination. Of course, Krushevan's belief in the mysterious power exerted by the movement was grossly exaggerated, but there was testimony, indeed right there in Kishinev, on which he could draw to substantiate his fears.[57]

Fears of Zionism's dangerously ambitious aspirations found their echo in official circles too. On the one hand, officials sought to use the Zionist movement as a wedge against radicalism, as a way to deflect the Jewish hope for reform in the empire to distant Palestine; hence the permission given to Russia's Zionists to convene the 1902 conference. On the other hand, Herzl's grandiosity, his frequent (if also unfounded) intimations of his movement's wealth, and particularly the launching of a Jewish colonial bank in 1901—accompanied by efforts to establish a branch in Russia—quickly soured officials on the prospect of cooperation. Indeed, such suspicions would only deepen in the wake of the Minsk conference (a condition of its legality was that police attend and take notes), where talk of cultural revival and nationalist education dominated the agenda rather than calls for emigration. The items highlighted at the conference struck officials as uneasily familiar, tinged as they were with subversion and the prospect of political activism.[58]

Thus not only did Russia's Zionists sound eerily similar to radicals, but Herzl himself, with his claims of great wealth and the prospect of support from English, Ottoman, or German authorities, seemed on the verge of an epochal diplomatic victory. It seemed certain—as attested by numerous articles appearing in Russia's right-wing periodicals—that Zionism was on the cusp of acquiring for itself vast chunks of the Holy Land. All such claims were either untrue or greatly overstated, but they were taken deadly seriously by the Russian Right, whose apprehensions grew to fever pitch once Zionism petitioned for authorization to establish a branch of the colonial bank in Russia so as to garner investors. This transformed Zionism from a project with the benign goal of emigration to an effort intent on acquiring Christianity's most sacred places and then, no doubt, far more.[59]

The looming prospect of an English-sponsored Jewish settlement in East Africa and Herzl's Russia trip soon after the Kishinev pogrom, when he had audiences with both Plehve and Sergei Witte, heightened fear of the Zionists. This would only be accentuated after news spread of the wildly enthusiastic reception he received when, on visiting Vilna, the "Jerusalem of Lithuania," thousands greeted his train in the middle of the night. Circles close to Krushevan as well as the Russian government registered all this with mounting concern. The government made this clear in a book-length report on the Zionists that was produced soon after the Minsk conference by the police director Aleksei Lopukhin, a particularly well-informed bureaucrat. As portrayed by Lopukhin, this was an organization no less preoccupied with Russian domestic reform than were the regime's liberal and radical opponents; Zionism's calls for emigration were sidelined by a mounting interest in the thoroughgoing reform of Jewish life in Russia. Its message was, arguably, even more threatening than that of the radicals, if only because its potential impact was greater, with the resources at its disposal making it better equipped to conceal its subversive goals.[60]

Mentioned frequently in the Lopukhin report is the prominence of Kishinev's Bernstein-Kogan, with nearly as many references to him as to Herzl. Bernstein-Kogan was described as occupying a role unmatched in the Zionist hierarchy, the virtual "president" of the movement in Russia.[61]

This was a curious depiction, since Bernstein-Kogan was never more than a midlevel activist, a financially strapped cholera specialist whose communal activities outpaced his devotion to his practice. (Unable to make a living in Palestine, where he moved before World War I, he would return to Romania later, spending the last years of his life ministering to the medical needs of the Jewish agricultural colonies in Soviet Crimea.) The government as well as the Russian Right took special interest in him because of the populism of his youth and the eventual jailing of his Socialist Revolutionary brother. In reality there was little to worry about. His relations with Herzl were not close, indeed often contentious. He wielded little influence in the movement and had left his radicalism behind long ago.[62]

Still, though he was far from the darkly influential figure imagined by St. Petersburg officials or Kishinev's far Right, Bernstein-Kogan's role in catapulting the city's pogrom into a world-famous event was pivotal. His ability to spread word of the pogrom—and with breathtaking speed—to newspapers, organizations, and influential figures throughout Europe, the United

States, and elsewhere would consolidate the belief that he was at the epicenter of Jewry's worldwide machinations. Here was that rare moment when fantasy, or at least the previously unprovable, seemed to mesh seamlessly with reality, when long-held suspicions of Jewish sedition would now be pegged onto humdrum Kishinev as the headquarters of a meticulously coordinated effort to do harm to the Russian empire.

Bernstein-Kogan would be identified as the endeavor's mastermind. And at his disposal was the Zionist movement's Kishinev-based correspondence bureau, one of four offices performing different institutional tasks set up a few years earlier. The others were by now largely nonfunctional; Bernstein-Kogan, no longer at the helm of Kishinev's office, had set in motion a well-run (albeit one-man) operation, ensuring not only contact with the movement's branches but also ready dissemination of information about Jewish concerns inside and beyond the empire.[63]

Bernstein-Kogan's superb work as head of Kishinev's correspondence bureau, as well as the city's proximity to the notoriously porous Romanian border at Jassy, one hundred miles to the west, was the backdrop to his stumble into history. The reasons for this were, of course, far more mundane than imagined by the right-wing circle close to Krushevan. Nonetheless there was good reason for them to connect the dots as they did with Bernstein-Kogan's activities: Since he had already been identified as suspicious by the government, this was concrete proof of what they already believed was the terrible truth.

In the anxious weeks before the pogrom's eruption, Bernstein-Kogan's apartment was designated as a depot for guns that could be used for self-defense. It is unclear whether these weapons were really intended to be used. On the second night of the pogrom, when most of the city's streets were finally quiet,

Bernstein-Kogan went door-to-door to the city's wealthy Jewish families, collecting money for relief and for the cost of telegrams he intended to send to newspapers and other outlets, telling them news of the massacre.[64]

By the night's end he had collected 48,000 rubles in cash and 18,000 rubles in checks. (He says in his memoirs that, when he encountered resistance, he simply stood his ground and refused to leave until the donation was given.) His familiarity with smugglers, who had long serviced his correspondence bureau, and his knowledge of the movement's international contacts, whom he had cultivated for years, proved to be invaluable. He spent some 1,500 rubles, a large sum, on telegrams transmitted from Jassy.[65]

The messages yielded, as Bernstein-Kogan later recorded in his memoirs, 1.25 million rubles in immediate relief, the bulk of this money coming to Kishinev from as far away as rural Australia. The Hilfsverein der deutschen Juden in Berlin, German Jewry's central community relief organization, alone contributed 192,443 rubles, and nearly all Jewish communities in the world quickly responded with impressive sums. In the midst of this, the already-porous lines between philanthropy and journalism collapsed. The Hearst chain sent to Kishinev 100,000 rubles that Davitt personally handed over to Bernstein-Kogan. With some of the money Bernstein-Kogan oversaw the launching of a trade school to provide marketable skills to girls whose parents had been killed. A few days after transmitting news of the pogrom via Jassy, he was summoned to St. Petersburg, where he met with Russian Jewry's leading figures and saw government officials as well as sympathetic members of Russia's literary community and intelligentsia, including Maksim Gorky. There he was introduced, especially in meetings with officials, as "Herzl's right-hand man." Plehve would astonish Herzl at their meeting in

August (Herzl said, "I was secretly amazed at [his] knowledge of [Zionist] personalities") when he noted the following: "But take Kogan-Bernstein! . . . [We] know that he conducts a press campaign against us abroad."[66]

It was a telegram from Bernstein-Kogan that had alerted the London representative of the Hearst press to the pogrom, and it was his name that topped Davitt's list of Kishinev contacts. Davitt also had letters of recommendation to Bernstein-Kogan from the American Jewish leader Cyrus Adler and London's Sephardic chief rabbi, Moses Gaster. As soon as Bernstein-Kogan arrived in Odessa, he was summoned by the U.S. consul to meet with Davitt, and as described earlier, he then spent seven hours with the latter—and Meir Dizengoff as translator—relating the pogrom's details. Bernstein-Kogan describes in his memoirs how

Jacob Bernstein-Kogan.

he and Davitt nearly managed to purchase the original copy of the Plehve letter with a large sum provided by Hearst, though it then slipped between their fingers. (This could never have happened, of course, because the letter never existed.)[67]

By now rumors were circulating—fanned by Georgi Pronin and others—that Jews had gathered just before the riot's outbreak in a Kishinev synagogue to plot revolution. In the cosmology of the far Right, Kishinev was transmuted from an agricultural depot at the empire's edge into a place of dark designs, what they believed to be the command post of a Jewish conspiracy with Bernstein-Kogan as its general.

Bernstein-Kogan's celebrity among Jews would pass quickly. With deep roots in Kishinev—where his father had been a well-known Jewish community figure—he never quite found another home after he abandoned it following rumors that his life was endangered once his role in publicizing the massacre became known. But the imprint he would leave in the annals of antisemitism would be profound and lasting—far more so than anything else he achieved in his life either as an activist or as a doctor. A warmhearted man armed with little more than the addresses of foreign newspapers and the stamina to stay awake all night collecting money to pay for a pile of telegrams, Bernstein-Kogan provided the authors of *The Protocols of the Elders of Zion* with as close a glimpse of a real Jewish elder as they would ever get. So it was that an overweight, underpaid, midlevel political activist— someone known to Krushevan since boyhood, when both were clothed in the same gymnasium uniform—became the unlikely inspiration for the most terrifying Jew on the planet.[68]

Kishinev offered Krushevan a front-row seat to Jewry's international machinations. And there was just enough solid evidence to bolster his already ample suspicions: Bernstein-Kogan's role in transmitting news of the pogrom, its outsize notoriety in the world's press, the Plehve forgery.

In Krushevan's view, nothing rioters could ever do to Jews could match the terrible, secret horrors Jews had in store, with Kishinev the testing ground for such designs. In Bernstein-Kogan's memoirs, written decades after the pogrom, he described Kishinev as a place where chickens wandered onto its larger boulevards from nearby, rural-like lanes. Krushevan's Kishinev was, in contrast, a place packed with fiends poised to bring Christendom to its knees. What connection there was for Krushevan between the demons haunting his adolescence and those he later sought to vanquish as he fought the Jewish people remains unknowable. Haunted, however, he undoubtedly was. *The Protocols* likely provides, as he saw it, a glimpse as to why.

Bessarabets front page, May 12, 1903.

▪ 6 ▪

Remains of the Day

The Kishinev pogroms in 1905 marked another period of crisis when the community locally, and the Jews nationally, organized themselves into various bodies to protest the outrages.

—LOUIS WIRTH, *The Ghetto*

The American sociologist Louis Wirth first wrote those words in his University of Chicago doctoral dissertation, which, when published in 1928, was justly hailed as a landmark study of urban life. He was knowledgeable in Jewish history, with a large swath of *The Ghetto* providing a reliable summary of Jewry's past, and when he described Russia's pogrom wave of 1905–6, it was Kishinev that, for him, was the natural marker, the most transparent way to capture early-twentieth-century Russian violence against Jews. Kishinev was—as for many others—so synonymous with pogroms that simple fact-checking likely felt unnecessary.

America's obligation to free Russia from barbarism had preoccupied liberal and left-wing opinion in the United States and Britain for decades before the Kishinev pogrom. As early as

1891, George Kennan, a war correspondent and explorer (a distant cousin of the renowned diplomat George F. Kennan), wrote *Siberia and the Exile System*, which contrasted a senselessly vindictive, dark penal system with the decency of those caught up in its web, and with Russia's nihilists embodying the best of its qualities. In response to Kennan's revelations, for example, the *Philadelphia Ledger* insisted that "civilized nations should refuse to have anything to do with Russia until she abandons barbarous practices."[1]

Unsurprisingly, such denunciations would often bring to the surface the embarrassing question of the similarity between Russian oppression of Jews and others and American treatment of blacks or, for that matter, of Chinese and Native Americans. In the United States these issues arose with such regularity in discussions regarding Russia that, as one historian has observed, "comparisons of the problems in the United States to troubles in Russia became so common as to seem almost a reflex." In 1892 the platforms of both the Democratic and the Republican Parties denounced religious persecution in Russia amid widespread criticism of Russia's antisemitic practices—most recently a mass expulsion of Jews from Moscow the year before.[2]

A wide range of motives fed such preoccupations, including the inclination to emphasize Russian obscurantism, thus sidelining the alarmingly commonplace practice of lynching as well as urban antiblack riots. Another crucial ingredient was Protestant- and Catholic-inspired contempt for Russian Orthodoxy. On the Left, it was the protestations of figures like the London-based exiled anarchist Prince Peter Kropotkin, the most congenial of all Russian radicals, whose leadership inspired the "Free Russia" movement of the 1890s.[3]

Though it had lost much of its momentum by the turn of the

twentieth century, the critique of Russia's sins returned to the front pages of American newspapers with the Kishinev pogrom. "When refugees from Kishinev docked in [New York] harbor," as the historian Christine Stansell has written, "their saber wounds still festering, there were people from the Henry Street Settlement there to meet them and publicize their plight." Some feared at the time that Kishinev's impact on left-wing politics in the United States, centered on the Lower East Side but with ample spillage beyond it, could well overshadow attention to the spike in antiblack violence, including lynchings-turned-riots in Delaware and Indiana in May 1903. Others insisted that, with pogroms now entering the American lexicon as synonymous with race riots, Russia's horrors would sensitize Americans to the need to react with urgency to their own country's indignities as well.[4]

Denunciations became commonplace, as evidenced even a decade and a half later in *Forverts* in the wake of the St. Louis race riot of 1917: "Kishinev and St Louis—the same soil, the same people. . . . Actually twin sisters that could easily be mistaken for one another." The Jewish communal administrator Oscar Leonard, an immigrant from Russia, insisted that the Black Hundreds "could take lessons in pogrom-making from the whites in St. Louis."[5] It was Kishinev's horrors—followed soon afterward by the pogrom wave of 1905–6—that would propel a new cadre of activists, many of them Jewish, for whom the conflation of lynching and pogroms would be second nature. The belief that such travesties were born of similar causes—the connivance of authorities, the rightlessness of the victims—helped give the issue of black injustice a prominence it had not enjoyed before.

This intersection between the call for the protection of blacks from lynching and Jews from pogroms would provide the immediate backdrop to the launching in 1909 of the first major American organization for the promotion of black civil rights: the National Association for the Advancement of Colored People, or NAACP. The high visibility in the United States of pogroms in Kishinev's wake gave a new sense of urgency to calls for the protection of blacks. Kishinev's influence on the politics of the American left—with the Yiddish-inflected preoccupations of the Lower East Side suddenly overflowing well beyond its immediate confines—also helped create a lexicon for the condition of America's blacks with comparisons to that of Jews under the most barbaric of autocratic regimes.

■

For decades Americans had tended to see Russia either through the lens of a Protestant prism, lacerating its primitive Russian Orthodox Church, or through that of an abolitionist critique of serfdom. An example of how Kishinev's pogrom, too, was made to fit readily into a Christian framework was displayed in the first book to appear in any language on the massacre: W. C. Stiles's *Out of Kishineff: The Duty of the American People to the Russian Jew,* which was rushed into print in June 1903. A retired Congregationalist minister, Stiles acknowledged that the "widespread interest, not to say excitement" in the pogrom "indicates an opportunity to draw the lessons of the case." Such lessons from the massacre (which left, as he reported, 240 dead) included proof of a Russian people who beat old men "in the presence of their sons . . . delicate women [were] violated and killed in the sight of their own children."[6]

Such Protestant-inspired criticisms of Russia were represented by the Society of American Friends of Russian Freedom, a stepchild of Boston's antislavery movement, which had by then run out of steam. Starting in mid-May, it was the Plehve letter—more so than the Kishinev pogrom itself—that would galvanize the movement's sudden rebirth. Such efforts were pushed from the start by the Hearst press, which was publishing day after day Michael Davitt's harrowing reports from the streets of Kishinev; these were augmented by banner headlines in *Forverts* and the Jewish press nationwide. Protest meetings would be held in twenty-seven American states, and a petition with the names of more than twelve thousand dignitaries would be forwarded in June as part of a formal call on the Russian government to investigate the pogrom, sent by President Theodore Roosevelt with the request that it be presented to the foreign minister and the tsar.[7]

Amid this cacophony, political radicals marginalized in the wake of the 1901 assassination of President William McKinley by an anarchist found a new, increasingly resonant voice. Much of their activity would concentrate on relief for pogrom victims. At the same time the widespread empathy for the victims, with its attendant message that tsarist Russia was no better than a prison house for Jews, opened up a full array of new prospects for left-wing endeavors.

Emma Goldman's rise to national prominence would occur amid the furor surrounding Kishinev. Just a few years earlier she had found herself so browbeaten after the McKinley assassination that she took an alias and found it necessary to earn her living at a Madison Avenue facial and massage parlor. She managed to extricate herself—emerging as the first immigrant-born celebrity to rise to national fame from New York's teeming Jewish ghetto—initially in the role of a theatrical promoter for a Russian troupe, the first of its kind to tour the United States, showcasing a wildly successful production built around the Kishinev pogrom.[8]

To be sure, Goldman had previously achieved a considerable

reputation on the Lower East Side as an orator, and in 1897 had embarked on her first cross-country lecture tour. But it was only once she promoted, in the winter of 1905, the work of Pavel Orlenev's St. Petersburg Dramatic Company that she would be catapulted into widespread prominence. Just a few months earlier, in late 1904, Goldman had cut her teeth as a promoter of the speaking tour of Catherine Breskhovskaya, the "grandmother of the Russian revolution," who was the first Russian radical of real prominence to appear on the American lecture circuit. Breskhovskaya did much to popularize the plight of Russian radicals under tsarism; her message was all the more effective because of the nobility of her bearing and her combination of integrity and straightforward intelligence. She appeared onstage with Goldman at her side as an interpreter. The tour electrified liberal and left-wing audiences, introducing Goldman, too, well beyond immigrant circles.[9]

But it was Goldman's achievement—while still using the unlikely pseudonym Smith—in introducing the first Russian theatrical troupe to tour the United States, ushering them onto Broadway with the financial help of German Jewish donors, celebrities, and the literary elite, that made Goldman into a household name. The vehicle was a ragtag group of actors who had arrived in the United States with little more than a sheaf of supportive letters signed by Kropotkin and others, with no financial backing and essentially penniless. What they chose from their repertoire was a Kishinev-themed play—originally called *The Jews* and renamed *The Chosen People*—by Evgenii Chirikov. After a debut at New York's Herald Square Theater with the guarantee of just one performance, Goldman took them under her wing, first caring for the entire troupe in 1905 at her summer retreat on Hunter Island near Pelham Bay Park in the Bronx (they slept in tents) and eventually booking further Broadway performances. With the use of both charm and relentless drive, Goldman induced Ethel and John Barrymore, the actor-manager Henry Miller, a collection of German Jewish grandees, and other luminaries to join the audience. "Now that I had greater access to the American mind," Goldman wrote in *Living My Life*, "I determined to use whatever ability I possessed to plead the heroic case of revolutionary Russia." *The Chosen People* served, as she saw it, as the best of all ways to do just this, and she stepped into the roles of the troupe's manager, translator, and press agent.[10]

Chirikov's play had been written in 1904 and published, without the pogrom scene at the end, in Russia. It had been praised by Maksim Gorky but savaged by most Jewish critics as didactic, lacking in drama, and essentially dull. Still, because of its explosive content, it could not be performed in Russia until 1906, when censorship restrictions lessened in the wake of the 1905 revolution. It first appeared onstage as it toured abroad in Germany and the United States.[11]

The performance is built largely around a series of conversations about Jews and their fate. Its male characters are shown mostly as cool, rational, and blind to the feelings of its female characters, which are the source of true wisdom born of the heart. The lead character is Liia, a Jew expelled from the university because of her radicalism. The crisis brings her to a deep affiliation with Jews, born mostly out of awareness that it was ignoble to abandon one's own people under siege.

In the play the description of the Kishinev pogrom is given to a Zionist, and soon after his harrowing account the Jewish characters are overwhelmed by a mob. Facing the likelihood of rape, Liia takes her own life. In stark contrast to Liia's stalwart resolve are the male characters, all of them incapable of reacting adequately to the crisis; for example, one accidentally shoots Christian workers seeking to defend Jews. Others are too weak or uncertain to do anything at all. Audiences responded enthusiastically to the play's message that there was an undeniable dignity to Jewish victimhood as represented by the noble Liia. The play, as Goldman would describe it, took the New York stage—and, unsurprisingly, the audiences of the Lower East Side—"by storm."[12]

Once Goldman emerged from this episode, she quickly dropped most of her ethnic ties. She minimized, as Stansell observes, her Russian past, taking her first steps toward becoming an American cultural celebrity, "something that few immigrants . . . and no immigrant Jewish woman had yet done." Much like Eugene O'Neill, who managed at more or less the same time to move beyond the world of Irish American letters—the first writer from his background to make this transition—Goldman with the use of Kishinev managed to shed, by and large, the remnants of her background. Leaning on the many useful contacts forged during her work with Orlenev—whose troupe soon fell apart because of rumors that some of its actors were, in fact, outspoken antisemites—Goldman found herself able to raise the funding to launch her remarkable magazine, *Mother Earth*, the freshest voice at that moment on the American Left.[13]

■

For others on the American Left, the Kishinev pogrom—and the widespread outbreak of attacks on Jews in the wake of Russia's constitutional crisis in the fall of 1905—moved them to recalibrate the issue of American blacks. Conflation of the sins of Kishinev with those of American lynching would surface as an item of paramount concern on the American Left, with pogroms and lynching increasingly viewed as evil twins.

The explosive interest surrounding Kishinev prompted surprise in some of the black press, with several outlets noting the stark contrast between an overall indifference to the mistreatment of American blacks and concern about the treatment of Russia's Jews. Hence applause for the American petition decrying Kishinev—an effort supported by many in the South and elsewhere who had publicly justified lynching—was scorned in several black newspapers. Such criticism appeared in a cluster of independent newspapers, especially those that had rejected the moderating influence of Booker T. Washington; these papers were mostly small and poorly funded but nonetheless likely representative of a significant swath of black public opinion.

That the mayor and city council members of Evansville, Illinois, had signed the Kishinev petition in June, and then in early July defended those who attacked blacks in the same city—the riot forced thousands to flee into the woods from their homes— elicited angry responses. Many black papers were infuriated by Booker T. Washington's expressed sympathy for Kishinev's Jews ("the horrors of Kishineff were shocking to the last degree") but unwillingness to condemn antiblack violence close to his own home. Chicago's *Broad Axe* attacked his "hypocrisy [that] . . . is more than enough to shame the very devil and all his imps in hell."[14]

Jewish leaders were also subjected to accusations of hypocrisy by black newspapers. One of the heads of the Philadelphia branch of B'nai B'rith, the organization responsible for drawing up the Kishinev petition, rejected any comparison between the pogroms and lynching, saying that "with rare exceptions [lynching] originates in crimes committed by Negroes." Reactions in black newspapers were fierce. Still, comparisons between Kishinev and lynching were commonplace in the black press. As the *Cleveland Gazette* stated on May 23, 1903, "The terrible massacres of Jews last week in Kishineff . . . are only what have taken place many times in the south." True, the numbers killed in Russia were larger, but the similarities outweighed the differences, since "the inhuman brutes of the southern part of this country are actuated by the same miserable motives"; their actions were "the dirtiest blot upon the world's escutcheon."[15]

Yet the same newspaper, known for its iconoclasm, also drew on the findings of a prominent French antisemite who disparaged the American public over its reaction to Kishinev while showing general indifference to lynching. There were no greater scoundrels, the paper insisted, than those Jews who campaigned for the rights of Russia's Jews while ignoring the mistreatment of American blacks. "Of all the morally wretched defenders of this crime . . . the American Jew who defends lynchers while denouncing Russian massacres—as some do—is the most contemptible."[16]

The first to formulate concrete proposals, however, drawing on the comparison between the treatment of blacks and Russia's Jews, was a married couple, once darlings of the American Left: William English Walling, the founding chairman of the NAACP, and his Russian-born Jewish wife, Anna Strunsky. Before surfacing as leading proponents of black civil rights, they—particularly Walling—had gained a national reputation as major interpreters of the Russian radical scene. Indeed, before John Reed's canonic evocation of the 1917 revolution, *Ten Days that Shook the World*, which was published in 1919, it was Walling's 1908 *Russia's Message: The True World Import of the Revolution* that provided the fullest account of the Romanovs as seen through the eyes of an American radical. The book was so influential that it would even be translated into Russian. Its treatment of Jewish suffering was extensive, if also unreservedly sympathetic, with considerable attention paid to the community's staggering poverty, government persecution, and anti-Jewish massacres and with Kishinev's pogrom described extensively. The couple spent nearly two years in Russia amid the turbulence of the 1905 revolution and its aftermath, interviewing scores of radicals, officials, and others. This work was aided greatly by Strunsky's native Yiddish and Russian.[17]

Their backgrounds could not have been more different. Walling was born into a wealthy Kentucky family; Strunsky, living first in New York and then in San Francisco, was born into a secular, left-leaning Jewish clan whose home figured among the liveliest of San Francisco's bohemian salons, attracting the likes of Jack London (who was, for a time, Strunsky's lover). Walling had long sought out—together with other patrician-born, left-wing friends—Jews on New York's Lower East Side, exploring, as one later recalled,

> . . . the teeming life down there. In those days when immigration poured countless thousands into the Lower East Side, most of them young, with political oppression behind them and new lives suddenly opening here, the whole vast region had become a melting pot for new ideas debated at a feverish heat in numberless cafés, large and small. Though in many the only drink was tea or coffee, and the men and boys

and girls who gathered there worked hard by day, most of them beginning at dawn, still those night discussions would run on till three or four o'clock. . . . We went to the Yiddish theater, too, . . . to meetings in Cooper Union and to Bowery barrooms.[18]

Unsurprisingly, Walling found just this exotic intensity in Strunsky, a remarkably intelligent, strikingly attractive Jew. By the time they met in 1905, Strunsky was in her late twenties and had already coauthored a book with London, *The Kempton-Wace Letters*, which explored the interplay between rationality and emotion in romantic love. Built out of a series of letters inspired by the couple's many conversations on the subject, it is a stilted, clotted volume, packed nonetheless with a fierce intensity. Since her late teens, Strunsky had won for herself a reputation as one of Northern California's most sought-after socialist speakers. She was chair of the local Friends of Russian Freedom and editor of the Berkeley-based journal *Russian Review*. Her autumn 1905 diary records lectures at the Sequoia Club, Ruskin Club, Oakland Socialist Branch, Jewish Council, and Socialist German Branch. She was a beautiful woman, and according to one admirer who knew her from her days as a Stanford student, had "soft brown eyes, a kindly smile and a throaty little voice that did something to your spine."[19]

At the time that Walling met Strunsky, as described by one historian, he was "an eclectic blend of European Marxism, the American equal rights movement and a romantic populism favored with a Russian Narodnik twist."* He counted among

---

* Russian peasant-oriented populists that by the time Walling wrote were associated mostly with the Socialist Revolutionary Party.

Anna Strunsky.

his ancestors from his storied Southern stock a democratic vice-presidential candidate and Daniel Boone. Lanky, broodingly handsome, a graduate of the University of Chicago at the age of nineteen who then worked as a factory inspector, he was convivial, a serial womanizer, and—as Strunsky wrote soon after his death—a man who carried with him always "a great loneliness." His books (there were five, including one on Walt Whitman) tended to be lengthy if also rather raw and pedantic. His energy seemed boundless; his writing was typically hastily done, though, until his sudden death, it continued to command a wide readership. Active in a broad array of progressive organizations, at the time of his death in an Amsterdam hotel room at the age of fifty-nine he had just rushed from Paris for still another meeting.[20]

Strunsky had none of his restless fluency. Her anticipated work on the Russian pogroms was left unfinished, as was a manuscript, tentatively called *Revolutionary Lives*, a series of well-observed and passionate sketches of the many inspiring radicals she and Walling had met during their Russian travels, beginning in 1906. It remained in manuscript even in 1917, when she sought, without success, finally to publish it.[21]

Strunsky retained a stalwart commitment to socialism, but, after marrying and giving birth to three children (following two miscarriages), she retreated as a public figure, becoming little more than a helpmate to her prominent husband. A novel, *Violette of Père Lachaise*, was completed in 1905 but would not be published for another decade. When the journalist and socialist activist Mary White Ovington described the founding meeting of what would become the NAACP, launched in Strunsky and Walling's New York apartment, she would characterize it as launched by "three people": a Jew (Henry Moskowitz), the descendant of an abolitionist (Oswald Garrison Villard), and the Southerner, Walling.[22]

Yet Strunsky had set much of this into motion. Amid the turmoil engulfing Russia in the first years of the twentieth century, Strunsky and Walling worked together to amass the information for *Russia's Message*. The book compared tsarist treatment of Jews to, no less, the St. Bartholomew's Day massacre, the Spanish Inquisition, and the workings of the Mafia. Russia's Jewish policy was, essentially, a "slow massacre system." It described in great detail attacks on Jews in Odessa and elsewhere, the connivance of authorities, and the indifference of the police, with the official explanation of the disturbances always blaming victims for incitement. The volume included two photographs of Krushevan, whom it decried as one of Russia's most vicious anti-Jewish leaders, responsible "for the first great massacre of recent years, Kishinev."[23]

While preparing notes for an article on the Gomel pogrom

of January 1906, Strunsky interviewed victims at a hospital. She described, for example, attacks on a woman who had been bayoneted and a girl with her eye gouged out. Strunsky visited the city's most dreadful slum, an enclave known as the Hole, and she collected photographs of shrouded dead. She interviewed authorities who insisted that the attack on Jews was little more than a Jewish scam to collect insurance money. Such claims left her speechless: "My arms trembled, my eyes swam. My pen began streaming ink over my notebooks." At Gomel's train station the next morning, amid Jews fleeing the city, she knew that she had to drop all pretense of dispassionate journalism, recognizing that "I felt I was seeing these people for the last time, and for the last time I belonged to them."[24]

Still, Strunsky bristled at the prospect of any special attention paid to Jewish political concerns: Her interest, she insisted, was in Jews as victims of oppression but not of special concern for any other reason. Particularly unimpressive were those promoting Jewish nationalism in the midst of revolution. In a draft of *Revolutionary Lives* dating to 1917 but based largely on interviews conducted a decade earlier, the only figure whom she took to task in an otherwise breathless paean to revolutionary devotion was the Jewish socialist activist and Bundist Mark Liber. She acknowledged his unstinting devotion as well as his intelligence but admitted her exasperation with his insistent preoccupation with Jews. Liber, she wrote, turned his back on "that romantic and highly varied result which comes out of the melting-pot of life." It was therefore all the more ironic "that Liber and hundreds of thousands like [him], having espoused Nationalism, forsook the vision which has inspired the revolutionary and democratic forces seeking to weld the world together!"[25]

Returning from abroad in early summer 1908 at the time *Rus-*

sia's Message appeared, Strunsky and Walling were immediately drawn to the eruption of antiblack violence in Springfield, Illinois. The birthplace of Abraham Lincoln, it was a city Walling had often visited. The riot broke out in August 1908, the first antiblack massacre in the North in half a century.

Visiting relatives at the time in Chicago, Strunsky sensed right away that this was an American version of what they had just witnessed in Russia. Explaining their sudden departure to their hosts, Walling wrote: "It was Anna's idea to begin with. She has been anxious for years to get an insight into one of these troubles and to write a broad, sympathetic and non-partizan [*sic*] account—as she did to the Homel massacre." Both arranged to publish articles: Strunsky promised to send reports to *Collier's*, and Walling committed to the liberal magazine *The Independent*, which had already published much of his just-released *Russia's Message*. Walling's piece, which appeared on September 3, created a veritable sensation, leading one year later to the creation of the NAACP; Strunsky, once again, never managed to finish hers.[26]

Taking the night train from Chicago, the couple arrived in Springfield the next morning to discover that "the rioting had been continuing throughout the night, and was even feared for the coming evening, in spite of the presence of nearly the whole militia of the State." What they found was that the town was all but unanimously committed to dislodging all of its blacks, hoping that those who had not already done so would "flee." Seven people died, forty homes and twenty-seven businesses were destroyed, and 107 indictments would be issued against rioters.[27]

Much like in Russia, where Jews themselves were as often as not blamed for attacks on them, Walling found this to be the case in Springfield. As expressed in the *Illinois State Journal*, there was "no other remedy than that applied by the mob. . . . [It was] the negroes' own misconduct, general inferiority or unfitness for free institutions that were at fault." Walling acknowledged that black criminality existed there and was encouraged by the bosses of both political parties. But, again much like in Russia, ultimate responsibility for the antiblack campaign was borne by the press, which had egged on the rioters and then justified their crimes.[28]

The similarities between how Walling and Strunsky would understand Russia's pogroms and the Springfield attack were striking. And both would now break ranks with the Socialist Party, which had avoided support of the nascent movement for black civil rights as sectarian and at odds with exclusionary unions. On arriving in Springfield the couple heard the riot explained away—by rioters and local officials alike—on the basis of the argument that blacks were on the cusp of taking over the city. Their incursions justified the riot, whose express goal was to run them out of Springfield. It was claimed that blacks had fired first—a standard charge in official reports on Russian pogroms as well—and that mob violence was revenge for the murder of whites.[29]

Walling ended his article with the warning that what Springfield revealed was that, unless checked, the heinous antiblack repression so characteristic of the South was certain to move northward: "What large and powerful body of citizens," he asked, "is ready to come to their aid?"[30]

Ovington responded immediately to Walling's call, pressing him in a letter to take the initiative to launch just such a "large and powerful body." A few days later, on September 12, at a public meeting in New York City's Cooper Union, Walling and Strunsky spoke about their travels in Russia with special attention to the suffering of Jews. There the first concrete moves were made toward creating a national black defense organization. And the call for its establishment was made in direct response to Strunsky's insistence—spontaneous, it seems, and formulated by her right on the spot—that the pogroms of Russia and the violence against blacks in the United States were horrors made of much the same stuff.[31]

Walling quickly countered that Springfield was, as he saw it, even worse than any pogrom. The rest of the meeting's program then shifted to a detailed airing of "comparative oppression," as an observer recalled, and as soon as it ended the couple sat with Ovington and several others late into the night, planning how best to launch an organization with the goal of putting a stop to the terrorizing of blacks. Over the next few weeks, as Strunsky and Walling continued their lecture tour to Indianapolis, Chicago, and elsewhere (which was slated originally to promote *Russia's Message*), they shifted its primary focus from Russia to the oppression of blacks. In a letter from Strunsky to her parents in California after Walling's first address in a black church, she said: "Great speech lasting two hours in a negro church. . . . All my family was there."[32]

Once back in New York, the couple rented an apartment on West Thirty-Eighth Street, and the meeting described earlier by Ovington, where the "Committee for the Advancement of the Negro" was created, finally took place on January 9, 1909. Strunsky's name appears among its founders. This set the stage for the first National Negro Conference—whose proceedings would be opened by Walling as the chair of its executive committee—on May 31, 1909. It was renamed, the next year, as the National Association for the Advancement of Colored People.[33]

Though so much of the impetus behind the launching of this initiative was Strunsky's, many close to Walling saw her as little more than an attentive spouse, a rather shadowy, even dowdy figure. The critical role she played, and so publicly, in fueling attention to the plight of blacks by linking it directly to the widely publicized persecution of Russia's Jews would recede from view. Suffering profoundly from two consecutive miscarriages—she may well have absented herself from the founding meeting at her home of the "Committee for the Advancement of the Negro" because she was feeling ill—she now retreated from the public stage and was quickly forgotten. She missed the May 1909 National Negro Conference meeting because of another miscarriage four days before.[34]

A socialist for the remainder of her life, Strunsky would never again achieve the prominence she enjoyed in her twenties. A great-nephew recalls how, as an elderly woman (she died at the age of eighty-seven in 1964), she was known in family circles as someone who would corner young relatives and relate lengthy tales of the famous people she had once known. She never managed to finish *Revolutionary Lives* (the manuscript was deposited eventually in Special Collections at Yale University), but its pages contain comments scribbled in pencil by her children with jottings of love for their mother and gratitude for the joys of her home. "I love Mother and Mother loves me, and we are the happiest people you would ever see."[35]

In October 1908, at much the same time that Walling and Strunsky were beginning to cobble together what would soon emerge as the NAACP, the biggest hit on Broadway was a play built around the Kishinev pogrom. This was Israel Zangwill's *The Melting Pot*, which debuted in Washington, DC, with Theodore Roosevelt in the audience; the president admitted in a letter to Zangwill a decade later that it still remained for him an abiding inspiration. "True Americanism" is what the play preached, as Roosevelt saw it. Zangwill likely saw the play somewhat differently, influenced as he was by an intermixture of beliefs that somehow combined Jewish nationalism and assimilation. Still, Zangwill's starkest message, as articulated most clearly at the close of his play, was evident to all: America represented that spot where "all races and nations come to look forward" in contrast to horrific Kishinev, the site of "crimes beyond human penalty . . . obscenities beyond human utterance."[36]

With the memory of Kishinev still fresh at the time of the play's premiere, the town's mention alone, according to one of Zangwill's biographers, was "enough to electrify an audience." Its protagonist is the violinist and composer David Quixano, a Kishinev orphan. His surname is meant to evoke noble Sephardic ancestry, with his profession intended—in this archly polemical production, more treatise than theater—as a refutation of Richard Wagner's essay "Judaism in Music" and its argument regarding the inability of Jews to create truly original compositions. High-strung, often hysterical, apparently brilliant but plagued by horrific recollections of Kishinev's brutality, Quixano is meant to be the voice of the new American:

America is God's Crucible, the great Melting Pot where all the races of Europe are melting and reforming! Here you stand, good folk, think I, when I see them at Ellis Island, here you stand in your fifty groups with your fifty languages and histories, and your fifty blood hatreds and rivalries. But you won't be long like that, brothers, for these are the fires of God. A fig for your feuds and vendettas! German and Frenchman, Irishman and Englishman, Jews and Russians—into the Crucible with you all! God is making the American. . . .

[T]he real American has not yet arrived. He is only in the Crucible. I tell you—he will be the fusion of the races, perhaps the coming superman.[37]

Zangwill wrote these words while also campaigning, oddly enough, as a fervent Jewish nationalist, a maverick in the Zionist movement, then at the helm of his own organization pressing for a Jewish home anywhere in the world—not excluding venues distant from Palestine. (The same year *The Melting Pot* debuted on Broadway, he admitted to the *Jewish Chronicle* that he was so busy running the London office of the Jewish Territorial Organization that he no longer considered himself a writer.) How he reconciled his play's unambiguous call for assimilation with his public Jewish activity he never managed to explain. And the play itself, while resoundingly successful at the time and the inspiration for the most resilient of all depictions of American exceptionalism, describes a phenomenon that never existed: "The point about the melting pot," wrote Nathan Glazer and Daniel Patrick Moynihan in their pathbreaking 1963 study, *Beyond the Melting Pot*, "is that it did not happen."[38]

In a dramatic work that, despite its title, had little if anything to do with the United States—it was, as Glazer and Moynihan rightly summed it up, "about Jewish separatism and Russian anti-Semitism"—Kishinev provided not so much a theme as scaffolding. Zangwill summed this goal up well, explaining that this theatrical work, much like his organizational activities, was little concerned with Russia "except as a place to escape from."[39]

■

This would become Kishinev's most salient of all lessons. The pogrom would serve for many as the final, definitive way in which the most nagging of all questions regarding the fate of Russia's Jews was put to rest. True, there would remain much to debate, with Jews divided, often furiously, over whether the best course was the fall of the Romanovs or flight from Russia to the United States, Palestine, or elsewhere, as the historian Ezra Mendelsohn insightfully captured in this conundrum: Here or there, and if there where?[40] What Kishinev made starkly clear, as its lessons would come to be absorbed over the next few years, was that Romanov Russia was beyond repair, now for Jews no more than, as Zangwill would put it, a springboard overready for flight.

It was the pogrom and the purported letter—these now meshed together irrevocably in the public mind—that provided the most indisputable of proofs. Kishinev was fodder for a host of stark, straightforward answers, the ideal focus for Bialik's fierce, brilliant poetic curse, for (albeit quickly discarded) synagogue liturgy, Jewish propagandist art, and the declamations of Israeli politicians to the present day.

The interplay between the wealth of readily accessible information regarding Kishinev's massacre—a veritable mountain of data—and the proliferation of distortions regarding it remains perhaps the saga's most profoundly intriguing legacy. A huge body of documentary evidence was readily available in the pogrom's wake, accompanied—indeed, as often as not overshadowed—by a stream of forgeries whose lessons retain their resonance still. The massacre would provide so many Jews as well as non-Jews with a conclusive sense of past and present. It would constitute for many the final nail in the coffin for the prospect of Russian Jewish integration, the ultimate verdict on the necessity for emigration to the United States or Palestine, the clearest of all clarion calls for revolution, and the starkest of all proof regarding Jewry's uncanny worldwide influence. It would be invoked as the grimmest of all modern Jewish humiliations, as evidence of the necessity for Jews to fight resolutely against their foes, and as evidence of a Jewish cunning so supremely manipulative that the benefits accrued from violence against Jews far outweighed its harm.

The city at the heart of this story, renamed Chişinău after the fall of the Soviet Union and the creation of an independent Moldova, is a place known mostly in recent years as one of the world's notorious depots for international prostitution, the capital of a fast-crumbling nation-state bedeviled by corruption, petty and grandiose, with an ambiguous identity readily absorbable either into that of Romania or, perhaps less likely, Russia.

Chişinău itself possesses a certain gray, tired grandeur: a few largish parks in the city center, an imposing arch just outside its main state buildings, a beautiful ethnographic museum situated in a leafy part of town, peppered with some of the city's more fashionable houses and embassies. To be sure, nearly all its streets are badly potholed and in need of repair; police corruption accompanied by shakedowns of foreigners are no less a fixture of the local scene than its undrinkable water. There are hints of gentrification in a cluster of the city's oldest neighborhoods, whose decrepitude the newly rich (their source of wealth at best legally ambiguous) have designated as enticing. Most of the city's Jews decamped long ago for Israel or the United States. A local literary scholar whose specialty is Krushevan's fiction—for which she had great admiration—explained to me as we were sitting at the local Jewish community library that, had Jews not left Chişinău in the 1990s, it would now be faring far better economically; yet she had insisted just a few moments earlier that the real reason for the outbreak of the 1903 pogrom was that the city was packed with far too many Jews, with this justly exasperating locals. Though pressed, she acknowledged no contradiction in what she had just said.

The city's grim past retains a palpable presence not only because of the pogrom's lingering infamy but also because so many of its original, crumbling buildings—despite a massive earthquake in 1940 and, of course, the devastation of its Jewish population in World War II—have survived largely as a result of Chişinău's chronic poverty. It is a shambling, unpretentious place, surprisingly lush, village-like in some of its corners, still bounded at its northern edge by the unassuming but harsh eyesore, the river Byk. A cement bridge stretches across this marshland, with the Old Town just around the corner, a quick walk from Azi-atskaia Street (now renamed), a tenement brushing up against the street's clapboard structures, which have weathered so much with no evidence, needless to say, that this was once and still remains one of the most storied sites of the recent Jewish past.

The dusty street is crowded in daytime with earnest, hard-working locals—women with their shopping bags, schoolchildren (there is an elementary school nearby), men lugging tools. Densely housed, a hodgepodge of Soviet-age construction and century-old piles, it is a place that has inspired lessons of heroism and shame, cowardice and militancy, loathing or trust for gentiles. As many would come to believe, it was here, in this crowded alleyway, where exile reached its sudden, bloody end.

ACKNOWLEDGMENTS

This book started as a cultural history of the Jews of Russia and Eastern Europe in the nineteenth and twentieth centuries. Accumulating material for that broad, synthetic work, I found myself so intrigued by evidence of the spillage from Kishinev's pogrom that, over time, the prospect of telling that story felt more pertinent: It offered a singularly revealing way of exploring how Jews of Russia and beyond would come to understand themselves and, in turn, came to be understood by others.

Two lengthy stints—a year at the Radcliffe Institute for Advanced Study, and five months as Jacob Kronhill Visiting Scholar at the YIVO Institute for Jewish Research—provided me with precious stretches of time and the incomparable resources of Harvard and YIVO. My thanks to Judith Vichniac at the Radcliffe and Jonathan Brent, Eddy Portnoy, and Lydmilla Sholokhova at YIVO. It was at YIVO that I had first embarked on my archival research as a graduate student, and it was a special pleasure to return daily again to that precious, intellectually boisterous institution.

I'm grateful to the following archives: Yale Special Collections; Manuscripts and Archives Research Library at Trinity College, Dublin; Hoover Institution Library and Archives; Bancroft Library, University of California, Berkeley; Tamiment Library and Robert F. Wagner Archives; New York Public Library of the Performing Arts; Central Zionist Archives; Gnazim Institute Archives; Beit Bialik, Tel Aviv; the Academy of Sciences of Moldova; and the State Archive of the Russian Federation (GARF). For research-related advice in Israel I thank Shmuel Avreri, Dan Porat, and Tali Tadmor-Shimoni; the suggestions of the literary scholar Avner Holtzman were invaluable. As always, I remain in the debt of Zachary Baker, assistant university librarian for collection development for the Humanities and Sciences and Reinhard curator of Judaica and Hebraica at Stanford.

I thank those who assisted me with a wide range of library and archival research as well as transliteration and translation tasks: Samuel Barnai (Jerusalem), Aleksandra Zolkina and Oleg Kaesch (Moscow), and California-based Heidi G. Lerner, Andrew Gay, Maria Greer, Eliza Davidson, Kristen Edwards, and Carnie Burns. The days I spent in Chişinău with graduate student Orest Dabija and Irina Shikova, director of the Jewish Heritage Museum of Moldova, in September 2016 helped greatly in firming up my sense of their city's topography. Special thanks to Tel Aviv's Asia Lev and retired Hoover Institution researcher Ron Basich (a truly extraordinary archival expert) for their patience and wisdom. Chişinău colleagues Igor Casu and Sergiu Musteata, both at Ion Creanga State University, unearthed invaluable material. Many of the photographs in this book were supplied by Chişinău researcher and archivist Iurie Svet.

As the writing of this book seemed to be drawing to a close, Mikhail Khazin generously provided me with an archival cache in his possession—the papers of Kishinev's most infamous antise-

Acknowledgments

mitic intellectual, Pavel Krushevan. This book would have been far different without this treasure-trove that has been acquired by the Hoover Institution.

Friends and colleagues have commented on drafts: Mitchell Cohen, Anita Shapira, Robert Alter, Eli Lederhendler, Derek Penslar, Joel Beinin, Jeffrey Shandler, Ken Moss, Sarah Abervaya Stein, and Andrew Ramer. John Efron read the manuscript in its entirety with great care. Writing side by side with my Stanford colleague Aron Rodrigue, now at work on a major book on the Jews of Rhodes, has been the source of uncommon intellectual inspiration. I've benefited from the help of many others, too, including Michael Hagemeister (whose pathbreaking work on *The Protocols of the Elders of Zion* has much influenced me), Carla King, Joe Lee, Sylvie Goldberg, Sidra Ezrahi, John Boylan, Christopher English Walling, Michael Strunsky, Leon Fink, Diane Everman, Patrick Phillips, Edward H. Judge, Mikhail Gluzman, Tony Michels, Anna Shternshis, Scott D. Seligman, Seth Perelman, ChaeRan Freeze, Norman Naimark, Amir Weiner, Bryan Cheyette, Hasia Diner, Gordon Chang, Abraham Socher, David Levering Lewis, David Fort Godshalk, Martha A. Sandweiss, C. S. Monaco, and David Fogelson. My conversations with University of California, Berkeley historian Yuri Slezkine have left a considerable imprint on these pages.

Julia Zafferano, for many years the managing editor of the journal *Jewish Social Studies: History, Culture, and Society*, for which I served as a senior editor, brought characteristic acuity and grace to an early draft of this book. Sue Llewellyn, my copyeditor at Liveright/W. W. Norton, proved no less astute if also memorably astringent. Barbara Roos, a splendid indexer, has worked with me since my first book in the 1980s.

The support of Stanford's dean of Humanities and Sciences,

Acknowledgments

Richard Saller, and associate dean for the Humanities—and my longtime friend—Debra Satz, proved crucial. I've benefited from suggestions and criticisms made at public presentations at the Radcliffe Institute; École des Hautes Études en Sciences Sociales (where I gave a series of lectures drawn from my research on this book as a visiting professor); Central European University, Budapest; Ion Creanga State University, Chişinău; Hebrew University of Jerusalem; YIVO Institute for Jewish Research; Columbia University; University of Chicago; Emory University; University of Wisconsin, Madison; University of Illinois, Champaign; National Yiddish Book Center, University of California, Santa Cruz; University of California, San Diego; and UCLA.

My tireless agent, Charlotte Sheedy, brought this work to the attention of my publisher, Robert Weil. He has proved to be a true collaborator and friend. I thank his staff, particularly his remarkably even-tempered editorial assistant, Marie Pantojan. At Stanford's History Department, I thank Monica Wheeler, Maria Van Buten, and Brenda Finkel for their kindnesses and patience.

■

Most of this book was written in the downstairs study of my Berkeley home with my wife Susan Berrin's vegetable garden just outside the window and the editorial office of her magazine, *Sh'ma*, on the floor above. At lunchtime we'd meet at a small table on a veranda outside the kitchen. May this last forever.

NOTES

Preface

1. Peter Burke's introduction to Carlo Ginzburg, *The Enigma of Piero: Piero della Francesca* (London, 2000), 4.
2. See Ben-Zion Dinur's comments in H. Shorer, ed. *Ha-pogrom bi-Kishenev bi-melot 60 shanah* (Tel Aviv, 1963), 243–259.
3. Serge Dmitreyevich Urussov, *Memoirs of a Russian Governor* (London, New York, 1908), 14.
4. On pogroms see Hans Rogger, *Jewish Policies and Right-Wing Politics in Imperial Russia* (Berkeley, CA, 1986), John D. Klier, *Russians, Jews, and the Pogroms of 1881–1882* (Cambridge, UK, 2011), and a thoughtful local study, Darius Staliūnas, *Enemies for a Day: Antisemitism and Anti-Lithuanian Violence Under the Tsars* (Budapest and New York, 2015). For comparative work see Donald L. Horowitz, *The Deadly Ethnic Riot* (Berkeley, CA, 2001), and Roger D. Petersen, *Understanding Ethnic Violence: Fear, Hatred, and Resentment in Twentieth-Century Eastern Europe* (Cambridge, UK, 2002).
5. Gur Alroey, *Zionism Without Zion: The Jewish Territorial Organization and Its Conflicts with the Zionist Organization* (Detroit, 2016); Jonathan Frankel, *Prophecy and Politics: Socialism, Nationalism, and the Russian Jews, 1862–1917* (Cambridge, UK, 1981); Adam Rovner, *In the Shadow of Zion: Promised Lands Before Israel* (New York, 2014).

Chapter 1. Age of Pogroms

1. *The Economist*, November 22, 2014.
2. Bernard Malamud, "The Jewbird," *The Complete Stories* (New York, 1997), 323; Carol Brightman, ed., *Between Friends: The Correspondence of Hannah Arendt and Mary McCarthy, 1949–1975* (New York, 1995), 149; Woody Allen and Marshall Brickman, *Annie Hall*, directed by Woody Allen, 1977 (MGM Home Entertainment, January 24, 2012); Hugh Trevor-Roper to Bernard Berenson, in Richard Davenport-Hines, ed., *Letters from Oxford* (London, 2007), xxi; Ian Whitcomb, *Irving Berlin and Ragtime America* (Pompton Plains, NJ, 1988), 19.
3. Nekula Marek, *Franz Kafka and His Prague Contexts* (Prague, 2016), 208; Arthur Koestler, *Thieves in the Night* (London, 1947), 217.
4. *Report of Kahan Commission Report* (Jerusalem, 2012); *New York Times*, June 1, 1993; *Homeland*, season 6, episode 4, "A Flash of Light," directed by Leili Linka Glatter (Bonanza 2017).
5. Malamud, "The Jewbird," 323.
6. Leo Motzkin, ed., *Die Judenpogromme in Russland* (Leipzig and Cologne, 1910); Abraham Ascher, *The Revolution of 1905: Authority Restored* (Stanford, CA, 1992), 145–154; Lamed Shapiro, "The Cross," in Leah Garrett, ed., *The Cross and Other Stories*, (New Haven, CT, 2007), 8.
7. Oleg Budnitskii, *Russian Jews Between the Reds and the Whites*, trans. Timothy J. Portice (Philadelphia, 2012).
8. *Correspondence Respecting the Treatment of Jews in Russia*, nos. 1–2, Papers, vol. 81 (London, 1882); Harold Frederic, *The New Exodus: A Study of Israel in Russia* (New York and London, 1892).
9. David G. Roskies, *Against the Apocalypse: Responses to Catastrophe in Modern Jewish Culture* (Cambridge, MA, 1984), 82–92; A. R. Malachi, "Pera'ot Kishinev be-aspaklaryat be-'ivrit ve-yidish," *Al admat Bes'arabyah* 3 (1963–1964), 64–98; *Australian Jewish Historical Society* 11 (1992): 821.
10. Benjamin Harshav, *Language in Time of Revolution* (Berkeley, CA, 1993), 4; K. Baedeker, *Russland: Handbuch für Reisende* (Leipzig, 1901), 31–40.
11. Steven J. Zipperstein, *The Jews of Odessa: A Cultural History, 1794–1881* (Stanford, CA, 1986), 9–40; Rogger, *Jewish Policies*, 25–40.

12. Jeffrey Veidinger, *Jewish Public Culture in the Late Russian Empire* (Bloomington, 2009); Steven J. Zipperstein, "Inside Kishinev's Pogrom: Hayyim Nahman Bialik, Michael Davitt, and Burdens of Truth," in ChaeRan Freeze et al., eds., *The Individual in History: Essays in Honor of Jehuda Reinharz* (Waltham, MA, 2015), 376–382; Gregory Freidin, "Isaac Babel," in George Stade, ed., *European Writers: The Twentieth Century*, vol. 2 (1885–1914), (New York, 1989), 1885–1914.

13. Steven J. Zipperstein, "Fateless: The Beilis Trial a Century Later," *Jewish Review of Books* (Winter 2015).

14. John Moore, *A Journey from London to Odessa* (London, 1833), 69–70.

15. Ibid., 74–75, 87–88.

16. *Times*, December 7, 1903, reprinted in *Jewish Chronicle*, December 11, 1903; Sam Johnson, *Pogroms, Peasants, Jews: Britain and Eastern Europe's "Jewish Question," 1867–1925* (New York, 2011), 85–88; Sam Johnson, "Use and Abuses: 'Pogrom' in the Anglo-American Imagination," in Eugene M. Avrutin and Harriet Murav, eds., *Jews in the East European Borderlands* (Boston, 2012), 158–166. See also David Engel's superb "What Is a Pogrom? European Jews in the Age of Violence," in Jonathan Dekel-Chen et al., eds., *Anti-Jewish Violence: Rethinking the Pogrom in Eastern Europe* (Bloomington, 2011), 19–37.

17. *Times*, December 7, 1903.

18. Ibid.

19. Peter Steinfels, "Beliefs; A century ago, in what is now Chisinau, hundreds fell victim to a pogrom. Yesterday, a day of healing, Christians and Jews Remembered," *New York Times*, May 30, 1998; Anita Shapira, *Land and Power: The Zionist Resort to Force, 1881–1948*, trans. William Templer (Stanford, CA, 1992), 34.

20. Anita Shapira, *Yosef Haim Brenner: A Life*, trans. Anthony Berris (Stanford, CA, 2015), 42; *Forverts*, May 10, 1903.

21. Edna Nahshon, ed., *From the Ghetto to the Melting Pot: Israel Zangwill's Jewish Plays* (Detroit, 2006), 211.

22. Cyrus Adler, ed., *The Voice of America on Kishineff* (Philadelphia, 1904), xvii. On the Kishinev pogrom: Edward H. Judge, *Easter in Kishinev: Anatomy of a Pogrom* (New York, 1992) is a first-rate monograph without, however, the use of Hebrew or Yiddish-language

sources. See also Monty Penkower, "The Kishinev Pogrom of 1903: A Turning-Point in Jewish History," *Modern Judaism* 24, no. 3 (October 2004): 19–43; *Kishinevskii pogrom, 1903 goda: Sbornik dokumentov i materialov* (Chişinău, 2000); Heinz-Dietrich Löwe, *The Tsars and Jews: Reaction and Anti-Semitism in Imperial Russia* (Chur, Switzerland, 1993), 139–166.

23. *New York American*, May 14, 15, 17, 18, 19, 20, 1903; David Nasaw, *The Chief: The Life of William Randolph Hearst* (Boston, 2000), 163.

24. Frankel, *Prophecy and Politics*, 463–484; Yisrael Halperin, *Sefer ha-gevurah: 'antologyah historit-sifrutit* (Tel Aviv, 1949–1950), vol. 3, 4–35.

25. *Bund: Dokumenty i materialy* (Moscow, 2010), 215–308; J. L. Keep, *The Rise of Social Democracy in Russia* (Oxford, 1963), 117–122; H. Shukman, "The Relations Between the Jewish Bund and the RSDRP, 1897–1903" (PhD diss., London University, 1961).

26. Yitshak Maor, *Ha-tenuah ha-Tsiyonit be-rusyah* (Jerusalem, 1973), 244.

27. James Boyland, *Revolutionary Lives: Anna Strunsky and William English Walling* (Amherst, MA, 1998), 136.

28. Edward H. Judge, *Plehve: Repression and Reform in Imperial Russia, 1902–1904* (Syracuse, NY, 1983), 94–101.

29. See the excellent analysis of now-discredited explanations regarding the authorship of *The Protocols* by Michael Hagemeister, "'The Antichrist as an Imminent Political Possibility': Sergei Nilus and the Apocalyptic Reading of *The Protocols of the Elders of Zion*," in Richard Landes and Steven T. Katz, eds., *The Paranoid Apocalypse: A Hundred Year Retrospective on The Protocols of the Elders of Zion* (New York, 2012), 79–91.

30. *Bikher-velt* 3–4 (1923), 241–242.

31. Chaim Weizmann, *Trial and Error: The Autobiography of Chaim Weizmann* (New York, 1949), 254, 343; Jehuda Reinharz, *The Making of a Zionist Leader* (Oxford, 1985), 149–152, 156–157.

32. Noam Chomsky, "Interview with Amy Goodman," Democracy Now!, National Public Radio, January 13, 2014.

33. Ari Shavit, *My Promised Land: The Triumph and Tragedy of Israel* (New York, 2013), 102–104.

34. Ibid., 108.
35. Ibid., 131.
36. Ibid., 132.
37. A. I. Solzhenitsyn, *Dvesti let vmesti (1795–1995)*, vol. 1 (Moscow, 2001), 321–338.
38. Steven J. Zipperstein, "Benjamin Netanyahu's Favorite Poet—and Ours," *Forward*, July 7, 2014.
39. Igor' Petrovich Shornikov, "Obshchestvenno-politicheskaia i litera-turnaya deiatelnost' P. A. Krushevana" (PhD diss., Pridnestrovskii Gosudarstvennyi universitet im. T. G. Shevchenko, Tiraspol, 2011).
40. *Forverts*, April 28 and May 1, 1903.
41. "Why Netanyahu refuses to 'turn the other cheek,' in his response to the UN Vote," *Times of Israel*, December 27, 2016.
42. Aleksandar Hemon, *The Lazarus Project* (New York, 2008),

Chapter 2. Town and Countryside

1. T. J. Binyon, *Pushkin: A Biography* (New York, 2002), 119.
2. Iulian Brescanr, "Karl Schmidt—Geschichte eines deutschen Humanisten aus Bessarabien," *Jahrbuch der Deutschen aus Bessarabien*, vol. 64, 201–204.
3. *New York Times*, June 6, 1903.
4. Keith Hitchins, *The Romanians, 1774–1866* (Oxford, 1996), 285–289.
5. Michael F. Hamm, "Kishinev: The Character and Development of a Tsarist Frontier Town," *Nationalities Papers* 26, no. 1 (1998) 24–27. On the paucity of archival sources on Kishinev's early years see V. I. Zhukov, *Goroda Bessarabii, 1812–1861* (Moscow, 1964), 21.
6. *Bessarabia: Handbook Prepared Under the Direction of the Historical Section of the Foreign Office*, No. 51 (London, 1920), 4–5; Zhukov, *Goroda Besarabii*, 62; V. S. Zelenchuk, *Naselenie Bessarabii i podnestrov'ia v XIX v.* (Kishinev, 1979), 148–160.
7. Hamm, "Kishinev," 22–23; Zhukov, *Goroda Besarabii*, 71, 98; George F. Jewsbury, *The Russian Annexation of Bessarabia, 1774–1828* (New York, 1976), 7–54.

8. *Bessarabia: Handbook*, 36–38.

9. Y. Zlatova and V. Kotel'nikov, *Across Moldova* (Moscow, 1959), 26–27; *Istoriia Kishineva* (Kishinev, 1966), 83–87.

10. *Bessarabia: Handbook*, 30; S. Konstaninov, *Kishinev: ekonomicheskii ocherk* (Kishinev, 1966), 22–23.

11. Judge, *Easter in Kishinev*, 26–27; *Bessarabia: Handbook*, 30–32; Miriam Bernshtain and Yitshak Koren, eds., *Sefer Bernshtain-Kogan* (Tel Aviv, 1946), 101.

12. Shlomo Hillels, *Har ha-keramim* (Tel Aviv, 1930), 7–8, 16–17.

13. Ibid., 57–58.

14. *Bessarabia: Handbook*, 6; Urussov, *Memoirs of a Russian Governor*, 113–118.

15. Hamm, "Kishinev," 25.

16. *Bessarabia: Handbook*, 28–29; Robert Edelman, *Gentry Politics on the Eve of the Russian Revolution* (New Brunswick, 1980), 34, 224; Rogger, *Jewish Policies*, 212–232.

17. Michael Davitt, *Within the Pale: The True Story of the Anti-Semitic Persecutions in Russia* (New York, 1903), 158–159; *Istoriia Kishineva*, 49, 101.

18. Zhukov, *Goroda Bessarabii*, 45.

19. *Bessarabia: Handbook*, 26–27; Konstaninov, *Kishinev*, 11–12.

20. Binyon, *Pushkin*, 123–124.

21. Ibid., 120.

22. Urussov, *Memoirs of a Russian Governor*, 13–14.

23. *Istoriia Kisheneva*, 49, 101; Judge, *Easter in Kishinev*, 20.

24. Michael Davitt, "Diary, Kishineff, 1903," folder 6, Davitt Papers, Trinity College, Dublin.

25. Judge, *Easter in Kishinev*, 34–35; Urussov, *Memoirs of a Russian Governor*, 30–31; Davitt Diary, Ms. 9578, folder 16; Konstantin Korolev, *Leninskaia v "Iskra" Kisheneve* (Kishinev, 1970); Keep, *The Rise of Social Democracy*, 95.

26. *Kishinevskii pogrom*, 35.

27. Pavel Krushevan, *Bessarabiia* (Moscow, 1903), 7–40.

28. Urussov, *Memoirs of a Russian Governor*, 12–14.

29. Yaakov Goren, ed., *'Eduyot nifga'e Kishenev, 1903: kefi she-nigbu 'al-yede H. N. Byalik va-haverav* (Tel Aviv, 1991), 82–160.

30. Davitt Diary, Ms. 9578, folder 11.

31. Wolf Moskovich, "Kishinev," *YIVO Encyclopedia of Jews in Eastern Europe* (New Haven, CT, 2008). On Jewish population statistics, see Yitshak Koren, *Yehude Kishinev* (Tel Aviv, 1940), 17.

32. Yosef Arokh, *Der tsen yor'riger kalendar'*, 1901/2–1910/11 (Kishinev, 1901).

33. Information on Jewish occupations in the late 1880s can be found in Koren, *Yehude Kishinev*, 211–212.

34. Ibid.

35. Simon Geissbühler, *Like Shells on a Shore: Synagogues and Jewish Cemeteries of Northern Moldavia* (Bern, Switzerland, 2010).

36. Ibid., 28–32.

37. Koren, *Yehude Kishinev*, 165–202.

38. Yosef Rubin, ed., *Dubossary: sefer zikaron* (Tel Aviv, 1965).

39. A selection of documents on the Dubossary affair in the State Archive of the Russian Federation (GARF, f 102, 3) has been translated in ChaeRan Y. Freeze and Jay M. Harris, eds., *Everyday Jewish Life in Imperial Russia: Select Documents* (Waltham, MA, 2013), 536–550.

40. Ibid., 536–538.

Chapter 3. "Squalid Brawl in a Distant City"

1. The most detailed eyewitness account can be found in the transcript of Bialik's interviews, *'Eduyot*, and the documentary volume *Kishinevskii pogrom 1903 goda*. For an edited version of the trial transcripts see Isidore Singer, *Russia at the Bar of the American People* (New York, 1904), 248–283. The reports of Pesach Averbach in the St. Petersburg Hebrew-language daily *Ha-Zeman* (Averbach would soon assist both Bialik and Davitt with their investigations) are particularly useful in their detail and likely the first published eyewitness descriptions of the massacre. See also S. M. Dubnov and G. Ia. Krasnyi-Admoni, eds., *Materialy dlia istorii antievreiskikh pogromov v Rossii*, vol 1 (Petrograd and Moscow, 1919); M. B. Slutskii, *V skorbnye dni* (Kishinev, 1930); A. Beilin, *Der Kishinyever pogrom* (Warsaw, 1932); and Judge, *Easter in Kishinev*, 107–133.

2. G. A. Pronin's court testimony, April 29, *Kishinevskii pogrom*, 262–263; Singer, *Russia at the Bar*, 249.

3. Dubnov and Krasnyi-Admoni, *Materialy dlia istorii*, vol 1, 210; Judge, *Easter in Kishinev*, 49.

4. Singer, *Russia at the Bar*, 10; *Times*, April 25, 1903.

5. *Ha-Zeman*, April 10, 1903; *Kishinevskii pogrom*, 226–228; Singer, *Russia at the Bar*, 11, 16.

6. Judge, *Easter in Kishinev*, 50; *Sefer Bernshtain-Kogan*, 127; *Sankt Petersburg Vedomosti*, May 8, 1903.

7. *Jewish Chronicle*, May 8, 1903; Urussov, *Memoirs of a Russian Governor*, 45–49; Davitt, *Within the Pale*, 97–100; Singer, *Russia at the Bar*, 3: "One single man succeeded in making a break in these tolerable conditions [in Kishinev]. . . . To him mainly are due the horrors of the April days of 1903. Six years ago a journalist by the name of Kroushevan started in a newspaper . . . ."

8. *'Eduyot*, 66; Davitt Diary, 9578, Davitt Papers, folder 17.

9. *'Eduyot*, 65–66; *Ha-Zeman*, April 14, 1903; *Jewish Chronicle*, December 16, 1903.

10. *'Eduyot*, 65; Motzkin, ed. *Die Judenprogromme in Russland*, vol. 2, 11; *Ha-Zeman*, April 10 and April 12, 1903.

11. *'Eduyot*, 65–66; Singer, *Russia at the Bar*, 252; Judge, *Easter in Kishinev*, 50.

12. Davitt, *Within the Pale*, 125; *'Eduyot*, 65–67.

13. Ibid., 76–78.

14. Singer, *Russia at the Bar*, 13; *New York Times*, August 13, 1903; Judge, *Easter in Kishinev*, 49.

15. *Sankt Petersburg Vedomosti*, May 8, 1903; *New York American*, May 17, 1903.

16. *'Eduyot*, 107.

17. Ibid., 110; Davitt, *Within the Pale*, 118.

18. *'Eduyot*, 87.

19. *Kishinevskii pogrom*; *Ha-Zeman*, May 8, 1903.

20. *'Eduyot*, 98; *Kol shire H. N. Byalik* (Tel Aviv, 1956), 364. The best English translation is Atar Hadari, ed. and trans., *Songs from Bialik: Selected Poems of Hayim Nahman Bialik* (Syracuse, NY, 2000), 1.

21. *'Eduyot*, 99.

22. Ibid., 100–101.

23. See Singer, *Russia at the Bar*, 11–13.

24. *'Eduyot*, 69–72.

25. Ibid., 91–92.
26. V. H. C. Bosanquet and C. S. Smith, *Dispatch from His Majesty's Consul-General at Odessa, Forwarding a Report on the Riots at Kishinev* (London, 1903). A summary was published in the *New York Times* on August 13, 1903.
27. *'Eduyot*, 100, 135.
28. Ibid., 133; Davitt Diary, Ms. 9578, folder 21, 1 v.
29. Davitt Diary, Ms. 9578, folder 19, r.
30. *'Eduyot*, 80–81; Michael Gluzman, "Pogrom and Gender: On Bialik's Unheimlich," *Prooftexts* 25 , nos. 1 and 2 (Winter-Spring 2005): 45–46.
31. Urussov, *Memoirs of a Russian Governor*, 147; Davitt Diary, Ms. 9578, folder 39.
32. V. G. Korolenko, "Dom No. 13-yi: epizod iz kishevskago pogroma" (Berlin, 1904).
33. *'Eduyot*, 82–83, 139.
34. Slutskii, *V skorbnye dni*, 35; *'Eduyot*, 85–93.
35. *'Eduyot*, 122–124.
36. Ibid., 131.
37. Ibid., 141.
38. Korolenko, "Dom No. 13-yi"; Slutskii, *V skorbnye dni*, 146.
39. Slutskii, *V skorbnye dni*, 146.
40. Urussov, *Memoirs of a Russian Governor*, 13.
41. Roskies, *Against the Apocalypse*, 84.
42. Halperin, *Sefer ha-gevurah*, vol. 3, 15.
43. *'Eduyot*, 159–160.
44. Ibid., 160–161.
45. Ibid.
46. Ibid., 76.
47. Boris Tarnopolsky, "The Gomel Pogrom of 1903: A Case Study in Russian-Jewish Relations in the Pale of Settlement" (MA thesis, University of Haifa, 2007).
48. Michael Stanislaswski, *Zionism and the Fin de Siècle: Cosmopolitanism and Nationalism from Nordau to Jabotinsky* (Berkeley, CA, 2001), 178–202.
49. *'Eduyot*, 92, 109–110.
50. Ibid., 93–94.

51. Pronin argued in an article published in *Novoe Vremia* on October 16, 1903, that Jewish aggression was the cause of the pogrom. It is reprinted in *Kishenevskii pogrom*, 148–150. Much the same charge was leveled by the procurator of the Odessa Chamber of Justice, ibid., 151–152, and the Kishinev chief of police, ibid., 216–221.

52. *'Eduyot*, 113–14, translated in Gluzman, "Pogrom and Gender," 43–44.

53. *Sefer Bernshtain-Kogan*, 127–128,

54. I draw for my analysis from William C. Fuller Jr.'s excellent *Civil-Military Conflict in Imperial Russia, 1881–1914* (Princeton, NJ, 1985), 109–110; see also *Kishinevskii pogrom*, 22–26, 224.

55. Fuller, *Civil-Military Conflict*, xviii.

56. Ibid., 77–98.

57. Urussov, *Memoirs of a Russian Governor*, 15–18; Judge, *Easter in Kishinev*, 46, 62–68.

58. Judge, *Plehve*, 96.

59. *Times*, May 6, 1903. For examples of how news of the Plehve letter now comes to dominate Jewish coverage of Kishinev, see *Forverts*, May 14 and 15, 1903, and *Jewish Chronicle* (London), May 29, 1903: "That the riots were pre-arranged down to the smallest detail there is no longer the slightest reason to doubt." A detailed sketch of Plehve appeared in the *Jewish Chronicle*, June 5, 1903.

60. *Times*, May 6, 1903.

61. Judge, *Easter in Kishinev*, 120–133; A. A. Lopukhin, *Otryvki iz vospominanii* (Moscow, 1923), 15, 16.

62. Rogger, *Jewish Policies*, esp. 40–55 and 188–211.

63. *Kishinevskii pogrom*, 67–68, 121–134.

64. Singer, *Russia at the Bar*, 4–9; Urussov, *Memoirs of a Russian Governor*, 45–47.

Chapter 4. Burdens of Truth

1. *New York Times*, May 12, 1903.

2. Scott D. Seligman, "The Night New York's Chinese Went Out for Jews: How a Chinatown Fundraiser Event for Pogrom Victims United Two Persecuted Peoples," *Forward*, January 26, 2011; *New York Tribune*, November 19, 1903.

3. *New York American*, May 18, 1903; Adler, *The Voice of America on Kishineff*, 334.

4. Malachi, "Pera'ot Kishinev," 24–64; Roskies, *Against the Apocalypse*, 83–86; Monty Penkower, "The Kishinev Pogrom of 1903," 192–193; J. B. Weber, *The Kishineff Massacre and Its Bearing upon the Question of Jewish Immigration into the United States* (New York, 1903).

5. Frankel, *Prophecy and Politics*, 473–474.

6. *New York Times*, May 17, 1903.

7. Taylor Stults, "Roosevelt, Russian Persecution of Jews, and American Public Opinion," *Jewish Social Studies* 33, no. 1 (1971): 15.

8. "Kishineff," NCOF+p.v.344, *New York Public Library for the Performing Arts*.

9. Philip Ernest Schoenberg, "The American Reaction to the Kishinev Pogrom," *American Jewish Historical Quarterly* 63 (March 1974): 264–265.

10. Mark Bornstein, *The Colors of Zion: Blacks, Jews, and Irish from 1845 to 1945* (Cambridge, MA, 2011), 125; Lawrence Marley, *Michael Davitt* (Dublin, 2007), 256–259; Carla King, "Michael Davitt and the Kishinev Pogrom," *Irish Slavonic Studies* 17 (1996): 19–44; Dermott Keogh, *Jews in Twentieth-Century Ireland* (Cork, 1998), 27–32.

11. Davitt Papers," Ms. 9501/5296–5396; Jonathan D. Sarna, *JPS: The Americanization of Jewish Culture, 1888–1988* (Philadelphia, 1989), 64, 69.

12. See Dan Miron, "Me'ir ha-haregah," in Michael Gluzman, Hanan Hever, and Dan Miron, eds., *Be-'ir ha-haregah ve-hala—bikur me'uhar* (Tel Aviv, 2005), 154. Biographies in Hebrew and English have appeared, both written by Avner Holtzman: *Hayyim Nahman Bialik* (Jerusalem, 2009) and *Hayim Nahman Bialik: Poet of Hebrew* (New Haven, CT, 2017).

13. Miron, "Me'ir ha-haregah," in Michael Gluzman et al., eds., *Be-'ir ha-haregah ve hala—bikur me'uhar*, 152–154; Moshe Ungerfeld, *Byalik ve-sofre doro* (Tel Aviv, 1974), 277. Perlman's critical essay is reprinted in Gluzman et al., eds., *Be'ir ha-hagirah*, 181–187; on Davitt's arrival in Kishinev, see *Sefer Kogan-Bernshtain*, 135–136.

14. Chaim Tchernowitz [Rav Tsa'ir], *Masekhet zikhronot* (New York, 1945), 116–125.

15. Steven J. Zipperstein, *Elusive Prophet: Ahad Ha'am and the Origins of Zionism* (Berkeley, CA, 1993), 21–66.

16. Ibid.

17. Ibid., 105–169.

18. Ibid., 195–199.

19. Ibid.

20. Holtzman, *Hayyim Nahman Byalik*, 74–130.

21. Steven J. Zipperstein, "Odessa," *YIVO Encyclopedia of Jews in Eastern Europe*, vol. 2 (New Haven, CT, 2008); Guido Hausman, *Universität und städtische Gesellschaft in Odessa: 1865–1917* (Stuttgart, 1998).

22. Zipperstein, *Elusive Prophet*, 72–73.

23. *Kol shire*, 156; Atar Hadari, ed. and trans., *Songs from Bialik: Selected Poems of Hayim Nahman Bialik* (Syracuse, NY, 2000), 11; Dan Miron, *The Prophetic Mode in Modern Hebrew Poetry and Other Essays on Modern Hebrew Literature* (New Milford, CT, 2010), 91.

24. Robert M. Seltzer, *Simon Dubnow's "New Judaism": Diaspora Nationalism and the World History of the Jews* (Leiden, 2014), 133–226.

25. Yeruham Fishel Lachower, *Byalik*, vol. 2 (Tel Aviv, 1934–1935), 424–426; *Kol shire*, 158.

26. For the text of Bialik's "Be'ir ha-harigah" see *Kol shire*, 364–376. An insightful analysis can be found in Alan Mintz, *Hurban: Responses to Catastrophe in Hebrew Literature* (New York, 1984), 141–154.

27. Pesach Averbach, "H. N. Byalik ve-'ir ha-harigah," in *Ha-pogrom be-Kishinev*, 28; Miron in *Be-'ir ha-haregah*, 80–85; Holtzman, *Bialik: Poet of Hebrew*, 91.

28. Simon Dubnow, *Kniga zhizni*, vol. 2 (Riga, Latvia,1934), 240–243.

29. *Ha-Zeman*, April 10, 1903; Zipperstein, *Elusive Prophet*, 203–208; Eric Zakim, *To Build and Be Built: Landscape, Literature, and the Construction of Zionist Identity* (Philadelphia, 2006), 23–26.

30. Zipperstein, *Elusive Prophet*, 205–207.

31. Ibid., 203, 207.

32. Halperin, *Sefer ha-gevurah*, vol. 3, 17–20.

33. Ibid., 19.

34. Ibid., 19–20.

35. King, "Michael Davitt," 10–60; Richard Ellmann, *James Joyce* (Oxford, 1982), 25.

36. Marley, *Michael Davitt*, 256–259. The banner headline above a pho-

tograph of Davitt in the *New York American*, May 15, 1903, reads: "I am going, resolved to find the truth."

37. Michael Davitt, *The Boer Fight for Freedom* (New York, 1902), 28; Davitt, *Within the Pale*, ix, 89.

38. H. H. Hyndman, *Further Reminiscences* (London, 1912), 52.

39. Ibid., 55. On Hyndman's views of Jews, see Colin Holmes, *Anti-Semitism and British Society, 1876–1939* (London, 1979), 22, 69. I thank Bryan Cheyette for this reference.

40. Davitt, *Within the Pale*, 86–87, 91–93, 126–127, 199; Keogh, *Jews in Twentieth-Century Ireland*, 27–32.

41. Davitt, *Within the Pale*, 103–104, 111; *Sefer Bernshtain-Kogan*, 135–136.

42. Davitt Papers, Ms. 9578, Ms. 9501/5301; Davitt, *Within the Pale*, 17–27; King, "Michael Davitt," 29–30. See Pesach Averbach's obituary in *Davar*, April 4, 1945.

43. Davitt, *Within the Pale*, 101.

44. Gluzman, "Pogrom and Gender," 39–59; Holtzman, *Bialik: Poet of Hebrew*, 92.

45. Gluzman, "Pogrom and Gender," 50–54.

46. Ibid., 52.

47. Ziva Shamir, *Li-netivah ha-ne'elam: ikvot parashat Ira Yan bi-yetsirat Byalik* (Tel Aviv, 2000), esp. 7–50; Holtzman, *Bialik: Poet of Hebrew*, 92–112. The director of Beit Bialik, Moshe Ungerfeld, marked the ninetieth birthday of Manya Bialik in a commemorative article in *Davar*, December 31, 1965.

48. Lachower, *Byalik*, 442–443; Holtzman, *Bialik: Poet of Hebrew*, 96–97.

49. Lachower, *Byalik*, 442–443; Holtzman, *Bialik: Poet of Hebrew*, 104–105.

50. Ariel Hirschfeld, *Kinor 'arukh* (Tel Aviv, 2011); Holtzman, *Hayim Nahman Byalik*, 116.

51. Ben-Zion Katz, *Zikhronot* (Tel Aviv, 1963–1964), 133–137.

52. *Kol shire*, 364; Hadari, *Songs from Bialik*, 1.

53. Miron, *Be-'ir ha-harigah*, 103.

54. *Kol shire*, 365; Hadari, *Songs from Bialik*, 2.

55. *Kol shire*, 368; Hadari, *Songs from Bialik*, 4.

56. *Kol shire*, 370; Hadari, *Songs from Bialik*, 5.

57. Dan Miron, "Hayim Nahman Bialik's Poetry: An Introduction to *Songs from Bialik*," in Hadari, *Songs From Bialik*, 38.

58. "Listovka Odesskoi organizatsii bunda po povodu pogroma v Kishineve," *Kishinevskii pogrom 1903 goda*, 60–62.

59. *Kol shire*, 367; Hadari, *Songs from Bialik*, 3.

60. *Kol shire*, 365–66; Hadari, *Songs from Bialik*, 3.

61. See, for example, Shlomo Dubinsky's article on self-defense during the Kishinev pogrom in *Ha'aretz*, August 10, 1928.

62. Roskies, *Against the Apocalypse*, 89.

63. Michael Davitt Papers, Ms. 9577/5.

64. Ibid.

65. Ibid.

66. Ibid.

67. Ibid.; King, "Michael Davitt and the Kishinev Pogrom," 30.

68. Davitt, *Within the Pale*, 170. On the impulses behind Bialik's poem, see Olga Litvak's provocative article, "The Post in Hell: H. N. Bialik and the Cultural Genealogy of the Kishinev Pogrom," *Jewish Studies Quarterly* 12, no. 1 (2005): 101–128.

69. *Moznayim* 45, no. 1 (1967–1968).

70. Ungerfeld, *Byialik ve-sofre doro*, 277; Stanislawski, *Zionism and the Fin de Siècle*, 178–202; David Ben-Gurion, *Mikhtavim* (Tel Aviv, 1972), vol. 1, 127; Holtzman, *Bialik: Poet of Hebrew*, 84.

71. Y. T. Helman, *As'arah perakim le-shire H. N. Byalik* (Tel Aviv, 1953–1954), 13–48.

72. Tali Tadmor-Shimony, *Shi'ur moledet: ha-hinukh ve-khinun medinah* (Beersheba, 2011); Leora Y. Bilsky, "When Actor and Spectator Meet in the Courtroom: Reflections on Hannah Arendt's Concept of Judgment," *History and Memory* 8, no. 2 (Fall-Winter 1996): 137–173.

73. *Al Ha-Mishmar*, August 13, 1967; *Di presse* (Buenos Aires), August 4, 1976.

74. *Ha-Hinukh*, July 23, 1967.

Chapter 5. Sages of Zion,
Pavel Krushevan, and the Shadow of Kishinev

1. V. I. Lenin, "The Second Duma and the Second Revolutionary Wave," in *Lenin Collected Works*, vol. 12 (Moscow, 1962), 113–118. Reference to Krushevan in Anna Shternshis and Psoy Korolenko, collectors and recorders, *"Lost" Yiddish Songs of World War II* (2017),

was discovered recently by Moshe Beregovsky and his colleagues at the Kiev Cabinet for Jewish Culture. I thank Anna Shternshis of the University of Toronto for this information.

2. Benjamin W. Segel, *A Lie and a Libel: The History of The Protocols of Zion*, Richard S. Levy, trans. and ed. (Lincoln, NE, 1995); Norman Cohn, *Warrant for Genocide: The Myth of the Jewish World-Conspiracy and the Protocols of the Elders of Zion* (London, 1967), 108. See also Richard S. Levy, "Setting the Record Straight: Regarding *The Protocols of the Elders of Zion*: A Fool's Errand," in William Collins Donahue and Marthe B. Helfer, eds., *Nexus: Essays in German Jewish Studies*, vol. 2 (Rochester, NY, 2014), 43–62.

3. *American Hebrew and Jewish Tribune*, June 15, 1934.

4. *Chemu uchit nas pokuyshchenie Pinkhusa Dasheshskago?* (n.p., 1903); *Ha-Zeman*, June 13, 1903; Michael Hagemeister, *Die "Protokolle der Weisen von Zion" vor Gericht* (Zurich, 2017), 543. Biographical material on Krushevan may be found in GARF, Fond 102, Opis 231 (October 1903).

5. Michael Hagemeister, "Zur Frühgeschichte der *Protokolle der Weisen von Zion*, I: Im Reich der Legenden," *Die Fiction von der jüdischen Weltverschwörung* (Göttingen, 2012), 140–160.

6. D. I. Storov, introductory essay in Pavel Krushevan, *Znamia Rossii*, ed. O. A. Platonov (Moscow, 2015), 5–60.

7. Ibid., 35–55.

8. Michael Hagemeister, *The Protocols of the Elders of Zion*: Between History and Fiction," *New German Critique* 35 (2008); Cesare G. De Michelis, *The Non-Existent Manuscript: A Study of the Protocols of the Sages of Zion* (Lincoln, NE, 2001). The linguist Henryk Baran is at work on a comprehensive study of *The Protocols*.

9. Krushevan, *Bessarabiia*, and Krushevan, *Delo Artabanova* (reprint, Moscow, 1995); S. Reznik, *Krovavaia karusel'* (Moscow, 1991); Umberto Eco, *The Prague Cemetery* (Boston, 2011), 192; Krushevan, *Znamia Rossii*; Urussov, *Memoirs of a Russian Governor*, 46.

10. Irving Howe and Ruth R. Wisse, eds., *The Best of Sholem Aleichem* (New York, 1979), 115–119.

11. Krushevan Papers, item 1, 1–5, now deposited at the Hoover Institution, Stanford, CA.

12. Ibid.

13. Mikhail Khazin, *Kostiuzheny i vokrug* (Boston, 2015), translated in Khazin, "The Forgery," 6.

14. See the eulogy for Krushevan in *Moskovskie Vedomosti* 7, June 13, 1909; Urussov, *Memoirs of a Russian Governor*, 116.

15. Khazin, *Kostiuzheny*, 167–169; Krushevan Papers, item 29.

16. Krushevan's nephew's memoir manuscript in the Krushevan Papers; Khazin, *Kostiuzheny*, 158.

17. Ibid., 159–160.

18. Arkadii Mazur, *Stranitsy istorii sorokskikh evreev* (Chişinău, 1999); Zhukov, *Goroda Bessarabii*, 38.

19. *American Hebrew and Jewish Tribune*, June 14, 1934.

20. Rogger, *Jewish Policies*, 188–211.

21. "Sestra Krushevana—Evreika" appeared on December 21, 1933, probably in *Novoe russkoe slovo*; the longer, more fanciful version, translated from the Yiddish report in *Forverts*, appeared as "Krushevan's Kin Now a Jewess: Sister of Infamous Instigator of Kishinev Pogroms (Here Interviewed) Does Penance for Him in Hebrew Prayers," *American Hebrew and Jewish Tribune*, June 14, 1934.

22. Ibid.

23. Krushevan Papers, item 24.

24. P. A. Krushevan, *Chto takoe Rossiia? putvyia zamietki* (Moscow, 1896), 355.

25. Ibid., 356.

26. Ibid., 356–357.

27. Ibid., 357.

28. Ibid., 358.

29. Ibid.

30. Ibid.

31. Ibid., 359.

32. Ibid.

33. Ibid.

34. See the list of *Bessarabets* columns in Krushevan Papers, item 12.

35. Judge, *Easter in Kishinev*, 40.

36. Krushevan Papers, item 23; Urussov, *Memoirs of a Russian Governor*, 10.

37. Krushevan Papers, items 31, 33.

38. De Michelis, *The Non-Existent Manuscript*, 73–86.

39. Richard Landes and Steven T. Katz, eds., *The Paranoid Apocalypse: A Hundred-Year Retrospective on The Protocols of the Elders of Zion* (New York, 2012).

40. Michael Hagemeister, "'The Anti-Christ as an Imminent Political Possibility': Sergei Nilus and the Apocalyptical Reading of *The Protocols of the Elders of Zion*," in Landes and Katz, *The Paranoid Apocalypse*, 79–91.

41. L. Wolf, *The Jewish Bogey and the Forged Protocols of the Learned Elders of Zion* (London, 1920).

42. De Michelis, *The Non-Existent Manuscript*, 33–34.

43. Ibid., 23–45.

44. Michael Hagemeister, "The American Connection: Leslie Fry and the Protocols of the Elders of Zion," 68; Marina Ciccarini et al., eds., *Kessarevo Kesarju: Scritti in onore di Cesare G. De Michelis* (Florence, 2014), 157–168.

45. De Michelis, *The Non-Existent Manuscript*, 2.

46. Ibid., 8–9.

47. Ibid., 65.

48. Ibid., 80–82.

49. The Russian text can be found reprinted in De Michelis, *The Non-Existent Manuscript*, 285–290.

50. Ibid.

51. Ibid.

52. Ibid.

53. Ibid., 369–370.

54. Ibid., 64–66; Yosi Goldshtain, *Ben Tsiyonut medinit le-Tsiyonut ma'asit: ha-tenuah ha-Tsiyonit be-Rusyah be-reshitah* (Jerusalem, 1991), 40–41, 98–99.

55. Khazin, *Kostiuzheny*, 157.

56. Mordekhai Nurock, *Ve'idat Tsiyonei Rusyah be-Minsk* (Jerusalem, 1963–1964); Moshe Cohen, "Ahad Ha'am bi-kenesyat Minsk," *Netivot* 1 (1913): esp. 11–13.

57. Zipperstein, *Elusive Prophet*, 187–193; A. J. P. Taylor, introduction to John Reed, *Ten Days That Shook the World* (London, 1977), ix.

58. Maor, *Ha-tenuah ha-tsiyonit*, 149–161.

59. De Michelis, *The Non-Existent Manuscript*, 47–50, 113–114.

60. *Tazkir Lopuhin: duah ha-mishtarah haha'it ha-Russit 'al tenu'ah*

ha-Tsiyonit, 1897–1902 (Jerusalem, 1988), trans. Yael Ha-Russi, 133–154.

61. Ibid., 28–29. For a detailed description of Bernstein-Kogan's Zionist activity, see Goldshtain, *Ben Tsiyonut medinit*, 30–40.
62. *Sefer Bernshtain-Kogan*, 79–92.
63. Ibid., 122–125.
64. Ibid., 127.
65. Ibid., 129.
66. Ibid., 131; Raphael Patai, ed., *The Complete Diaries of Theodor Herzl* (New York, 1960), 1526.
67. Davitt Papers, Ms. 95–1/5305; *Sefer Bernshtain-Kogan*, 136–137.
68. Khazin, *Kostiuzheny*, 166.

Chapter 6. Remains of the Day

1. David S. Foglesong, *The American Mission and the "Evil Empire"* (Cambridge, UK, 2007), 21.
2. Ibid., 21, 24–25.
3. Martin Miller, *Kropotkin* (Chicago, 1976), 160–173.
4. Christine Stansell, *American Moderns: Bohemian New York and the Creation of the New Century* (New York, 2000), 65.
5. Jonathan Kaufman, "Blacks and Jews: The Struggle in Cities," *Struggles in the Promised Land: Toward a History of Black-Jewish Relations* (New York, 1997), 108; Charles L. Lumpkins, *American Pogrom: The East St. Louis Riot and Black Politics* (Athens, OH, 2008), 127.
6. W. C. Stiles, *Out of Kishineff: The Duty of the American People to the Russian Jew* (New York, 1903), 21. See the review in the *Jewish Chronicle* (London), July 24, 1903.
7. Foglesong, *The American Mission*, 28; Adler, *The Voice of America on Kishineff*, passim.
8. Valleri J. Hohman, *Russian Culture and Theatrical Performance in America, 1891–1933* (New York, 2011), 41–45; Stansell, *American Moderns*, 123–125; Emma Goldman, *Living My Life*, vol. 1 (New York, 1931), 359, 369–370.
9. Hohman, *Russian Culture*, 40–48.
10. Stansell, *American Moderns*, 123–124; Goldman, *Living My Life*, vol. 1, 367.

11. E. N. Chirikov, *Evrei* (Munich, 1910); Christopher John Tooke, "The Representation of Jewish Women in Pre-Revolutionary Russia" (PhD diss., University College London, 2011), 114; Hohman, *Russian Culture*, 41.

12. Tooke, "The Representation," 118–121; Goldman, *Living My Life*, vol. 1, 367; Stansell, *American Moderns*, 124.

13. Ibid., 125.

14. *Broad Axe*, June 20, 1903.

15. *Cleveland Gazette*, May 23, 1903.

16. Ibid., August 15, 1903.

17. Boyland, *Revolutionary Lives*; Leon Fink, *Progressive Intellectuals and the Dilemmas of Democratic Commitment* (Cambridge, MA, 1997), 114–146.

18. Ernest Poole's essay in *William English Walling: A Symposium* (New York, 1938), 25; Earle Labor, *Jack London: An American Life*, 130.

19. Labor, *Jack London*, 146–147, 154–155.

20. Fink, *Progressive Intellectuals*, 122.

21. Walling (Anna Strunsky) Papers, Ms. 1111, Box 32, Folders 387–388, Manuscripts and Archives, Yale University Library, New Haven, CT.

22. Mary White Ovington, "William English Walling," *Crisis*, November 1936; Charles Elliot Kellogg, *NAACP: A History of the National Association for the Advancement of Colored People* (Baltimore, 1967), 12.

23. William English Walling, *Russia's Message: The True World Import of the Russian Revolution* (New York, 1908), 46, 52, 56–58, 61–65.

24. Anna Strunsky Walling, *The Homel Massacre: An Address Delivered Before the New York Section Council of Jewish Women* (New York, 1914).

25. Walling (Anna Strunsky) Papers, Ms. 111, Box 32, Folders 387, 235, Yale University Library, New Haven, CT.

26. Boyland, *Revolutionary Lives*, 152.

27. William English Walling, "The Race Riot in the North," *The Independent*, July–December 1908.

28. Ibid.

29. I thank David Fort Godshalk, author of *Veiled Visions: The 1906 Atlanta Riot and the Reshaping of American Race Relations* (Chapel Hill, 2005), for sharing his typescript "African Americans, American

Jews, and the Pogroms: How Russian Ethnic Violence Transformed American Racial Politics Between 1903–1909."

30. Walling, "The Race Riot."

31. Mary White Ovington, *How the National Association for the Advancement of Colored People Began* (New York, 1914), n.p.

32. Boyland, *Revolutionary Lives*, 156.

33. Kellogg, *NAACP*, 19.

34. Boyland, *Revolutionary Lives*, 159–160.

35. Strunsky Papers, File 387, n.p.

36. Aviva F. Taubenfeld, *Rough Writing: Ethnic Authorship in Theodore Roosevelt's America* (New York, 2008), 16.

37. Nahshon, *From the Ghetto to the Melting Pot*, 363; Leftwich, *Israel Zangwill*, 256; Nathan Glazer and Daniel Patrick Moynihan, *Beyond the Melting Pot: The Negroes, Puerto Ricans, Jews, Italian and Irish of New York City* (Cambridge, MA, 1963), 289.

38. Alroey, *Zionism Without Zion*; Glazer and Moynihan, *Beyond the Melting Pot*, v.

39. Leftwich, *Israel Zangwill* (New York, 1957), 255.

40. Ezra Mendelsohn, *On Modern Jewish Politics* (New York, 1993), 18.

BIBLIOGRAPHY

Archives

American Academy of Sciences of Moldova (Chişinău)
American Jewish Historical Society (New York)
Archives and Research Library at Trinity College, Dublin
Bancroft Library, University of California at Berkeley
Beit Bialik (Tel Aviv)
Central Zionist Archives (Jerusalem)
Gnazim Institute Archives (Tel Aviv)
Pavel Krushevan Papers
Public Library of the Performing Arts (New York)
State Archive of the Russian Federation (Moscow)
Tamiment Library and Robert F. Wagner Archives (New York)
Yale Special Collections (New Haven)
YIVO Institute for Jewish Research (New York)

Newspapers and Journals

Al Ha-Mishmar (Tel Aviv)
American Citizen (Kansas City, KS)
American Hebrew and Jewish Tribune (New York)
Appeal (St. Paul, MN)
Bessarabets (Kishinev)

Bibliography

Bikher-velt (Warsaw)
Broad Axe (Chicago)
Colored American (Washington, DC)
Commercial Advertiser (New York)
Die Welt (Vienna)
Evreiskaia starina (St. Petersburg)
Forverts (New York)
Ha'aretz (Tel Aviv)
Ha-Shiloach (Odessa; Warsaw)
Ha-Zeman (St. Petersburg)
Herut (Tel Aviv)
Indianapolis Freeman
Iskra (London)
Jewish Chronicle (London)
La Revue Russe (Paris)
New York American
New York Times
New York Tribune
Novoe Vremia (St. Petersburg)
Odesskii listok (Odessa)
Odesskie novosti (Odessa)
Osvobozhdenie (Stuttgart)
San Francisco Examiner
Sankt Petersburg vedomosti
Savannah Tribune
St. Louis Palladium
The Times (London)
Voskhod (St. Petersburg)
Wisconsin Weekly Advocate (Milwaukee)

Secondary Sources

Adler, Cyrus, ed. *The Voice of America on Kishineff*. Philadelphia, 1904.
Allen, Woody, and Marshall Brickman. 1977. *Annie Hall*. Directed by Woody Allen. MGM Home Entertainment, January 24, 2012.
Alroey, Gur. *Zionism Without Zion: The Jewish Territorial Organization and Its Conflict with the Zionist Organization*. Detroit, 2016.
Arokh, Yosef. *Der tsen yor'riger kalendar', 1901/2–1910/11*. Kishinev, 1901.

Bibliography

Ascher, Abraham. *The Revolution of 1905: Authority Restored*. Stanford, CA, 1992.

Averbach, Pesach. "H. N. Byalik ve-'ir ha-harigah." In *Ha-pogrom be-Kishinev bi-melot 60 shanah*, edited by H. Shorter, 28. Tel Aviv, 1963.

Baedeker, K. *Russland: Handbuch für Reisende*. Leipzig, 1901.

Beilin, A. *Der Kishinyever pogrom*. Warsaw, 1932.

Bernshtain, Miriam, and Yitshak Koren, eds. *Sefer Bernshtain-Kogan*. Tel Aviv, 1961.

Bessarabia: Handbook Prepared under the Direction of the Historical Section of the Foreign Office. No. 51. London, 1920.

Bilsky, Leora Y. "When Actor and Spectator Meet in the Courtroom: Reflections on Hannah Arendt's Concept of Judgment." *History and Memory* 8, no. 2 (Fall-Winter 1996).

Binyon, T. J. *Pushkin: A Biography*. New York, 2002.

Bornstein, Mark. *The Colors of Zion: Blacks, Jews, and Irish from 1845 to 1945*. Cambridge: MA, 2011.

Bosanquet, V. H. C., and C. S. Smith. *Dispatch from His Majesty's Consul-General at Odessa, Forwarding a Report on the Riots at Kishinev*. London, 1903.

Boyland, James. *Revolutionary Lives: Anna Strunsky and William English Walling*. Amherst, MA, 1988.

Brescanu, Iulian. "Karl Schmidt—Geschichte eines deutschen Humanisten aus Bessarabien." *Jahrbuch der Deutschen aus Bessarabien* 64 (2013): 201–204.

Budnitskii, Oleg. *Russian Jews between the Reds and the Whites*. Translated by Timothy J. Portice. Philadelphia, 2012.

Bund: Dokumenty i materialy. Moscow, 2010.

Chirikov, E. N. *Evrei*. Munich, 1910.

Chomsky, Noam. "Interview with Amy Goodman," *America Now! National Public Radio*, January 13, 2014.

Ciccarini, Marina, et al., eds. *Kessarevo Kesarju: Scritti in onore di Cesare*. Florence, 2014.

Cohen, Moshe. "Ahad Ha'am be-kenesyat Minsk," *Netivot* 1 (1913).

Cohn, Norman. *Warrant for Genocide: The Myth of the Jewish World-Conspiracy and the Protocols of the Elders of Zion*. London, 1967.

Correspondence Respecting the Treatment of Jews in Russia, nos. 1–2, Papers, vol. 81. London, 1882.

Davenport-Hines, Richard, ed. *Letters from Oxford*. London, 2007.

Bibliography

Davitt, Michael. *Within the Pale: The True Story of the Anti-Semitic Persecutions in Russia*. New York, 1903.

———. *The Boer Fight for Freedom*. New York, 1902.

De Michelis, Cesare G. *The Non-Existent Manuscript: A Study of the Protocols of the Sages of Zion*. Lincoln, NE, 2001.

Documenty po razledovaniiu Gomel'skogo pogrom. N.p., 1906.

Dubnow, Simon. *Kniga zhizni*, vol. 2. Riga, Latvia, 1934.

———, and G. Ia. Krasnyi-Admoni, eds. *Materialy dlia istorii anti-evreiskikh pogromov v Rossii*, 2 vols. Petrograd and Moscow, 1919, 1923.

Eco, Umberto. *The Prague Cemetery*. Boston, 2011.

Edelman, Robert. *Gentry Politics on the Eve of the Russian Revolution*. New Brunswick, NJ, 1980.

Ellmann, Richard. *James Joyce*. Oxford, 1982.

Engel, David. "What Is a Pogrom? European Jews in the Age of Violence." In *Anti-Jewish Violence: Rethinking the Pogrom in Eastern Europe*, edited by Jonathan Dekel-Chen et al., 19–37. Bloomington, IN, 2011.

Feigina, D. Ia. *Kishinevskii pogrom, 1903 goda: Sbornik dokumentov i materialov*. Chişinău, 2000.

Fink, Leon. *Progressive Intellectuals and the Dilemmas of Democratic Commitment*. Cambridge, MA, 1997.

Foglesong, David S. *The American Mission and the 'Evil Empire.'* Cambridge, UK, 2007.

Frankel, Jonathan. *Prophecy and Politics: Socialism, Nationalism, and the Russian Jews, 1862–1917*. Cambridge, UK, 1981.

Frederic, Harold, *The New Exodus: A Study of Israel in Russia*. New York and London, 1892.

Freeze, ChaeRan Y., and J. M. Harris, eds. *Everyday Jewish Life in Imperial Russia: Select Documents*. Waltham, MA, 2013.

Freidin, Gregory "Isaac Babel." In *European Writers: The Twentieth Century*, vol. 2, *1885–1914*, edited by George Stade. New York, 1989.

Fuller, William C., Jr. *Civil-Military Conflict in Imperial Russia, 1881–1914*. Princeton, NJ, 1985.

Geissbühler, Simon. *Like Shells on a Shore: Synagogues and Jewish Cemeteries of Northern Moldavia*. Bern, Switzerland, 2010.

Glatter, Leili Linka, director. "A Flash of Light," *Homeland*, Season 6, Episode 4. Bonanza, 2017.

Bibliography

Glazer, Nathan, and Daniel Patrick Moynihan. *Beyond the Melting Pot: The Negroes, Puerto Ricans, Jews, Italian and Irish of New York City.* Cambridge, MA, 1963.

Gluzman, Michael. "Pogrom and Gender: On Bialik's Unheimlich," *Prooftexts* 25, nos. 1–2 (Winter-Spring 2005): 39–59.

Gluzman, Michael, et al., eds. *Be'ir ha-haregah—bikur me'uhar.* Tel Aviv, 2005.

Godshalk, David Fort. *Veiled Visions: The 1906 Atlanta Race Riot and the Reshaping of American Race Relations.* Chapel Hill, 2005.

Goldman, Emma. *Living My Life*, vol. 1. New York, 1931.

Goldsthain, Yosi. *Ben Tsiyonut medinit le-Tsiyonut ma'asit.* Jerusalem, 1991.

Goren, Yaakov, ed. *'Eduyot nifga'ei Kishenev, 1903: kefi she-nigbu 'al-yede H. N. Byalik va-haverav.* Tel Aviv, 1991.

Hagemeister, Michael. *Die "Protokolle der Weisen von Zion" vor Gericht: Der Berner Prozess 1933–1937 und die "antisemitische Internationale."* Zurich, 2017.

———. "The American Connection: Leslie Fry and the *Protocols of the Elders of Zion.*" In *Kesarevo Kesarju: Scritti in onore di Cesare G. di Michelis*, edited by Marina Ciccarini et al., 217–228. Florence, 2014.

———. " 'The Antichrist as an Imminent Political Possibility': Sergei Nilus and the Apocalyptic Reading of the Protocols of the Elders of Zion." In *The Paranoid Apocalypse: A Hundred Year Retrospective on The Protocols of the Elders of Zion*, edited by Richard Landes and Steven T. Katz, 79–91. New York, 2012.

———. "The *Protocols of the Elders of Zion*: Between History and Fiction," *New German Critique* 35 (2008): 83–95.

Halperin, Yisrael. *Sefer ha-gevurah: antologyah historit-sifrutit*, vol. 3. Tel Aviv, 1949–1950.

Hamm, Michael F. "Kishinev: The Character and Development of a Tsarist Frontier Town," *Nationalities Papers* 26, no. 1 (1998): 24–27.

Harshav, Benjamin. *Language in Time of Revolution.* Berkeley, CA, 1993.

Hausman, Guido. *Universität und städtische Gesellschaft in Odessa: 1865–1917.* Stutgart, 1998.

Helman, Y. T. *Asara perakim le-shire H. N. Byalik.* Tel Aviv, 1953–1954.

Hemon, Alesandar. *The Lazarus Project.* New York, 2008.

Hillels, Shlomo. *Har Ha-keramim.* Tel Aviv, 1930.

Hirschfeld, Ariel. *Kinor 'arukh.* Tel Aviv, 2011.

Bibliography

Hitchins, Keith. *The Romanians, 1774–1866*. Oxford, 1996.

Hohman, Valleri J. *Russian Culture and Theatrical Performance in America, 1891–1933*. New York, 2011.

Holtzman, Avner. *Hayyim Nahman Byalik*. Jerusalem, 2009.

———. *Hayim Nahman Bialik: Poet of Hebrew*. New Haven, CT, 2017.

Howe, Irving, and Ruth R. Wisse, eds. and trans. *The Best of Sholem Aleichem*. New York, 1979.

Hyndman, H. H. *Further Reminiscences*. London, 1912.

Istoriia Kishineva. Kishinev, 1966.

Jewsbury, George F. *The Russian Annexation of Bessarabia, 1774–1828*. New York, 1976.

Johnson, Sam. *Pogroms, Peasants, Jews: Britain and Eastern Europe's "Jewish Question," 1867–1925*. New York, 2011.

———. "Use and Abuses: 'Pogrom' in the Anglo-American Imagination." In *Jews in the East European Borderlands*, edited by Eugene M. Avrutin and Harriet Murav, 158–166. Boston, 2012.

Judge, Edward H. *Easter in Kishinev: Anatomy of a Pogrom*. New York, 1992.

———. *Plehve: Repression and Reform in Imperial Russia, 1902–1904*. Syracuse, NY, 1983.

Kahan Commission Report. Jerusalem, 2012.

Katz, Ben-Zion. *Zikhronot*. Tel Aviv, 1963–1964.

Kaufman, Jonathan. "Blacks and Jews: The Struggle in Cities." *Struggles in the Promised Land: Toward a History of Black-Jewish Relations*. New York, 1997.

Keep, J. L. *The Rise of Social Democracy in Russia*. Oxford, 1963.

Kellogg, Charles Elliot. *NAACP: A History of the National Association for the Advancement of Colored People*. Baltimore, 1967.

Keogh, Dermott. *Jews in Twentieth-Century Ireland*. Cork, 1998.

King, Carla. "Michael Davitt and the Kishinev Pogrom," *Irish Slavonic Studies* 17 (1996): 19–44.

Koestler, Arthur. *Thieves in the Night*. London, 1947.

Kol shire H. N. Byalik. Tel Aviv, 1967–1968.

Konstaninov, S. *Kishinev: ekonomicheskii ocherk*. Kishinev, 1996.

Koren, Yitshak. *Yehude Kishinev*. Tel Aviv, 1940.

Korolenko, V. G., "Dom no. 13-yi: epizod iz kishevskago pogrom." Berlin, 1904.

Bibliography

Korolev, Konstantin. *Leninskaia "Iskra" v Kisheneve*. Kishinev, 1970.

Krushevan, Pavel. *Bessarabia*. Moscow, 1903.

———. *Znamia Rossii*. Edited by O. A. Platonov. Moscow, 2015.

———. *Delo Artabanova*. Reprint, Moscow, 1995.

———. *Chto takoe Rossiia? putevyia zamietki*. Moscow, 1896.

Lachower, Yeruham Fishel. *Byalik*, vol. 2. Tel Aviv, 1934–1935.

Landes, Richard, and Steven T. Katz, eds. *The Paranoid Apocalypse: A Hundred-Year Retrospective on* The Protocols of the Elders of Zion. New York, 2012.

Leftwich, Joseph. *Israel Zangwill*. New York, 1957.

Lenin, V. I. "The Second Duma and the Second Revolutionary Wave." *Lenin Collected Works*, vol. 12. Moscow, 1962.

Levy, Richard S. "Setting the Record Straight: Regarding *The Protocols of the Elders of Zion*: A Fool's Errand." In *Nexus: Essays in German Jewish Studies*, vol 2, edited by William Collins Donahue and Marthe B. Helfer, 43–61. Rochester, NY, 2014.

Litvak, Olga. "The Post in Hell: H. N. Bialik and the Cultural Genealogy of the Kishinev Pogrom," *Jewish Studies Quarterly* 2, no. 1 (2005): 101–128.

Löwe, Heinz-Dietrich. *The Tsars and Jews: Reaction and Anti-Semitism in Imperial Russia*. Chur, Switzerland, 1993.

Lumpkins, Charles L. *American Pogrom: The East St. Louis Riot and Black Politics*. Athens, OH, 2008.

Malachi, A. R. "Pera'ot Kishinev be-aspaklariat ha-shirah be-ivrit ve-yidish," *Al admat Be'sarabyah*, vol. 3. Tel Aviv, 1963–1964.

Malamud, Bernard. *The Complete Stories*. New York, 1997.

Maor, Yitshak. *Ha-tenuah ha-Tsiyonit be-Russiyah*. Jerusalem, 1973.

Marek, Nekula. *Franz Kafka and His Prague Contexts*. Prague, 2016.

Marley, Lawrence. *Michael Davitt*. Dublin, 2007.

Mazur, Arkadii. *Stranitsy istorii sorokskikh evreev*. Chişinău, 1999.

Miller, Martin. *Kropotkin*. Chicago, 1976.

Mintz, Alan. *Hurban: Responses to Catastrophe in Hebrew Literature*. New York, 1984.

Miron, Dan. *Bodedim be-mo'adam*. Tel Aviv, 1987.

———. *From Continuity to Contiguity: Toward a New Jewish Literary Thinking*. Stanford, CA, 2010.

———. *The Prophetic Mode in Modern Hebrew Poetry*. New Milford, CT, 2010.

Bibliography

————. "Hayim Nahman Bialik's Poetry: An Introduction." In Atar Hadari, ed. and trans., *Songs From Bialik: Selected Poems of Hayim Nahman Bialik*, xvii–lxiv. Syracuse, NY, 2000.

Moore, John. *A Journey from London to Odessa*. London: Privately printed, 1833.

Motzkin, Leo, ed. *Die Judenpogromme in Russland*. Leipzig and Cologne, 1910.

Nahshon, Edna, ed. *From the Ghetto to the Melting Pot: Israel Zangwill's Jewish Plays*. Detroit, 2006.

Nasaw, David. *The Chief: The Life of William Randolph Hearst*. Boston, 2000.

Nurock, Mordekhai. *Ve'idat Tsiyonei Rusyah be-Minsk*. Jerusalem, 1963–1964.

Ovington, Mary White. *How the National Association for the Advancement of Colored People Began*. New York, 1914.

————. "William English Walling," *Crisis*, November 1934.

Patai, Raphael, ed. *The Complete Diaries of Theodor Herzl*. New York, 1960.

Penkower, Monty. "The Kishinev Pogrom of 1903: A Turning-Point in Jewish History," *Modern Judaism* 24, no. 3 (October 2004): 187–225.

Reinharz, Jehuda. *The Making of a Zionist Leader*. Oxford, 1985.

Rogger, Hans. *Jewish Policies and Right-Wing Politics in Imperial Russia*. Berkeley, CA, 1986.

Roskies, David G. *Against the Apocalypse: Responses to Catastrophe in Modern Jewish Culture*. Cambridge, MA, 1984.

Rovner, Adam. *In the Shadow of Zion: Promised Lands Before Israel*. New York, 2014.

Rubin, Yosef, ed. *Dubossaryi: sefer zikaron*. Tel Aviv, 1965.

Schoenberg, Philip Ernest. "The American Reaction to the Kishinev Pogrom," *American Jewish Historical Quarterly* 63 (March 1974): 262–283.

Segel, Benjamin W. *A Lie and a Libel: The History of the Protocols of the Elders of Zion*. Translated and edited by Richard S. Levy. Lincoln, NE, 1995.

Seligman, Scott D. "The Night New York's Chinese Went Out for Jews: How a Chinatown Fundraiser Event for Pogrom Victims United Two Persecuted Peoples," *Forward*, January 26, 2011.

Bibliography

Seltzer, Robert M. *Simon Dubnow's "New Judaism": Diaspora Nationalism and the World History of the Jews*. Leiden, The Netherlands, 2014.

Shamir, Ziva. *Li-neivah ha-ne'elam: ikvot parashat Ira Yan bi-yetsirat Byalik*. Tel Aviv, 2000.

Shapira, Anita. *Land and Power: The Zionist Resort to Force, 1881–1948*. Translated by William Templer. Stanford, CA, 1992.

———. *Yosef Haim Brenner: A Life*. Translated by Anthony Berris. Stanford, CA, 2015.

Shapiro, Lamed. *The Cross and Other Stories*. Edited by Leah Garrett. New Haven, CT, 2007.

Shavit, Ari. *My Promised Land: The Triumph and Tragedy of Israel*. New York, 2013.

Shonikov, Igor' Petrovich. "Obshchestvenno-politicheskaia i literaturnaya deiatelnost' P. A. Krushevana." PhD diss., Pridnestrovskii Gosudarstvennyi universitet im. T. G. Shevchenko, 2011.

Shorer, H., ed. *Ha-pogrom bi-Kishenev bi-melot 60 shanah*. Tel Aviv, 1963.

Shukman, H. *The Relations between the Jewish Bund and the RSDRP, 1897–1903*. PhD diss., London University, 1961.

Singer, Isidore, ed. *Russia at the Bar of the American People: A Memorial of Kishinev*. New York, 1904.

Slutskii, M. B. *V skorbnye dni*. Kishinev, 1930.

Solzhenitsyn, A. I. *Dvesti let vmesti (1795–1995)*, vol. 1. Moscow, 2001.

Stanislawski, Michael. *Zionism and the Fin de Siècle: Cosmopolitanism and Nationalism from Nordau to Jabotinsky*. Berkeley, CA, 2001.

Stansell, Christine. *American Moderns: Bohemian New York and the Creation of the New Century*. New York, 2000.

Steinfels, Peter. "Beliefs; A Century Ago, in what is now Chisinau, hundreds fell victim to a pogrom. Yesterday, a day of healing, Christians and Jews Remembered," *New York Times*, May 30, 1998.

Stiles, W. C. *Out of Kishineff: The Duty of the American People to the Russian Jew*. New York, 1903.

Strunsky Walling, Anna. *The Homel Massacre: An Address Delivered Before the New York Section Council of Jewish Women*. New York, 1914.

Bibliography

Stults, Taylor. "Roosevelt, Russian Persecution of Jews, and American Public Opinion," *Jewish Social Studies* 33, no. 1 (1971): 15.

Tarnopolsky, Boris. "The Gomel Pogrom of 1903: A Case Study in Russian–Jewish Relations in the Pale of Settlement." MA thesis, University of Haifa, 2007.

Tadmor-Shimony, Tali. *Shi'ur moledet: ha-hinukh ve-khinun medinah.* Beersheba, 2011.

Taubenfeld, Aviva F. *Rough Writing: Ethnic Authorship in Theodore Roosevelt's America.* New York, 2008.

Taylor, A. J. P. Introduction to *Ten Days that Shook the World* by John Reed. London, 1977.

Tazkir Lopukhin: Duah ha-mishtarah ha-shait ha-Russit 'al tenu'ah ha-Tsiyonit, 1897–1903. Translated by Yael Ha-Russi. Jerusalem, 1988.

Tchernowitz, Chaim [Rav Tsa'ir]. *Masekhet zikhronot.* New York, 1945.

Tooke, Christopher John. "The Representation of Jewish Women in Pre-Revolutionary Russia." PhD dissertation, University College, London, 2011.

Ungerfeld, Moshe. *Byalik ve-sofe doro.* Tel Aviv, 1974.

Urussov, Serge Dmitreyevich. *Memoirs of a Russian Governor.* London, New York, 1908.

Veidinger, Jeffrey. *Jewish Public Culture in the Late Russian Empire.* Bloomington, 2008.

Walling, William English. "The Race Riot in the North," *The Independent*, July-December, 1908.

Weber, J. B. *The Kishineff Massacre and Its Bearing upon the Question of Jewish Immigration into the United States.* New York, 1903.

Weizmann, Chaim. *Trial and Error: The Autobiography of Chaim Weizmann.* New York, 1949.

Whitcomb, Ian. *Irving Berlin and Ragtime America.* Pompton Plains, NJ, 1998.

Wolf, Lucien. *The Jewish Bogey and the Forged Protocols of the Learned Elders of Zion.* London, 1920.

Zakim, Eric. *To Build and Be Built: Landscape, Literature, and the Construction of Zionist Identity.* Philadelphia, 2006.

Zelenchuk, V. S. *Naselenie Bessarabii i podnestrov'ya v XIX v.* Kishinev, 1979.

Zhukov, V. I. *Goroda Bessarabii, 1812–1861.* Moscow, 1964.

Bibliography

Zipperstein, Steven J. *Elusive Prophet: Ahad Ha'am and the Origins of Zionism*. Berkeley, CA, 1993.

———. "Fateless: The Beilis Trial a Century Later," *Jewish Review of Books* (Winter 2015): 22–27.

———. "Inside Kishinev's Pogrom: Hayyim Nahman Bialik, Michael Davitt, and Burdens of Truth." In *The Individual in History: Essays in Honor of Jehuda Reinharz*, edited by ChaeRan Freeze et al., 365–383. Waltham, MA, 2015.

———. "Benjamin Netanyahu's Favorite Poet—and Ours," *Forward*, July 7, 2014.

———. *The Jews of Odessa: A Cultural History, 1794–1881*. Stanford, CA. 1986.

Zlatova, Y., and V. Kotel'nikov. *Across Moldavia*. Moscow, 1959.

INDEX

Page numbers in *italics* refer to illustrations.

Index

Index

Black Hundreds (Union of Russian Peoples), 4, 37, 147, 172, 187
blacks, American:
  civil rights, xv, xix, 14, 188, 194–95, 198, 200–203
  mistreatment compared with pogroms, 187–88, 192–94, 202
  newspapers of, 193–94
  violence against, xix, 14, 186–88, 192–94, 200–201
blood libel, xiv
  see also ritual murder accusations
B'nai B'rith, 193–94
Boer War for Freedom, The (Davitt), 120–21
Bolgarskaia Street, Kishinev, 88
Bolshevism, 4, 13, 21, 149, 167–68
  Lenin, 13–14, 145
Borenstein, Efim/Efraim, 158
Boxer Rebellion, China (1900), 171
Brenner, Joseph Hayyim, 11
Breskhovskaya, Catherine, 190
British:
  Davitt election to Parliament, 120
  immigration restrictions, 92
  Jewish settlement in East Africa supported by, 14, 177
  on Kishinev pogrom, 67
  Labour Party, 120
  Mandate period, 2–3, 19
  on Moldavians (1920), 36
  Parliament's *Correspondence Regarding the Treatment of Jews in Russia*, 5
  and Russia's barbarism, 185–86
  see also England; Ireland
Broad Axe, Chicago, 193
Broadway theater, 12, 190–92, 205
Brody, descriptions of, 6, 8
Bruvarman, Hannah, 72
Buber, Martin, 19
Butmi, G., 171–72
Byk river, xv–xvi, *xvi*, 42, 208

calendar, Yiddish-language, 53
carpet makers, Bessarabia, 33

Catholics, contempt for Russian Orthodoxy, 186
Chamberlain, William Houston, 148
Chew Mon Sing (Joseph Singleton), 101–2
Chicago:
  Broad Axe, 193
  The Lazarus Project, 24
China, Boxer Rebellion (1900), 171
Chinese Americans, 101–3, 186
Chinese Theater, New York City, 101, 104
Chirikov, Evgenii, 190–92
Chişinău (Kishinev's current and pre-Russian name), xiii, 21, 38, 64, 207–8
Chomsky, Noam, 18–19
Choral Synagogue, Kishinev, 55
Chosen People, The (Chirikov), 190–92
Christianity:
  contempt for Russian Orthodoxy, 186, 188
  Jewish threat to, 174, 177, 183
  see also blood libel
"Christian socialism," 22, 148
Chto takoe Rossiia (What Is Russia?), Krushevan, 159
Ciuflea Church, Kishinev, 61, 63
Civil-Military Conflict in Imperial Russia, 1881–1914 (Fuller), 222n54
civil rights, black, 188, 194–95
  NAACP, xv, xix, 14, 188, 194, 198, 200–203
Cleveland Gazette, 194
Cohn, Norman, 146–47
Collier's, 200
Committee for the Advancement of the Negro, 202–3
  see also National Association for the Advancement of Colored People (NAACP)
Communism, Transdniestria, 21
conservatism:
  Russian, 12, 15, 22, 37, 95, 157

Index

Index

Index

Index

Index

Index

Index

Index

Poland, 6, *160*
police:
  Lopukhin, 95, 177–78
  during pogrom, 63, 66, 88–89
  Russian secret police (Okhrana),
    22, 104–5, 147, 169, 170
politics:
  activists stirring up riots, 96–97
  anarchists, 19, 186, 189
  Bolshevism, 4, 13–14, 21, 145,
    149, 167–68
  Kishinev pogrom impact, 6, 20, 21
  see also civil rights; conservatism;
    Left; liberalism; radicalism;
    Right; Social Democratic Party;
    socialism; Zionists
Popov (local activist), 97
population/numbers:
  Bessarabia, 34, 36, 37
  Jewish immigrants from Russian
    empire to U.S., 103
  Kishinev, 37, 40, 43, 50
  Kishinev rioters, 65, 68, 134, 137
  pogrom rapes, 73, 135
*Portrait of the Artist as a Young Man,
  The* (Joyce), 120
Prague Cemetery, The (Eco), 150
prayer:
  dried up value, 141
  Moldavian outlawed (1870s), 36
press:
  Berkeley *Russian Review*, 196
  Kishinev pogrom, 11, 17–18, 91,
    149, 178–83
  Mother Earth magazine, 192
  Odessa, 114
  responsibility for violence, 201
  see also Jewish press; Krushevan,
    Pavel; newspapers; *Protocols of
    the Elders of Zion*
Pridnestrovian Moldavan Republic
  (Transdniestria), 21–23
Principles of Sociology (Spencer), 91
"Program of World Conquest by Jews,
  The" (World Union of Freema-
  sons and Sages of Zion), 167,
  172–74

Pronin, Georgi A., 62, 97, 98, 182
Prophecy and Politics (Frankel), xx,
  103–4
"Prophet, The" (Pushkin), 109–10
Protestants, contempt for Russian
  Orthodoxy, 186, 188
protest meetings, U.S., 12, 189
Protocols of the Elders of Zion, The, xv,
  147, 167–72
  Bernstein-Kogan and, 182
  Bern trial and, 147, 169
  Butmi version, 171–72
  De Michelis annotated translation,
    170
  Die Protokolle der Weisen von Zion
    (Segel), 170
  Egyptian television series, 148
  forgery, xvi–xvii, 99, 168–69
  Krushevan version, xvi–xvii, xviii–
    xix, 16, 22, 99, 146–50, 153,
    159, 167–71, 183
Die Protokolle der Weisen von Zion
  (Segel), 170
Purishkevich, V., *144*
Pushkin, Alexander, xi, 28, 40–41,
  109–10

Raaben, R. S. von (Governor General
  of Bessarabia), 44–45, 48, 68,
  71, 87, 90–91
rabbis, Kishinev, 53
race:
  Davitt and, 120–22
  U.S. and, xix, 14, 186–88, 192–94,
    200
  see also antisemitism; blacks; ethnic
    and religious groups
Rachkovsky, Piotr, 169, 170
radicalism:
  American, 189, 194–95
  Russian, 6, 157, 176–78, 186, 189,
    190, 194–95, 197–98
Radziwill, Catherine, 170
rapacity of Jews, 15, 22, 123
rapes:
  anti-Jewish violence in Russia
    (1918–1920), 4

Index

Index

Index

Index